My Three Mothers and Other Passions

Sophie Freud

 New York University Press
NEW YORK AND LONDON

Copyright © 1988 by New York University
All rights reserved
Manufactured in the United States of America

Library of Congress Cataloging-in-Publication Data
Freud, Sophie, 1924–
    My three mothers and other passions / Sophie Freud.
        p.   cm.
    Includes bibliographies.
    ISBN 0-8147-2588-0
    1. Freud, Sophie, 1924–   . 2. Mothers and daughters. 3. Freud,
Anna, 1895–   . 4. Psychoanalysts—Biography. I. Title.
II. Title: My 3 mothers and other passions.
BF173.F857F74   1987
616.89'0092'4—dc19   87-29803
c 10 9 8 7 6 5 4 3 2   CIP

New York University Press are Smyth-sewn and printed
on permanent and durable acid-free paper.
Book design by Ken Venezio

While I honor the memory of my three mothers with the book's title, I would like to thank two living women with my dedication.

This book is dedicated to my American mother of thirty-five years, Constance Rathbun, and to my British mother of eight years, Gillian Parker, who have been loving friends, mentors, and models. Their caring, courage, and affirmation of life sustain me in pursuing the uncertain road that lies ahead.

Contents

Acknowledgments

IT is with eagerness that I take this opportunity to thank the many women and men without whom this book could never have been conceived. Many of the essays in this book were first written in response to some organization and/or person which honored me by asking me to contribute to a conference or to a collection of writings. Although these essays may have changed shape, in the rewriting and editing work, it was, in most cases, the certainty of an assured audience that sparked the core ideas.

The essay "My Three Mothers" was written in response to Aida Press, editor of the *Radcliffe Quarterly* (December 1984) asking me to contribute some reflections on the mother/daughter experience. I am happy she thought of me when planning the *Quarterly* issue on mothers and daughters.

My research on passion was made possible by the 700 women who generously contributed their most private experiences to my research. Many of these women were students and friends, as well as friends of friends, in expanding networks. I am pleased that this book might finally mirror back some of their experiences. I also wish to acknowledge Jerold Harmatz who tried to help me organize my data so they could be fed into a computer. It was not his fault that this enterprise came to naught. Carol Landau greatly encouraged me by asking me to report on my research at the Butler Hospital Grand Rounds (Fall 1977) in a talk entitled "Passion as a Mental Health Hazard," and then accepting the talk in written form as a chapter in her edited book *The Evolving Female* (Human Sciences Press, New York 1980). I also much appreciated an early opportunity created by Dr. Nancy Downey, Director of the Radcliffe Seminars who arranged a colloquium to present some preliminary findings to a responsive audience (April 1977). Nancy Downey had generally facilitated my teaching in the Radcliffe Seminars Program, and it was above all the participants in those seminars who contributed through our discussions to my study of passions in women's lives.

"The Last Sabbatical" was written for a conference *In Celebration of Life Transitions* (November 1980) organized by Dr. Vivian Rogers, then director of the Adult Life Resource Center of the University of Kansas. Her role was one of enabler. "Learning to Heal" was written for the thirteenth annual conference of the National Association of Social Workers in New Jersey (October 1982) in response to their request for a paper dealing with the experience of being a psychotherapist. I owe special appreciation to two of their board members, Edythe Deiches Gutman ACSW, and Betty Levin ACSW, in their facilitating roles.

"The Passion and Challenge of Teaching" was read in its first draft at an annual Asquith Symposium (April 1979) organized by the Harvard University Graduate School of Education. It was then rewritten for publication in the *Harvard Educational Review,* and published in an issue on women and education which had a special editorial board of all women (February 1980; copyright © 1980 by President and Fellows of Harvard College). I owe special thanks to Emily Hancock and Gloria Garfunkel who encouraged me throughout this process and gave me much editorial assistance in rewriting the article for publication.

The essay on "Work and Love: The Divided Self" was written for a conference organized by the Harvard Medical School, Department of Continuing Education (June 1982). The theme of the conference was the "Process of Change in Psychotherapy." I thank Dr. Douglas Jacobs and his committee who invited me to participate in the conference. The essay titled "Making a Difference as a Therapist" was prepared for the same organization, contributing to the theme of "Psychotherapy: Long and Short Term Approaches: A Clinical Dialogue" (June 1986). The invitation for participation was extended by Dr. Judith Reiner Platt who was most understanding about my difficulty in meeting their deadline.

The essay titled "The Paradoxes of Parenthood: On the Impossibility of Being a Perfect Parent" was sparked by discussions with

Professor Philip J. Davis of Brown University. He generously invited me to contribute an essay for the book *No Way: The Nature of the Impossible* of which he is coeditor. (W. H. Freeman, New York 1987) Philip Davis not only suggested the idea of this essay, but was persistent and patient in encouraging me to write it. His editorial comments as well as those of Hadassah Davis greatly enriched the essay. I gained new understanding about life from our encounter.

"Making a Difference" was written for a plenary talk of the Annual Convention of the National Association of Social Workers (November 1985). I am grateful to the committee members who selected me, and most specifically to my own Dean, Diana Waldfogel who participated in this selection process. I also owe to Diana Waldfogel, coeditor of the *Handbook of Clinical Social Work* (Jossey-Bass, San Francisco 1983) as well as to my former colleague and friend Elizabeth C. Lemon, section editor, the privilege of having been asked to contribute "A Feminist Perspective" to the *Handbook*. A part of this chapter forms the core to this volume's chapter "What Does Woman Want?" I seize this opportunity to express my gratitude to Dean Waldfogel in more general terms. Her furthering a familylike setting at the Simmons School of Social Work creates an atmosphere which enhances the creativity of individual faculty members, including my own.

"On Daughters and Fathers" was written for a German radio series on that subject (1981) and later published in a book called *Vatersein* (Being a Father) and edited by Hans J. Schultz (1982). I thank Mr. Schultz for inviting me to contribute to this series, and Dr. Helm Stierlin for suggesting my name to him. I further extend my deep appreciation to Helm Stierlin whose writing on parental delegations has illuminated my own experience.

I am greatly indebted to Professor Maurice DuQuesnay of the University of Southwestern Louisiana who selected me as the lecturer for the Flora Levy Annual Lecture in the Humanities (March 1984) in memory of Flora Levy. Dr. DuQuesnay asked me to discuss the work of Anna Freud, giving me a much-welcomed incentive to absorb myself in my aunt's life work, resulting in the essay "The Legacy of Anna Freud."

Even "Mother and Daughter: An Epitaph" was written initially in response to a speaking engagement. I had promised the American Jewish Committee to talk on the subject "The Jewish Woman Today: Her Changing Options," when my mother died a few days before that talk was scheduled. I decided to deliver an epitaph for my mother on that occasion (November 1980) and I want to express my deep thanks to the women and men in the audience for helping me to mourn my mother. Many of us shared our tears on that occasion. I also want to thank Don Bloch then editor of *Family Process* for accepting the epitaph for publication (March 1981) allowing me to share my feelings with a wider audience.

Robin Ohringer who shares my appreciation for the roundness of life, presented me with a favorite quote, which I chose for the epigraph for my book. In thanking Robin, who has been my doctoral student, and my thesis advisee, I think of all my other students who are far too numerous to name individually, yet who are inextricably woven into the very texture of this book. My students from Simmons, from the Harvard Extension Program, and from the Radcliffe Seminars of some years ago, give meaning to my identity as educator; they are my inspiration and my inner audience for much of my writing. I cannot think of my writing or even of my life, as separate from my students. I especially would like to mention the women in the Radcliffe Seminar class of 1978. We have sustained each other through our regular meetings during these last nine years, and they are always my first somewhat uncritical audience for each new short story that I write.

Dr. Fredelle Maynard edited "On Time" and "Cowardice" in a most helpful way, and contributed much to their final shape. Her keen interest in my ideas has been gratifying. I was also pleased and encouraged when editor Dr. Trude Weiss-Rosmarin accepted my story "Cowardice" for publication in the *Jewish Spectator* (Winter 1983). Professor Milton Ford's positive response to my short stories and to my writings and his unceasing support through these last seven years have been very important to me. Andrea Fleck Clardy did some editing of my articles in relation to an earlier publishing plan. Although the venture failed, I appreciated her belief in my writings and we profited from her editing comments.

Robert S. Weiss has been for almost twenty years a sympathetic and helpful critic of my essays and short stories. His steady encouragement and his respect for me, in colleagueship and friendship has meant a great deal to me.

I would like to thank my three children, Andrea Freud Loewenstein, Dania Jekel, and George Loewenstein for teaching me about hope, joy, passion, grief and anxiety, all the emotions that led me to my writing. I want to thank them for the respect and affection they continue to demonstrate to me. I want to thank them for not being too angry when they appear in my stories. I want to express most profound gratitude to my oldest daughter, Andrea. Since I am in awe of her talent as a novelist, her encouragement of my writing short stories has been a most precious and meaningful gift. I could never have sustained that particular voice if she had not declared it important. Her editing of my short stories has been invaluable, uniquely enhancing whatever merit they may have.

I am extremely grateful to Dr. Jeffrey Berman for his sustaining friendship and his appreciation of my work as well as his occasional gentle criticism from which I profit. His enthusiastic wish to be helpful led him to introduce me to his own editor, Kitty Moore, senior editor of the New York University Press. I am most fortunate to have found an editor who is willing to take risks with some of my unconventional forms of writing. I especially appreciate her agreeing to include my imperfect short stories in the manuscript. Kitty Moore has been a steady voice at my side, spurring me on without pressure or impatience, encouraging me to do extensive rewriting without insisting that I do so. Only a writer can appreciate the vital indispensible role of an enabling editor in completing a book.

Among the passions in my life, I have acknowledged my mothers in the title, my social work mentor in the dedication, my children, and my students in the above paragraphs. It is important that I also acknowledge the two men who taught me about passion, however inadvertently. Let their names be Pierre and the British Don. Without their appearance in my life, I could not have found the creative spark that led me to write a book about passions.

LINCOLN, JULY 1987

Introduction

I have lived many lives. I have been a slave and a prince. Many a beloved has sat upon my knees, and I have sat upon the knees of many a beloved. Everything that has been shall be again.

W. B. YEATS

IN the chapter "The Passion Experience" I try to draw you, dear reader, into my long story by confessing to my own passion experiences, and then I choose to hide behind other women's voices. Indeed, many of the women in this essay speak for me as well. Am I being a coward and excessively self-protective? I think not. You will find that each "story" in this book is about my search for, and conquest of (or defeat by) the passion experience, in one form or another. Perhaps it was my attempt to make peace with my passions that led me to write many of the chapters in this book during the last eight years which started with my "Last Sabbatical" and is ending as I approach after all another sabbatical. Coming to terms with my passions is perhaps the essence of my midlife attempt to "Learning to Heal" myself, a form of bearing witness to the good and hard parts of my life. While you will get to know me perhaps all too well, if you choose to come along on this midlife journey, you deserve to know more directly about the passion experiences in my own life, since they gave rise to this book.

The most indelible passion of my life, as is true for most human beings, was my mother. My mother and I had such an undifferentiated relationship that her presence filled me with dread. I could meet her only through an anxiously guarded emotional and geographic distance. I felt responsible for her unhappiness, and I experienced her pain at least as intensely as she did herself. As the years wore on I became frozen toward her, and a simple friendly exchange took more and more effort. I was able to mourn her death by writing an epitaph for her, entitled "Mother and Daughter." I found in the writing of this piece that her death had released some of my deep love for her, which I had buried as early as my late childhood when the burden of sharing her pain became too great. I would have preferred to have a reconciliation with my mother while she was still alive, even at the last moment, but I could not manage it. Still, it has been very important that I have made peace with my mother in my heart, because mysteriously, perhaps since my divorce, I feel that I have taken on her identity and it allows me to be relatively at peace with myself. It would be disastrous to carry an unforgiven and unforgiving mother within oneself.

The intense yet painful bond with my own mother led me to search for better mothers all my life, and some of the deepest passions of my life were with other women, my second mother, my daughters, my first social work mentor, and my aunt. You will meet all these women in these pages.

Forgiving one's parents is an urgent midlife task. I believe it was my third mother who led me toward forgiving my father. I describe in "The Last Sabbatical" how I went to London, perhaps in an unconsciously planned effort to make peace with my family. In "Silk Yarn" I try to share the profound love I felt for my aunt. That sabbatical visit became a watershed in my life. By writing "Daughters and Fathers" and "The Heirloom" and perhaps even "The Legacy of Anna Freud," which is the study of a passionate father-daughter relationship, I tried to come to terms with the passion and betrayal that I experienced in relation to my father.

I married a man whom I respected and loved, yet at the age of twenty-one I was quite innocent of passion. It was the birth and the passion I felt for my first child that made the first breach in my relationship with my husband. I wish he had intruded upon our mother-infant love affair, but instead he retreated as a defeated rival; such was his way. As time went on, I allowed him to carry the passion between us for both of us. In due time this marriage of an overloving man and an underloving woman took on a rigid and corrupt pattern. I am a woman who would rather love than be loved. I think my own lack of passion was like an insidious chronic disease that slowly spread until it choked the relationship to death. But this is only one frame. At other times my husband's passion, with its typical anxiety, suffering, and elations, was exclusively reserved for his work. It is, of course, also possible that his passion for me was his private experience that had little to do with my true self. It became a lonely marriage. I think ours was an extremely undifferentiated relationship. As the years wore on, I became frozen toward him and a simple friendly exchange took more and more effort. We got a divorce. It need not have happened that way, but so it went.

Nothing prepared me for the intense, fierce, tender, and passionate feelings that the birth of my first child unleashed in me. There was much suffering as well. Our love for each other became a chronic passion that caused us both difficulties for many years. Yet, while life is round, patterns need not repeat themselves in exactly the same way. My daughter is a more courageous woman than I have been. She started important conversations with me. Honest dialogue leads toward differentiation. Our love for each other has not become frozen. It continues to be difficult, but it is fierce and alive. While my passion for my first child had a special tormenting quality, my passions for my other two children were also deep and often turbulent. I have tried to speak about my struggles as a parent in "The Paradoxes of Parenthood," and in "On Time" and "Cowardice." It should be said here that my short stories, albeit autobiographical to some extent, are also fiction. The events in these stories may or may not have happened in quite this way. All the names in both essays and stories are of course fictional.

It was a short time after the birth of my second child and in a new job that I fell in love with my social work mentor. At that time, I was not able to label my feelings. I still keenly remember my preoccupation with her and my constant yearning to be in her presence. Eventually my passion abated and developed into a loving friendship that has lasted thirty-five years. This woman taught me much about social work and even more about love.

She demonstrated that passionate love, when handled with acceptance and without fear, can sometimes turn into lifelong affirming friendship. She contracted a crippling chronic illness and I still look forward to my regular visits to her home through all these many years. We have adopted each other as mother and daughter. I am happy that I have learned to listen to people's pain without cutting them off, reassuring them and cheering them up too quickly, or doing similar disconfirming things. My loved friend feels free to tell me about her fears of going blind, losing her voice, and other such major disasters. "You are the only person in my life with whom I can share my very deepest feelings," she has said to me gratefully. "You have taught me how to be more open and loving. You are the most important person in my life. I love you very deeply." This was my only happy love story. I dread and fear her approaching death.

I shall tell you in "Reunion" about the sense of bewilderment when I fell in love at the age of forty-seven with a much younger man. Again, I had just started on my academic career, an important life transition. Since the object of my passion was finally a man, albeit a much younger one, I found this time a label for my feelings: I had fallen in love!

You will hear in "The Last Sabbatical" and in "The Visit" how I succumbed to a second unrequited passion in late midlife. Each of these midlife passions was accompanied by intense suffering, and indeed the moments of joy were quite rare compared to the months and years of anguish. At times my two nonmutual passions for these men felt like tortures, narcissistic assaults, emotional catastrophes. They were deeply threatening to my pseudoindependence, reawakening the vulnerable little child in me who used to burst into tears whenever anyone hurt her feelings. Moreover, getting more fully in touch, quite late in life, with the capacity to love deeply and violently led to the demise of my marriage, because it had been good enough only as long as I had defined myself as a woman who did not have strong feelings.

Do I regret these passions in my life? Will I live differently "next time around"? Perhaps in some ways. On the whole I feel quite satisfied with the mixture of turmoil and tranquility, safety and risk, love and work, suffering and joyfulness that has crossed my path. Neither would I wish any part of my life away, past, present, or future. It is, after all, the only life I have.

I also have the impression that my three "midlife passions" sparked a new kind of creativity that is extremely precious to me, because ultimately I found that the truest, deepest, most lasting, and most rewarding passion of my life has been my work. If each human being were only allotted a single passion in her life, I would choose the passion of work. I try to celebrate my passion for work in "The Passion and Challenge of Teaching," "Making a Difference," "Making a Difference as a Therapist," and "Silences." In many ways, it has been work, rather than love, that has been easier for me. Yet, while I have a passion for work, it is the people that I work with, my students, my colleagues, the friends all over the world to whom work has led me, who make this work so deeply rewarding. I have tried to talk about the interconnection and conflicts between love and work in my life and in women's lives in general, in "Work and Love: the Divided Self" and in "Seduction," perhaps trying to answer my grandfather's famous question, "What does woman want?" Then, in the chapter that bears the title of that question, I try to answer him once again, more formally.

I am happy that "My Three Mothers" could be in the title of my book. My passions for them, in childhood, adolescence, and midlife shaped and punctuated my life. My other passion experiences enriched my life, and each changed its course; they shaped my identity as therapist and educator in crucial ways. My life would have been very different without them. I treasure these experiences as the highlights of my life. I would like this book to be a celebration of passions.

References

Yeats, W. B. (1908). "The Pathway." In *The Collected Works of William Butler Yeats*. Stratford-on-Avon: Shakespeare Head Press.

1 / My Three Mothers

*I*T is not true that I had only three mothers. I have spent much of my life recruiting mothers, seeking and craving the advice, protection, support, and comfort of older, wiser women. One part of my self-image is that of a triumphant queen, the direct descendant of three powerful, talented women, and a prized adopted daughter of other distinguished women. The other part of my divided self is that of an orphan child, roaming the streets in search of a mother who might approve of me and want to get to know me. Orphans, I imagine, are people who have to earn love through hard work, rather than receive it unconditionally. Orphans, I also imagine, are people who continue to need mothers to take care of them, because they missed out on some care taking when they needed it most. It is in these ways that I sometimes feel myself to be an orphan.

I did have three mothers who were of my own kin, who thought of me, at least for a time, as their own daughter, who each in her own way taught me what is important in life, and who each left me a legacy. They were the mother of my childhood, the mother of my early adolescence, and the mother of my late midlife. I would like to understand more deeply how my three mothers shaped my life. I especially want to explore the mutual care taking that went on between each of my three mothers and myself, because I think it lies at the root of my own ability and failure to nurture my own daughters and to be a "good enough" mother to the young women who in turn recruit me for their own needs.

I think of my first mother as the mother of my childhood. She was my biological mother, and our relationship continued throughout her life, but it became static in my adolescence, undifferentiated and distant until her recent death at the age of eighty-six. Later in life, it became quite difficult for me to recapture how deeply attached I must have been to my first mother, but I have numerous childhood photographs in which I melt into her body, while she, always beautifully dressed, stares into the camera. I continue to feel anguish, puzzlement, and guilt about my frozen feelings toward this first mother who seems to have loved me so much. This relationship has set the stage for my constant yearning to be intensely loved, while I remain terrified of the costs should this ever really happen.

First Mother

My first mother grew up as the oldest of three daughters in a well-to-do middle-class Viennese Jewish family. I persuaded her to write her autobiography when she was eighty-two years old, and here are her own words about her childhood: "I did not have a happy childhood at all; most of the time I was terrified of my mother's harsh punishments. I was convinced that my mother hated me, and I suffered very much from her unjust treatment. I was an easy and friendly little girl, but because of what I thought loveless treatment, I became a difficult and morose teenager, made even more unhappy by constant nagging and slapping, and scenes verging on the hysterical made for trifles by my mother."

After the fateful Kristallnacht in November 1938, which escalated the terror against German and Austrian Jews, my mother's widowed mother, initially left behind in Vienna, joined her daughters in Paris. Unlike her three daughters, who all managed to escape from France to America, my maternal grandmother was deported from France to Terezin, which is all we ever learned about her death. My first mother and I never discussed her mother's tragic fate. Neither could I discuss the matter with my second mother, my first mother's youngest sister, who probably never recovered from the guilt of leaving her mother behind when she and her family left France in good time. It became part of my family legacy that daughters rescue their own lives at their mother's expense.

My first mother must have hoped as fervently as I later hoped as a young mother to give her daughter all the love that she had missed. I never experienced her as harsh, nagging, or critical, perhaps because such treatment was reserved for my less favored brother. Besides, as a working woman, she never did attend that closely to my daily activities. I was a much loved and favored child, yet, I think, largely unseen. My first mother was (or became in her disastrous marriage) an unhappy and bitter woman. She married a fairy tale prince, a son of Sigmund Freud, a handsome charming knight whose shiny armor quickly tarnished. Quarrels, tears, and violent hysterical scenes were the background music of my childhood. Later I would enter my own marriage with the tacit agreement never to fight. It is quite sad to realize that the suppression of rage and tears also tends to choke deep love and tenderness. The physical demonstration of intense emotions is inaccessible to me except through written words.

My first mother gave me a model of an ambitious, goal-oriented, and disciplined worker. I also learned from her that relationships to husband, children, and friends lead to betrayal, disappointment, and disaster, while one can count on the satisfactions derived from one's own efforts and accomplishments.

I watched my first mother's anxious and intense preoccupation with preserving her beauty; I secretly resolved, one evening after she had departed in a cloud of scents and adornments, never to paint my face, dye my hair, use perfume, and generally to avoid most other feminine accoutrements. I must have been about six years old.

In spite of her beauty, intelligence, and multiple talents, my first mother was torn and tormented by massive inferiority feelings that encompassed both her personal and her professional life. "Mirror, mirror on the wall, who is the most beautiful of all?" My first mother's life was spent proving that she was a woman of greater beauty, status, intelligence, knowledge, and achievement than her disrespectful, slighting enemies seemed to assume.

My first mother looked to me from early childhood on for solace against the daily injuries of life. She cried in my arms, asked for company at unexpected lonely moments when I was playing with friends, rehearsed her recital pieces under my eight-year-old tutelage. Together we worried acutely whether the audience for her poetry recital would be large enough; whether enough private clients would ask for help with their speech problems; whether she would be included in some important occasion; whether someone of importance would accept an invitation to her party; whether my father would remember to send her red roses for their wedding anniversary. Why did my first mother want red roses from a man who regularly read the newspaper during the one daily meal that he shared with her? After Austria was occupied by the Germans, I remember one early dawn watching my mother and father leave the house together. This image has stayed with me for forty-six years, because their going out together was the most unusual happening in those days of strange happenings. I think they were summoned by the Gestapo to be interrogated.

Was it perhaps my first mother's immense needfulness and my despair about my inability to comfort her that eventually moved me to close my heart to her suffering? Later I would have a daughter who needed to share the unhappiness of a child's daily life with me. I could not bear it; I transformed my pain into anger against her.

After the Anschluss my brother, my father, and his whole family went to London, while my mother and I moved to Paris, where her youngest sister and her family had come from Berlin a few years earlier. I lost overnight a father, albeit an emotionally distant one, an older brother, friends, relatives, my governess, my home, my school, favorite and hated teachers, and a familiar language. This drastic occurrence has become a commonplace twentieth century event for millions of people around the world.

Second Mother

It was at this frightening moment in my life, when I had decided not to become engulfed in my first mother's desperation but to abandon her to her fate, that I found in my maternal aunt my second mother of early adolescence.

My mother's self-doubts sparked a tormenting jealousy. "Who is your favorite grandmother?" she would ask my children, perhaps with sinking heart. Although she matched her youngest sister in beauty and talent and surpassed her in worldly success, she was consumed with envy toward this charming charismatic sister who collected hearts without seeming effort.

My second mother had been, I think, quite intimate with my father, and now she would steal my affection as well. My first mother must have suffered a great deal, but she did not interfere in the relationship. Perhaps she was ready to submit to a fate that had destined her sister to be universally loved, while she was meant to live in emotional isolation. Yet I have a second, more compelling explanation. My first mother was generous toward me and wished me well. I think she hoped that her sister would teach me the art of being loved.

The two sisters, one forever unloved, the other universally loved (or so it seemed), watched each other all their later lives from an unbreachable distance of five blocks in New York City. My aunt was stricken with extreme misfortune when her only son succumbed to mental illness. Although my brother did not speak to his mother for fifteen angry years, she had, after all, raised two children who were able to negotiate life. My first mother must have secretly felt some righting of the fates. My second mother, however, viewed the fates as highly capricious and unfair. "Why did your mother have such luck with her children in that miserably quarrelsome household in which you grew up, while I protected my son from such ugliness?" she would ask me. But that happened much later.

When my second mother received me with open, loving arms as the daughter she had always longed for, she was a vital, passionate woman who presided over a court full of men and women who pleaded for her love, her friendship, her patronage. I stepped from the confining Victorian environment in which I had been raised by a governess into the dazzling, colorful world that this joyous, warm-hearted woman was ready to share with me.

Perhaps it will be a special feast for Freud's numerous historians to learn that his own granddaughter grew to be thirteen and one-half years old without the slightest idea how babies start to grow inside their mothers. My first mother's information about sexual matters had been quite sparse, and I had apparently not been a very curious child. "Don't scratch yourself," she said to me when I was perhaps four years old, whenever my hand would wander below my waist. In my early teens she said to me: "Girls start to bleed at a certain age" after I had suddenly and inexplicably started to bleed and my governess had refused to discuss the matter, "and it means that they are becoming women." "You can always fake it," she said to me and blushed, when I was a young married woman. These were the only sexual conversations with her that I can recall.

In contrast, my second mother radiated sexuality. I would visit her on a late Saturday morning and find her having breakfast in bed, surrounded by disorder. While I threw away the empty whiskey bottles that had a mysterious way of accumulating under her bed and emptied dozens of overflowing ashtrays, she regaled me with exciting stories of love and intrigue.

Great Loves

My second mother's marriage was at least as unhappy as my first mother's, but in a very different way. While my first mother's passionate attachment to her hate-filled and stingy husband survived their forty years of marital separation, my second mother had only contempt tempered by pity for her husband. He was unable to relate to people, but was devoted to his wife and apparently grateful to live in her periphery. No doubt the drama and color that filled her life helped him to forget the deadness within him. While my first mother had turned to a professional career as a source of satisfaction, my second mother found an outlet for her passionate nature in a series of great love affairs. She chose her lovers with great care; I could mention a handful of internationally distinguished men who were honored by having been intimate with her.

Although my second mother provided me with some factual sexual information, she was hardly inclined to drag me into a dishonorable life. She assured me that people who claimed that sex was enjoyable were simply lying. I will never know whether she was acting protectively or sharing her own truth with me. She also vigorously interfered with my timid sexual experimentation. Both of my mothers, sisters after all, were united in wishing to preserve my virginity, guiding me unspoiled to a suitable marriage. Cultural myths about marriage as the solution to a woman's life problems outweighed these two women's private experiences.

At times my second mother would also talk about disappointments. There were short stories she had written that were inevitably returned in the mail; there were tasteful collages out of seashells that could not be marketed; there were the plans for an interior decorating business that never quite took off. Yet these failures were treated with a touch of humor and shrugged off as temporary set-backs. My second mother was not dependent on her earnings and did not share my first mother's starvation fantasies. She had a husband who was adept at earning a great deal of money, which she spent as fast as he could earn it.

Do all mothers prefer to use their daughters rather than their sons as confidantes, in the manner of my first and second mothers? My second mother once had a growth in her breast that needed to be removed. While she confided in me from the very beginning all the anxieties surrounding this fearful event, her son of the same age was never informed of the operation until its benign outcome. Are sons so fragile that they need to be protected from their mothers' emotional and physical vulnerabilities? It could also be true that sons do not make understanding or sympathetic listeners.

The role of confidante has thus become part of my identity, imprinted in childhood and adolescence. Whenever someone comes to the house to repair the refrigerator, or when I go for job interviews, or even in the course of a mere business telephone call, I become the recipient of some significant information about that person's life. As you can see, I am ready in turn to share of myself. Actually I am always hoping that other people might ask me good questions and wait long enough for the answer.

My second mother, just like my first, also wished me a better life than she was leading herself. When I started to smoke she raised such a ruction, imploring me not to follow her nicotine-addicted path, that I desisted smoking forever.

While I was too symbiotically fused with my first mother to

experience love for her, my second mother, who had other close relationships as well, left me enough room to breathe. I think it was my deep feelings for my second mother that laid the seeds for my occasional capacity to love deeply and passionately.

Yet again, I would betray this second mother who had appeared in my life at a moment of extreme need and who had nurtured me with such generosity. Or perhaps we betrayed each other; it is hard to be certain.

After our separate war odysseys, the families reassembled in New York City with children grown into young adulthood. My second mother's son began to court me and I explained to him that I thought of him as a brother, not a lover. Within a few years my second mother's life became absorbed in his illness. She came to visit my young family in Boston and called her son as soon as she arrived, then left after a few hours. "He loved you" she said. "His doctors have told me that your rejection precipitated his illness. I wanted you to marry him; you are a strong woman and could have sustained him." There was a visit in which my second mother watched my oldest daughter, my *Sorgenkind*—the child I had chosen to overlove and worry about, and said, "This child's labile moods are just like your cousin's when he was her age. They seem to have quite similar personalities." After that I never again asked my second mother, whom I had once loved with such great passion, to visit us. I did not see her again before she choked to death, dying of emphysema ten years before my first mother, who was eight years older than she. My second mother did not remember me in her will, yet she left me executor of her son's estate, knowing that she could count on me, her only daughter.

Third Mother

I had failed my first mother in crucial ways and forfeited my second mother, believing that I could hold on to my own life only by forsaking them. But since the gods have favored me in extraordinarily outrageous ways, I found a third chance to redeem myself. I found a third mother who allowed me to help her die, harmoniously, without guilt or betrayal. At the age of fifty-five I journeyed to London for a year, apparently to recruit this third mother for my middle life. She was my grandfather's youngest child, my father's youngest sister, my famous aunt, Anna Freud.

My first mother would never learn of my great love for my paternal aunt, and indeed, that love would bear fruition only after her death. While my first mother had been defeated in her rivalry with her younger sister for the love and admiration of men, she was even more jealous of her sister-in-law's immense worldly recognition, which would have meant so much to her.

My love for my aunt might have seemed an act of treason to her. It is, however, more likely that my mother wanted me to repair the rift created forty years earlier between us and the Freud family. Why else would she have told me so often through the years, frequently in anger and sometimes in admiration, that I looked and acted like a typical Freud?

As a last act of generosity my first mother waited to die until I had returned from my sabbatical. I was too frozen to thank her fully for always having wished me well, but I was able to bid her good-bye, and she did not seem to hold grudges against me. Until her death, she nurtured me the best she could.

The image of my third mother had accompanied me all through life. I worked in a field related to hers, and I regularly read her books and articles and went to lectures that she sometimes gave in the Boston area. We exchanged yearly holiday greetings, but I felt too timid and unworthy to approach her more closely even when we lived temporarily in the same town. My aunt in turn treated me coldly, like a stranger or worse, on our occasional encounters.

As I had listened to her lecturing, simple and modest in her demeanor yet speaking with great force and clarity and without notes, she had evoked my intense admiration. Simply dressed and mostly unadorned, she always struck me into her old age and even after her stroke as the most beautiful woman I had ever met. I wanted to become such a woman. When I was a young woman her words were gospel to me; later I lost my faith in that religion, but I remained tactful and cautious about expressing different opinions. It is perhaps fortunate that we met at a point when theories hardly mattered any longer.

I do not know what mysterious forces suddenly compelled me

at such a late age to seek out this stern and distant aunt and ask her blessing before she died. Was I merely carrying out my mother's mission? Was it perhaps my last chance to repair the broken relationship with my long-dead father? Or did I want to make up for the hurt of having been excluded from my grandfather's last year and death? My mother had bequeathed me her self-doubts as well as a determination to defeat them. Perhaps I needed this third and deeply admired mother's love as a victory over my self-doubts.

My campaign to win my eighty-two-year-old aunt's well-guarded heart could never have been deliberately designed. The relationship developed like a sequence of movie shots, in which I played my assigned part from day to day without clear knowledge of the plot or the outcome. Only in retrospect am I able to admire my skillful strategies, my tenacity, the infinite guile and bribery that I deployed during that year. Some of my friends have said that it should not be so hard to win someone's love. Yet athletes train for years to win an Olympic medal and do not feel that they worked too hard for the prize.

Our first meeting was in Grandfather's large calcified office-museum. We both sat in semisilence and shivered with cold. "I am tired" she said. "I am sorry to disturb you," I answered. However, that winter her life companion died, and I found it possible to move into that empty space in her life. Occasional visits, which I always had to initiate, slowly turned into daily ever-longer evenings in which I sat next to her bedside and listened to her reminiscences of the war years. Sometimes we would simply sit together in silence and attend to our individual knitting. "Look, I finished this baby sweater," I said. She examined the piece carefully. "You forgot to reverse one of the cables," she said kindly. "I always unravel my knitting whenever I discover a mistake." Often we laughed together. I realized with delight that my worldly third mother was also a child at heart.

I found my readjustment after the sabbatical very difficult and was often sad that year, and our active correspondence became my greatest source of comfort. I still weep with longing when I think of her willingness to get to know me: "I am worried that you write that you are depressed and that painful things are happening. Will you let me know what they are? I would like to share them with you." My third mother, not unlike myself, found it easier to say loving things at a distance. Her verbal expressions of affection would remain forever cautious, momentary, and indirect, leaving me yearning and uncertain. Yet they would reach me.

She regularly advised me to comfort myself by becoming absorbed in my work. It was the way she herself had coped with sorrow in her life. My first and third mother have taught me self-discipline and an appreciation of the pleasures of work. My second mother introduced me to passion. None of my three mothers could teach me how to be a loving wife or a wise mother. No wonder I never excelled in those skills, nor did I find it easy to teach them to my daughters. I hope they find other mothers to teach them what I could not.

I carried my third mother's letters with me, like talismans to be read over and over in quiet moments. In turn, I wrote her passionate love letters. "It is quite inconvenient for you," she wrote back "to be in love with such an old aunt."

I could explain that I fell so passionately in love with my third mother because she became so kind and accepting toward me; or because she would share with me memories of her life; or because she showed such spontaneous childlike pleasure with the gifts that I always found for her; or because she bore her illness and approaching death with such great courage; or because I was awed by her worldly fame; but it would miss the essence of my love, which could not be explained by reason.

I visited my third mother two more summers in London, and as she became increasingly ill and eventually semiparalyzed by a stroke, she allowed me the privilege of helping to take care of her during those visits. I peeled grapes for her and held her shaking head as she tried to drink. I sat next to her chaise-longue and read her a very dull book sent to her for comments, and she invariably fell asleep. Then she woke up and said: "Continue reading, I am listening, I love your voice and I love your accent." She always smiled at me when she woke up, and sometimes she laid her hand against mine. "Look," she said, "we have similar hands." As the sun moved, we moved the chaise-longue so that I could sit in the sun while she preferred the shade. We took care of each other.

After I left London with a most heavy heart that last summer, she wrote: "It was beautiful that you were here and your departure has left a hole. My thoughts accompany you in your life at home. Do not be sad and I wish you all the best." I returned to London a second time that summer and slept next to her room and we spent this last week fully together. "Now you have found a daughter after all," I said, and she smiled and nodded her head. I had certainly won my gold medal, many many gold medals.

My three mothers have all died. It is sad to be an orphan even when one is sixty years old. It is hard to pretend all the time that one is an independent grown-up woman. When my last mother died I was inconsolable. My great love for her and her reciprocal affection for me had given meaning to my life. I shall never quite recover from her loss.

I like to think that each of my three mothers has chosen me for her spiritual reincarnation. While my three mothers are physically dead, they are very much alive for me.

2 / The Last Sabbatical: "The Summer Before the Dark"

Was schert mich Weib, was schert mich Kind!
. . .Lasz sie betteln gehn, wenn sie hungrig sind—

(To hell with wife, to hell with child
. . .let them go begging, if they are hungry)

"DIE GRENADIERE," HEINRICH HEINE 1837

Much of our lives is taken up with separations and new beginnings, exits and entries, departures and arrivals. Transitions are an intrinsic part of development, but they are often painful.

LEVINSON 1980, p. 279

The private voice in the public sphere confirms our common experience through which we begin to assert ourselves.

METZGER 1976, p. 408

IN the middle of my life I packed my bags, left my family, friends, students, and job, and went three thousand miles across the sea. I did not desert my home, never to return, although admittedly that thought had crossed my mind. I left on a legitimate, socially sanctioned trip, a sabbatical duly earned after eight years of faithful academic service. Ever since adolescence I had worked while I went to school, worked while I raised children, and driven myself relentlessly in search of illusive recognition. Suddenly I was pre-sented with the fantastic, awesome gift of a whole year to do with as I pleased. I decided to leave town.

I left to escape the continuously escalating pressure of duties, ob-ligations, structures, and expectations that surround even a modest academic career. I left to learn some new clinical skills. I left in search of experiences and lessons different from those connected with my life as educator and guru. I left to reconnect with my European past and to gain experiences that I had missed in life. I left to claim the carefree adolescence that had escaped me in my own youth, overshadowed by war, emigration, poverty, and alienation.

Why should I write about an experience that touches only aca-demics, a small elitist group in our society? In our world of increas-ingly fluid and changing timetables (Neugarten, 1979) there are many people who have similar life experiences. Some, like Kate Brown in *The Summer Before the Dark*, have only one free summer. Others may convalesce after an illness (Schwerin 1976) or drop out in adoles-cence, go back to school as an adult, or have a similar "out of or-der" experience: a life interval in which daily routines are inter-rupted and a reflective turning inward is both permitted and even invited.

. . . many people declare moratoria. . . . They also declare periods for the consolidation of psychological gains, periods for resting upon laurels after success, periods for personal trial or probation, periods for expiation of sins, periods for contemplation, periods for prolonged self-search-ing. (Strauss 1962, p. 81)

Such an interval, however long or short, may recapitulate an en-tire life in microcosm. There is entrance into the new life, decisions about how to spend the available time, efforts to wring meaning from the chosen activities, and the eventual end of that interval, a form of death. Existential answers found during this time may al-low a glimpse of an alternate, more creative use of self, which may later become incorporated into one's "real life" or, more likely, re-main identified with that unique period of freedom.

I have used current theories to order my experiences. In one year I faced all the major issues that the social science literature attributes to midlife. I was very struck that literature on both male and female development seemed to fit my own experience, and I have freely drawn on both. I experienced the opposite yet similar pulls of work and love (Smelser and Erikson 1980); conflicts about use of time (Smelser 1980; Neugarten 1979; Levinson 1978, 1980); the need to recapture disowned aspects of the self (Fiske 1980; Levinson 1980; Gould 1980; Neugarten 1979); changing life priorities and commitments (Fiske 1980); changing identities (Strauss 1962); and changing defensive patterns (Gould 1980; Vaillant 1977); the struggle for self-love (Gould 1980; Levinson 1978); dealing with polarities such as intimacy versus freedom (Neugarten 1979), attachment versus separateness (Levinson 1978), getting old versus remaining young (Levinson 1978); and acknowledging both masculine and feminine aspects of the self (Levinson 1978). And perhaps we can add the polarity of loving versus being loved, and wooing versus being wooed.

I said that I was in the middle of my life when I left home, but that is not exactly true. I had already lived out two-thirds of my alloted life span. Thus, there was not only the problem of using one particular life interval creatively, but also the knowledge that this would be the last period in which I did not yet quite embody the identity of "an old woman," at least not in my own self-image. It was a last chance to realize the unlived adventures, to deal with the unsolved problems, to escape the multiple constraints of mature adulthood, a last chance to be young (Levinson 1978, p. 210). I invested this period with all the passion and poignancy such an experience calls for.

I spent my adolescence in three different language communities and as many continents, longing for a stable, secure, and settled life. For the many years that followed I had not wished to travel. It was more important to establish roots, a sense of being needed, belonging, and becoming a valued member of a family, a school, and even of a whole professional community. And then suddenly, after having attained those goals, I started to feel unbearably oppressed. I felt captured and imprisoned by all the people who loved and admired me, by the very people who had given meaning to my life. So I decided to leave them all—for a time.

Three days earlier he was still at home. In his house, with a woman both gentle and melancholy. And colleagues, some friendly, some envious. . . . The same burdens the same alibis. Suddenly he felt like leaving it all. Without a word. Leave. For a few days. Or a few years. And breathe. and remain silent; remain silent at last.   (Wiesel 1965 p. 107)

"I am going abroad for a sabbatical," I said in a voice loud and clear, never believing that I could do it. "Your place is with your husband and children," said my aged mother, whose place had never particularly been with her husband and children. "Please don't do anything crazy or irrational," wrote my brother, whose life had been impoverished by lack of enterprise. "Of course you won't do this," said my worst friend. "You are much too responsible to leave all the people here who depend on you." "Your regular visits have been the joy and comfort of these last ten years," said my increasingly paralyzed friend. "Far out," said my daughter, and while I did not know that expression, it sounded approving. My husband said nothing, being a man of few words. And in the midst of envious, disapproving, and encouraging colleagues, friends, and family members, I realized that all had taken my announcement seriously and would let me leave. My children were of course all adult and living their own lives. Please believe me, I have always been a painfully conscientious mother.

I don't know why I had to leave on this sabbatical. I had always been such an honorable woman, by which I mean doing what was expected of me, yet I longed to escape the personal and professional constraints of my daily life. Maybe my story will lead us to an answer.

Coming to a strange city always reminds me of the days when I was thirteen years old, having newly arrived in Paris after emigrating from Vienna. Overnight I had left an entire community of family and friends. It was a time when I transformed myself from a little girl, who cried every time someone looked crossly at her, to a determined survivor. It now seemed to me that I had gone through life so bent on raising children to the best of my ability, establishing a career, finding a respected place in society, that I had needed to put aside some of my deepest emotional needs. Perhaps not accidentally my return to Europe would revive the greater openness and vulnerability of my more passionate childhood self.

When I arrived in London at the age of fifty-six, I became once again a frightened little girl. I had to learn the value of foreign money and the secrets of a new transportation system. Even the intricacies of making a telephone call seemed difficult to master. Nevertheless, this time I entered the new setting armed with decades of emotional and intellectual resources. Part of my agenda had been to reexperience the old traumas of adaptation to a foreign culture, but under circumstances that I knew I could master.

For many weeks I watched myself walk around the big city, mechanically visiting places of interest, faithfully leading weekly seminars and attending conferences, but I felt nothing at all. In spite of the fact that my colleagues were friendly enough, they were also essentially indifferent strangers. I was unable to understand why I had abandoned a city full of friends and deliberately exposed myself to an alien environment. Yet my depersonalization was so great that it eclipsed ordinary feelings of loneliness. I missed no one, cared about no one, and seemed to need nothing.

Soon after I arrived I became ill. Fortunately, I was able to get out of bed every morning and attend the clinic where I had, in spite of being a marginal member, an assigned place and definite role. I could not have stayed abroad without membership in a social system.

Like the illness of the heroine of *The Summer Before the Dark*, mine was similarly mysterious, lingering, and debilitating.

. . . she was sure she would die, hoped that she would, and by the time she reached London was sustained only by thinking of her own bed, in her own room, with its flowered curtains. . . . oh she could not wait to be back in her own home, with possibly even one of the children back from somewhere and able to help her. (Lessing 1973, p. 133)

Kate Brown understood that she could not return home, and neither could I consider such a solution. I imagined that my extreme weakness and multiple system infections were an indication of leukemia, and I too was prepared to die. It was a possibility that I could somehow finally contemplate without unbearable anguish. It was certainly easier than going home with an abysmal sense of failure. Never again did I want to be a dependent little girl who needs other people to take care of her. Besides, at the time, I no longer remembered those people at home. It turned out I had mononucleosis, a diagnosis which served the two purposes of relieving my anxiety and helping me to get well.

Once we start counting time as "time left to live" (Neugarten 1968, p. 97) rather than time from the beginning, time becomes a most precious commodity, the starkest and most irrevocable constraint under which we live. The decision on how to use my sabbatical was invested with all the panic of contemplating the unaccomplished in view of a dwindling lifetime. I faced this panic a few weeks after settling down in my new community. I had taken twenty-five books with me, as well as the raw research data from a study from which I was to write a book. And suddenly I was faced with the realization that if I wanted to explore my new setting, I would have time neither to read my twenty-five books nor to write my own book; I would not even have time to become an expert in the professional skills that I had hoped to acquire in the overseas clinic. Besides, I found myself wanting to read different books, not the ones I had brought along, and not even books that would eventually be useful for my teaching.

For years I had led a life totally regulated by the clock, with an obsessive attempt to waste neither hours nor even minutes, and suddenly all that had changed.

The hours flew by. He wasn't aware of time. Before, it had filled him with anguish. Time-conscious? More than that: time-obsessed. Not any more. He was living outside time. No clock, no obligations. No need to pretend being busy, entertained, interested, moved. He would get up and go to sleep whenever he chose. (Wiesel 1965, p. 108)

For two weeks I wrestled with the option to return home and continue the path of frantic productivity that would eventually lead to achievement and glory, the ultimate proof that I was a worthwhile human being. Then, with the help of my assigned tutor at the clinic—oh, what joy to be able to turn to a woman who was older and wiser—I resolved *to be* rather than *to do*.

He lives more in the present and gains more satisfaction from the process of living—from being rather than doing and having. (Levinson 1978, p. 242)

If "being" was too alien to my accustomed life-style, I could at least experiment with new ways of "doing." I certainly did continue to write a few papers, teach some courses, and pursue the clinical work at hand, but these activities, compared to my usual tempo, amounted to taking one huge vacation. Essentially, I allowed myself to waste nine months of the fifty-sixth year of my life. It was the most generous and extravagant gift that I had granted myself in my life journey.

Only after I reached this decision did I find in myself the freedom to value and enjoy the many opportunities for learning that my new community could offer me.

When one has participated in a social system for a while, debts and credits become embedded in a network of mutual privileges and obligations. But when one enters a new system, decisions on how to pay one's way must be made. I had been accepted in a clinical training program and assigned a position halfway between staff and trainee. My teaching responsibilities in the program helped me to sustain my identity as an educator, but my double status also created some confusion and uncertainty for me. I felt myself to be a graciously accepted guest who was taking up one of a limited number of learning places. The need to repay my hosts for their hospitality and to establish myself as a contributing member, thereby justifying their generous welcome, was always in my mind.

I realize now that I was only replaying my customary life stance. I am used to keeping track of my debts, perhaps because of having incurred in adolescence the enormous debt of becoming a guest/refugee in the United States rather than being killed in the Holocaust. In my meetings in Europe with my brother, my old Fraeulein in Vienna, and friends from childhood and adolescence, I continued to marvel at the wonder and triumph of our having survived the war. We are a generation of survivors. This is an integral part of my identity.

On some level, I continue to be grateful to every institution that has given me a place, every school that has accepted me as a student or teacher. I try to "pay my way" within my abilities. It is not always admirable to pay one's way. Opposites tend to be the same and my mental bookkeeping has an ungenerous quality and clashes with my critical, rebellious, and revolutionary self. As a member of a social system, I pay my way through emotional engagement, manifested at the lowest level by my effort to keep everyone provoked, awake, and alive, perhaps to a fault,

While the wish and hope to be needed has been a driving force in my life, the fulfillment of this wish has created resentment and a sense of being exploited, used, and overused by my human community. I went abroad to escape being "used up" and, once established, I systematically started to relinquish the very anonymity I had sought out so eagerly.

A Woman of Power

My home and community have accorded me not only respect and affection, but a feeling that I am a woman of power, a most confidence-building and sustaining self-concept in midlife. I never experienced an antithesis between the exercise of power and love (Levinson 1978, p. 228) or even between power and femininity (Rubin 1979, p. 64), although others may view my need to take charge and "get things done" (Levinson 1978, p. 232) as a masculine trait. My concern about power was whether it was simply a loan from my community, or whether I could count on it as an integral part of myself.

I had sufficient self-doubts not to rely on being welcomed just for my personal qualities. In packing my bags, I needed to take along academic titles, publications, and famous maiden name. Some of this baggage I even sent ahead; I wanted to be well received by my new community.

Fortunately or unfortunately, such ornaments provide entrance, but no more. Recognition and respect need to be *earned* in each new setting. I was in a Gestalt workshop with a very effective woman leader of my age, and she turned to me and asked: "Why are you looking me over like that?" "I am interested in watching another woman guru in action," I replied. "Another?

How many do you meet?" "I am the other one," I said. There was much derisive laughter in the group. Clearly my unfair claim to power was creating resentment and incredulity.

Must I conclude that power is not something that I have, but rather something that my social network accords me, to be used as long as I serve it well? It is quite possible in life to sit back and hope that engaging things might happen. This is not my way. I am willing to work very hard to make things happen. I lend my energy to the people and activities that intersect with my life. By the time I left the clinic in which I worked I had reinstated myself as a woman of power. I had not realized that I would be able to do this. I shall never forget the generosity of that foreign community willing to accept and respect my contributions.

Paradoxically, however, my new role of trainee reminded me also of what it means to be a student, and of the risks this role entails. There is the risk of asking questions that might provoke resentment, the risk of making demands and being seen as a person with an excessive sense of entitlement, the risk that one's knowledge and experience may be resented as a threat, remain unrecognized, or become devalued. As a teacher of adult students, who come to study after some years of successful work, I found it enormously helpful to experience for myself what students confront: the sense of powerlessness, helplessness, fear of exposure, and fear of displeasing authority.

Having resolved the transitional crisis of adapting to a different use of time (or use of self), and feeling physically well again, I emerged with a renewed surge of energy and zest. If not all my life energy was going to be directed to a relentless schedule of work, I was ready to seek new challenges. I was about to validate the idea that work and love are after all not such very different life pursuits, requiring on the contrary, quite similar talents and investments.

In the light of these evident similarities between the processes of working and loving it might be appropriate to regard the two as different names for a very similar process of human adaptation, both involving a fusion of the different psychic forces—impulse, discipline or control, integration, and object attachment . . . in fact the two orientations are so inextricably meshed that it becomes difficult to distinguish between them. For example one can love one's work, and one can—indeed, is well advised to work at love. (Smelser 1980, p. 105)

Over the years I have built up a large and solid network of friendships with women. We dare to burden each other with fears and sorrows, offering reflection, support, and practical help in times of stress. We confide our murderous fantasies against our "loved ones," and we care about each other's physical well-being.

With one friend of my age we cheerfully exchange the worst symptoms and our black dreads as well. (Scott-Maxwell 1968, p. 31)

We even forgive each other our triumphs, gracefully expressing whatever envy gets aroused. However, with family, friends, and students all competing for limited time, I found neither time, energy, nor inclination to initiate new and perhaps challenging relationships. I had come to feel that my friendship was a coveted prize that would be honored and appreciated. I had become accustomed to being wooed. But deep down I am a woman who would rather woo than be wooed. My temporary unmet needs for human connections, affirmation, and caring allowed me to develop that part of myself, since it led me to take exceptional risks in reaching out to people. I approached the task of building a new network of human relationships with all the energy, talent, and passion that I had used in the working world.

It was an exciting challenge to practice wooing in foreign places, and my efforts were well rewarded. As I travel through the world, I have two important identities that facilitate my opportunity to connect with people. The first is my membership in the international social work community, a community whose interest and willingness to extend itself to me I deeply appreciate. The second is my identity as a woman able to accept and share most experiences that women face. I want to learn from them and am willing to ask them questions that they have hoped for a long time to be asked.

When I am with other people I try to find them, or try to find a point in myself from which to make a bridge to them, or walk on egg-shells of affection trying not to hurt or misjudge. (Scott-Maxwell 1968, p. 14)

Daughters and Sons

I found very soon that in my new community, as had been true at home, young women were seeking my friendship. "Some of the issues of middle age . . . include the need to nurture and to act as model, guide or mentor to the young" (Neugarten 1979, p. 890). Professional midlife women of my generation do not merely act as mentors for a few young people, as do professional men (Levinson 1978, pp. 251–255). We have to be guide, permission giver, and inspiration for a generation of young women who are seeking new models.

Who are the matriarchs—the Demeters? They can't be the mothers who socialized us to accept Pluto. Are they the lonely giants who shimmer mirage-like in the garbage heaps of male knowledge and acceptance? Anaïs Nin, Margaret Mead, Eleanor Roosevelt, Greta Garbo, Eva Curie? Who is there to be like? (Cooper 1979, p. 32)

Young women who have rejected their mothers' traditional life-styles need help in finding new ways to live in a changing, unpredictable society. Confused and ambivalent these women are often caught between their mothers' contradictory missions. They must justify and make up for the failures and disappointments in their mothers' lives, yet do so without showing contempt for their mothers' life-styles, without taking undue risks, and without flaunting the social order. "You can be anything you really want to be . . . [but] don't go too far" (Rich 1976, p. 248; Rubin 1979, p. 43; Stierlin 1972).

Women recognize in me that potential "counter-mother" who might give them permission and courage to lead a different life. Since I have long ago lost all convictions about the one and only good life that is to be found, I can sometimes meet their needs. However, I too feel myself to be a badly mothered daughter.

But the motherless woman may also react by denying her own vulnerability, denying she has felt any loss or absence of mothering. She may spend her life proving her strength in the "mothering" of others . . . mothering men . . . ., whose weakness makes her feel strong, or mothering in the role of teacher, doctor, psychotherapist. (Rich 1976, p. 24)

My mother's triple legacy has weighed heavily on me all my life. First, I had to earn the public recognition that she desperately wanted, without which she could not love herself. Second, I had to carry out her vengeance against her husband's famous name, and third, I had to honor this name, which was such a strong base for her own self-respect. I have been a dutiful daughter in these respects, but my yearning for a good fantasy mother has been a lifelong search. "I wanted another mother . . . when I was young. I wanted a mother who liked herself, who liked her body and so would like mine . . . my mother did not like herself . . . that is part of the definition of who she was and who I am. She was my mother" (MacDonald 1979, p. 13).

As always, establishing significant relationships with men who crossed my paths in my life abroad was much more difficult than making important connections with women. The lack of talent for friendship among many middle-class men has been frequently documented (Levinson 1978, p. 335; Schlossberg and Kent 1979, p. 280). "You seem to have made more friends in this city in half a year than I have in the last forty years," my brother said to me in an envious tone. Although he would like to be my friend and is faithful and loyal to me, he is unwilling, perhaps afraid, to know me. True friendship with him was therefore initially difficult. Yet, we are working on it and things are changing between us. I am hopeful.

My major emotional commitments have always been to women. Although I had worked with men as students and colleagues, few of my relationships with men had lived up to my requirements of mutual openness, caring, availability, and support, as had my relationships with women. I wondered whether friendship with men was possible for me.

We worked in small clinical teams, and I was assigned to work with two male colleagues and one male supervisor, all three of whom could have been my sons. I feel embarrassed to admit that I was not satisfied to take the role of equal colleague in that group. " . . . it was noticeable that when she was absent from the committee things did not go smoothly . . . for no other reason than that she was unable to switch herself out of the role of provider of invisible mana, consolation, warmth, sympathy. . . . She had been set like a machine by twenty odd years of being a wife and mother" (Lessing 1973, pp. 45, 46). Was it *my* needs or those of the three men that made me become responsible for the emotional welfare of this little family? I tried to create group solidarity, assured communication among members, and became their nurturing, supportive mother and their critical, praising, and challenging teacher. The men accepted my input, rewarding me with the affection and appreciation due to a good mother/teacher while being relatively oblivious to my separate identity, including my needs, hopes, fears, and wishes. Of course, they were even less sensitive to each others' needs. "Not having to maintain a rigid division between work . . . and personal relationship, he can combine work and friendship in various admixtures" (Levinson 1978, p. 237).

Being a woman in midlife I disrupted the rigid boundaries between work and friendship that these younger men had set up for themselves. There were times when the effort to reach out to these distant men wearied me. But the pleasure of taking care of three attractive, intelligent young men far outweighed other considerations. It was a sobering encounter with what I thought was my feminism when I found myself reaching out to *men* with more initiative and persistence than I usually display when starting friendships with *women*. "The gap between intellectual acceptance of new roles and emotional comfort is often a difficult one to close" (Lemkau 1980, p. 131; also Rubin 1979, pp. 63–64).

At the age of fifty-six, I still sought a woman who not only would be a model of intellectual achievement, but who might also show me that it is safe to become old, and that it might even be possible to die with a sense of inner peace. She would need to be a woman who loved herself well enough, and would love me as well, but not too much, since she had to remain comfortably distant and separate. Finding such a woman and wooing her with passion and wisdom became the most challenging and ultimately joyful pursuit of my sabbatical year.

It is possible to fall in love with children, women, men, activities, or ideas. I fell in love with two human beings during my sabbatical, and one of them was my eighty-two-year-old aunt, Anna Freud. I knew that if I could win her love and receive her blessing I could forgive my father and come to terms with the heavy legacy of the Freud family. "He may feel he was cheated or done in by the tribe during early adulthood. If as a youngster he broke away from his origins, he may now attempt some form of rapprochement" (Levinson 1978, p. 242).

Although neither my aunt nor I were aware of feeling disappointed or betrayed by the other, it turned out that there was much to be forgiven. I learned through others that she was bitter that I had not become a psychoanalyst or at least asked to study in her clinic. In turn, I felt that my powerful family had expelled me from its ranks and abandoned me during the war. Family therapists encourage family members to discuss their grievances so they can come to forgive each other. This was not the path we took.

My initial goals were modest: I wanted her to offer me a cup of tea and give me a kiss. The effort of telephoning her repeatedly when I felt like such an unwelcome burden caused me much anguish. But I brought to my quest a lifetime of being loved and accepted by many human beings, an optimism about my ability to reach people, and an inner conviction of the importance and purity of my mission. I seem to have planned the campaign of winning my old aunt's guarded heart with no less care than Napoleon must have planned the campaign of Waterloo, but Napoleon lost his campaign of destruction, while I won my campaign of love.

I also grew to love a man in my life abroad. I perceived him as both engaging and distant, sensitive to feelings and afraid of them, alternately confirming and disconfirming, and perhaps vulnerable in spirit and body. He seemed to me a complex and interesting human being. We met in mutual massive projections. I was his mother, sister, and mentor. He was my father, brother, son, and husband. He admired me with all the ambivalence that this entails. We occasionally worked together and exchanged creative ideas. I was charmed by his ability to hear sometimes what was meant rather than what was said. He did not ask me many questions, except now and then—important occasions. We also had some conflicting views, and the possibility arose that we might clash. I was older than he, and my voice was louder. As a solution to this conflict, I fell in love with him, and the danger passed. Voluntarily I took on the masochistic position of an aging woman who loves a man who is not there for her. He said, "It is useful to discuss one's work with an objective observer." He also said, "Some people come and go, but others leave a deep impact."

It would have made me extremely happy to experience with this man some mutual openness, a loving friendship, perhaps some expressions of tenderness. He did not allow any of these things to happen. Falling in love in such a ridiculous way two-thirds through my life caused me a piercing pain that lasts and lasts. Yet this love put me in touch with my passionate self, which I had lost through the years. I lived in a state of semiintoxication for many months. It was certainy worth the price. Is that the face of midlife love?

While relationships with men were thus somewhat problematic, there were also significant incidents during my travels that held out the possibility that the souls of men and women can sometimes meet.

The first day in a new town fills me not with joyous and curious enterprise but with dread and alienation. I am waiting for an evening conference, and a long and lonely afternoon stretches before me. I walk into a student cafeteria and settle next to the table of a young man who sits alone. "I am a stranger in this town," I say to him, "and I feel lost and lonely. Would you talk to me a little about yourself?" He is startled for only a minute, and then he comes to sit next to me. He is writing his dissertation on a subject close to my own field. We are both eager to exchange perspectives and information. He is delighted to be speaking to such an interesting American professor. The town has become a friendly place. A single person can humanize a whole city.

A letter comes to me in the mail from a Frenchman whom I had known in my youth. He had found me through a newspaper article. We agreed to meet. We had met during the war years in Casablanca, where he, a non-Jew, had escaped from the Germans. He was living there with a foster family who was hosting him until he could join the French forces abroad. He had to leave this family suddenly without ever thanking them, and this was now haunting him. Last year his son had died in a car accident. He had contracted a progressive bone disease and had chosen early retirement. He was a quiet man in profound despair. We spent a day together and I said little. But I did encourage him to contact his family in Morocco, which was easy enough. Later he writes to me, "I have gone to Morocco to thank Mr. and Mrs. L., eighty-five and ninety-five years old. We had a large and joyous family reunion. When I came back I felt so much better that I returned to work part-time. Meeting you again changed my life."

All of us have had experiences in which our presence in someone's life, or their presence in ours, however ephemeral, made a profound difference. Our interdependence for emotional survival is awesome.

While I worked and played with men during my stay abroad and fell in love with one of them, it was women who were there for me. There was my older advisor, who sustained me through the successive crises of arrival, illness, grief, and departure; there were my younger friends in the support group that we built for ourselves, who gave me the consensual validation that meant so much to me; and there was the beginning of a profound friendship with a German woman who has become my younger sister.

I used to think that it took years of acquaintance and many hours of being together to build a solid and lasting friendship. As my life rapidly gets shorter I realize that it need not take that long. It is possible for two people who trust each other to connect deeply in a short period of time, and when a certain critical point is reached, lasting bonds may be established. Through those multiple relationships in many parts of the world, I have renewed my world citizenship.

. . . a higher level of individuation both requires and allows a higher level of relatedness. . . . Progress in individuation demands, therefore, ever new levels of communication and reconciliation. (Stierlin et al. 1980, p. 17)

After traveling to Austria and Germany, I established deeply significant relationships with German colleagues and recaptured with intense pleasure the language of my childhood. Warm encounters in Israel strengthened my Jewish identity. My life space now encompasses the fate of many people in different countries, and my sense of world interdependence is no longer a theoretical concept.

I had solved the terror of my aloneness in late adolescence by finding a mate who was my kin in every way. As Jewish immigrants—he from Germany and I from Austria—we had already met in France, and we had a deep understanding of each other's cultural backgrounds. We formed a tight partnership and together we built quite a good life for ourselves, exorcising the ghosts of poverty, loneliness, and strangeness in a new country.

In middle life I longed for the experience of living alone. In our coupled society the needs for separateness are dangerous to express. They are taboo needs that married women must deny and suppress. I would feel even more guilty and deviant if I had not encountered similar feelings in other women, expressed in secrecy and with shame. "I wonder if living alone makes one more alive. No precious energy goes in disagreements or compromise. No need to augment others, there is just yourself, just truth—a morsel—and you" (Scott-Maxwell 1968, p. 33).

The freedom to plan one's life without consideration for another human being can be liberating: the freedom to come home in the evening, to stay out and see a movie, or to pay a visit to a friend; the freedom to eat an evening meal or skip it; to go to sleep at 7:00 p.m. without explanation or to stay up most of the night to finish writing a paper.

He would get up and go to sleep whenever he chose. No one would ask: Where were you? Or: Whom did you see? Or: Why are you late: No one would try to make him forget or remember. He would be alone at dusk and still alone at dawn. Not like a prisoner in his cell; like a fugitive in the forest. (Wiesel 1965, p. 108)

I treasured the time alone, the quiet evening after a busy day full of people. I was even glad when I found that I could not get a telephone, thus gaining even more protection for my solitude when I wanted it. As much as I had feared loneliness when I was young, I now needed aloneness in middle life. " . . . he can draw more upon his inner resources and is thus less dependent on external stimulation. He enjoys solitude more since he has internal company . . . " (Levinson 1978, p. 242). I was jealous of these nine

months of independence and asked my family and friends not to
visit me, although I appreciated our correspondence. I had taken
nine months of my life to be separate, and I wanted no one to
step on this piece of time that was all mine. I also valued my
single state because it gave me an opportunity to relate to the
world not as a couple, but as a woman who could meet others
on her own in face to face encounters. My single friends who
envy my married state tell me that I could enjoy my singleness
only because it was temporary and unreal. That is probable, since
it is of course both separateness and attachment that we need. I
have always admired de Beauvoir and Sartre as one couple who
managed both. I want to give honest testimony to my somewhat
ruthless and unwomanly drive for autonomy and independence
in middle life. Perhaps this drive for separateness may be a factor
in midlife divorces. Perhaps our society needs to make provisions
to meet these midlife needs without having to sever longtime human bonds (Neugarten 1979, p. 889).

By the time it was all over with, she would certainly not have chosen
it for herself in advance, for she did not have the experience to choose,
or the imagination . . . Choose? When do I ever choose? Have I ever
chosen?   (Lessing 1973, p. 6)

Once again I am in a strange town, but this time it is the one
where I have spent most of my adult life. I sit among the trees
while the gypsy moths are eating all their leaves and their bark,
the bushes, and the flowers. The trees are dying, and in the silence I can hear the crunching of the caterpillars and the falling
of their droppings like a continuous rain.

I am faced with the loss of a whole community of people in
which I had invested my emotions. I wait for the mail and I am
relieved when letters arrive. It is my only proof that I have not
invented the whole experience, that it was not a mere dream about
a reckless carefree vacation. Like other dreams, it is about to disappear. My friends tell me that they missed me and that I will
feel better soon. They are strangers and they do not understand
me.

I do not remember the joys and satisfactions that I found in my former life. Will life consist of teaching more and more courses and writing more and more papers? "When a man confronts the realization that his occupational career has peaked, not only is he likely to feel anxious and insecure, but he may be prompted to reflect on his work in terms of such questions as 'What was it all for?'" (Fiske 1980, p. 247).

The meaning of my life has escaped me and I cannot recapture it. I need to settle down and age with dignity, but it is hard to grow up. "Good things have gone, and some good things will always go when new things come and we mourn. We mourn rightly for the outlook is uncertain, perhaps very dark" (Scott-Maxwell 1968, p. 86).

References

Carruth, J. (1975). "Crises: An abstract model versus individual experience." In N. Datan and L. Ginsberg (Eds.). *Life-Span Developmental Psychology*. New York: Academic Press.

Cooper, B. (1979). "Notes from the fifty-ninth year." *Sinister Wisdom* 10:9–14.

Fiske, M. (1980). "Changing hierarchies of commitment in adulthood." In N. J. Smelser and E. H. Erikson (Eds.). *Themes of Work and Love in Adulthood*. Cambridge: Harvard University Press.

Giele, J. Z. (1980). "Adulthood as transcendence of age and sex." In N. J. Smelser and E. H. Erikson (Eds.).*Themes of Work and Love in Adulthood*. Cambridge: Harvard University Press.

Gould, R. (1980). "Transformations during early and middle adult years." In N. J. Smelser and E. H. Erikson (Eds.). *Themes of Work and Love in Adulthood*. Cambridge: Harvard University Press.

Heine, Heinrich. (1837). "Die Grenadiere." In *Heine's Saemtliche Werke*, 3d ed. Erster Band. Leipzig, Germany: Der Tempel Verlag.

Lemkau, J. P. (1980). "Women and employment: Some emotional hazards." In C. L. Heckerman (Ed.). *The Evolving Female*. New York: Human Sciences Press.

Lessing, D. (1973). *The Summer Before the Dark*. New York: Bantam.

Levinson, D. J. (1980). "Toward a conception of the adult life course." In N. J. Smelser and E. H. Erikson (Eds.). *Themes of Work and Love in Adulthood*. Cambridge: Harvard University Press.

——, et al. (1978). *The Seasons of a Man's Life*. New York: Knopf.

Loewenstein, S. F. (1980). "The challenge and passion of teaching." *Harvard Educational Review* 50 (1):1-12.

MacDonald, B. (1979). "Do you remember me?" *Sinister Wisdom* 10:9–14.

Mann, T. (1927). *The Magic Mountain*. New York: Knopf.

Metzger, D. (1976). "It is always the woman who is raped." *American Journal of Psychiatry* 133 (4):405–8.

Neugarten, B. (1968). "The awareness of middle age." In B. Neugarten (Ed.). *Middle Age and Aging*. Chicago: University of Chicago Press.

——. (1979). "Time, age and the life cycle." *American Journal of Psychiatry* 136(7):887–94.

Rich, A. (1976). *Of Woman Born*. New York: Norton.

Rubin, L. (1979). *Women of a Certain Age*. New York: Harper and Row.

Schlossberg, N., and Kent, L. (1979). "Effective helping with women." In S. Eisenberg and L. Patterson (Eds.). *Helping Clients with Special Concerns*. Chicago: Rand McNally.

Schwerin, D. (1976). *Diary of a Pigeon Watcher*. New York: Morrow.

Scott-Maxwell, F. (1968). *The Measure of my Days*. New York: Knopf.

Smelser, N. J. (1980). "Vicissitudes of work and love in Ango-American society." In N. J. Smelser and E. H. Erikson (Eds.). *Themes of Work and Love in Adulthood*. Cambridge: Harvard University Press.

Stierlin, H. (1972). *Separating Parents and Adolescents*. New York: Quadrangle.

——, et al. (1980). *The First Interview with the Family*. New York: Brunner/Mazel.

Strauss, A. (1962). "Transformations of identity." In A. Rose (Ed.). *Human Behavior and Social Process*. Boston: Houghton Mifflin.

Vaillant, G. (1977). *Adaptation to Life*. Boston: Little, Brown.

Wiesel, Elie. (1965). *One Generation After*. New York: Random House.

3 / The Passion Experience

I WAS 48 years old when I experienced the most amazing passion. I had not anticipated such an experience at that stage in my life, and for many months I did not understand what was happening to me. Later I realized that I must have fallen in love and that this was the experience so endlessly celebrated in world literature and art. Still later I also realized that I had felt identical feelings several times before, once for my oldest child and a second time for one of my social work mentors. But for these earlier experiences, I had had no label. The object of my later passion was a "happily" married man young enough to be my son. When I look back, I wonder if I needed to fall in love with a young man in order better to free my adolescent son to pursue his own life. Nothing much happened between myself and this man except that once my feelings were declared our warm friendship was broken up.

About two years later, after I had recovered my zest for life, I started a research study about the passion experience in women's lives. I interviewed former students, colleagues, friends, and strangers about their passion experiences, and I devised a "passion questionnaire" that I distributed to seven hundred women in my classrooms, audiences, and my friends' friendship circles. I cannot claim that I ever rigorously analyzed the data, yet much interesting material emerged.

I define passion as an intense and obsessive emotion. There is preoccupation with and yearning for a love object, with or without sexual desire. It is important to distinguish this kind of feeling from mature love, which exists, according to Harry Stack Sullivan, "when and only when the satisfactions and security of the loved one are approximately as important as one's own" (Mullahy 1952, p. 48). By contrast, passion is a dark and irrational force.

The Latin root of the work "passion" refers to suffering, and the German word "Leidenschaft" can be literally translated as "sufferingship." Passion thus inevitably involves anguish, doubts, and uncertainty, even where there is mutuality of feelings, and unrequited passion turns into dejection and despair.

Psychoanalysts (Bak 1973; Freud 1914; Kernberg 1976) and social scientists (de Beauvoir 1952; de Rougemont 1956) have emphasized two aspects of the passion experience: the wish for fusion of self with another, and the overevaluation of the love object. These aspects involve loss of ego boundaries and reality distortion, both potentially symptoms of mental illness. In addition, striking features of passionate love are its obsessive nature, frightening and exhilarating loss of control, and the loosening of inhibitions, as the ever-present obsession with the love object replaces habitual forms of obsessional preoccupations. One falls ill, one falls in love, fate has taken over one's destiny and the outcome may be uncertain. As one respondent said,

I lost interest in everything else. My mothering was affected.
I showed selfishness, immaturity, irresponsibility, loss of strength.
It was difficult to give up the intense happiness.

It never occurred to me to give a name to this exquisite confusion, the total breakdown of reason that I have experienced with some men. At such times nothing but feelings matters. Nothing else.

I learned that most women, although not all, have had at least one but usually several passion experiences that have shaped and sometimes reshaped their lives. Passions in one form or another, directed toward men, other women, one's children, psychotherapists, ideas, or activities, are a central factor in many women's lives, connected with the moments of the most intense ecstasy and/or the most bitter despair that they had experienced. These intense emotions have not only often changed the course of their lives, but the accompanying joy, pain, and turmoil have often led to new levels of maturity and depths of understanding of the human experience. It seems that while passion involves a loss of control, it curiously enough also often can lead to a greater feeling of control over life.

I feel more whole and rounded rather than going along with my life.

My major passion was very important to giving me a sense of myself and to my ability to feel both sorrow and joy. It provoked me to taking hold of my life's direction.

For these women, the memory of these passions was guarded like a precious jewel. As they said:

Passion on any level of involvement in people or causes is to me the essence of life. It gives me the motivation and sometimes zest to go on with living and it is the only source of satisfaction that is continual.

It felt like souls touched and doors to other worlds opened through someone else's eyes. It seems like living double-time, to be so very close to someone else. Like two lives that can be enjoyed and experienced beyond the range of your own imagination and comprehension.

I never thought that the passion and romance could involve me on such a great level. It was real and it made me feel beautiful and greatly increased my self-confidence . . . it was probably the most important experience of my life.

Ten percent of my respondents had not experienced passion. Competent women, who had felt other forms of intimacy and love, they had certainly read and heard about passion but felt they had never experienced it. They felt regret, ambivalence, disinterest, or outright contempt for the passion experience, as these comments indicate.

I feel as if I were seeing the world without my glasses on. Everyone is talking passion and I don't know if I ever feel it and don't know it.

I have spent a great many therapy hours trying to unearth me and maybe passion is part of this.

I feel uncomfortable with idealization, and tend to be more realistic.

I interpret all-consuming passion as an essential element of American romanticism which is proper for actors and actresses but not for adults aiming at self-actualization.

My definition of passion includes both sexual and nonsexual experiences. I do not want to equate passion with sexual lust, perhaps because my own deepest passions were not related to sexuality. One experience with passion involved my infant daughter; the other my very old aunt during the last two years of her life. Certainly, physical contacts, such as holding, kissing, and caressing were important ways in which I expressed my feelings in both situations. Freud taught us that all loving, tender, and passionate emotions are sublimated sexual feelings, but I think his repeated confounding of sensual and sexual feelings has clouded rather than clarified human relations. Current psychoanalytic literature, following Reik's (1944) and Sullivan's thinking (Carson 1969), tends to separate sexual desire and passionate love (Benedek 1976; Christie 1972) as two different emotions that frequently but not necessarily coincide. Yet for some women, love is intimately bound up with their sexuality and they seem unable to experience one without the other.

Passion for people . . . ultimately gets down to a desire to experience that sense of total combination with the object's body that one can sometimes experience in successful sexual union.

Sexuality and emotional intensity are the only things that really matter to me, that seem like good reasons for living.

Yet other women experience sexual lust and emotional passion as very different emotions that may or may not coincide. "Love gets you through times of no sex better than sex gets you through times of no love," writes one woman. And several women described how their passion terminated or at least cooled when sexual contact was initiated, one seemingly substituting for the other.

My passion ended when I just quit caring. It was then that I agreed to sleep with him. You could say the passion ended in an affair and later a terrible marriage, ending in divorce.

Walster (1978) pointed out that other unsatisfied needs can be as arousing as sex, and our respondents confirm that. "I was on my first trip to Europe—alone—in love with life—he was Paris for me." "He is artistic, sensitive and listens to feelings, unlike my husband."

It might actually make better sense to see sex as sublimated love, rather than the reverse. Sexual lust is after all a bodily appetite that can be quite divorced from any emotions. Most writers suggest, however, that obstacles to sexual consummation, at least in passions between adults, seem to heighten and maintain the yearning quality of the experience (Christie 1972).

The elements of romantic love, a concept closely related to passion, have been described as fourfold by Kremen and Kremen (1971):

1) Partial knowledge of the love object leading to idealization;
2) Obstacles to attaining the love object;
3) A period of discontent with self (or perhaps a time of transition?);
4) Objective value attributed to the love object.

There actually seems to be considerable variation on these factors. For example, not all passions necessarily include idealization. Also, there seems to be a large range in terms of the fourth factor, the objective value and even reality of the love object. While mature love involves mutuality, getting to know each other, and acknowledging and transcending differences, passion tends to involve the projection of fantasies upon the loved one. Some of the most celebrated passions in history resided exclusively in the fantasy of the lover. Dante, for example, never spoke to Beatrice, and he saw her only a few times in his life. He had a wife and several mistresses, but his true passion was reserved for an unknown woman (Hunt 1959). And, from Shakespeare, who can always be counted on to illustrate the complexity of the human soul, we have Titania in *Midsummer Night's Dream*, who falls in love with Bottom, a man who has been changed into an ass. It is Shakespeare's way of telling us that passion is blind, because it is a private experience.

Another example of this fantasy of the love object is found in the fairy tale of the Frog Prince. The love object here is an ugly frog, but after he is kissed by the princess, meaning after she has fallen in love with him, he becomes a beautiful prince—in her eyes. An alternate explanation is that the love of the princess actually transformed the ugly frog into a beautiful prince; this speaks to the transforming power of true love.

Finally the ancient Greeks, who invented love of every kind including passionate love (Hunt 1959), have their own example of projected love. Pygmalion was a sculptor who created a statue, Galatea, so beautiful that he fell in love with her, and through his love the statue came to life. This myth is a lovely symbol for the idea that all passions have some aspect of Narcissus' love, namely love with one's own image or own creation. And Narcissus, like other great lovers, died of his passion, albeit for himself.

The Roots of Passion

Beginning with Freud, most writers seem to agree that the potential for passion is created during infancy, in the intense love/ hate tie of the infant to his or her mother (Freud 1914; Bak 1973; Reich 1953; Reik 1944). Early psychoanalytic theory emphasized the little girl's passion for her father as fateful for her later love life. Later writers, such as Kernberg (1976) have viewed the pathological, irrational aspects of passion as a regression to infancy, and mature love, defined as "the normal integration of genitality with the capacity for tenderness and a stable deep object relation" (p. 82), is considered the successful resolution of the oedipal conflict. In a similar vein, Theodore Reik (1944) felt that it is the special and uncertain character of the early attachment experience and the anxiety about conditional love and separation that give rise to the later potential for passion.

According to Freud, only men were capable of true passions. He wrote, " . . . women love only themselves with an intensity comparable to that of the man's love for them. Nor does their need lie in the direction of loving, but of being loved; and *that* man finds favor with them who fulfills this condition" (1914, p. 113).

I want to challenge Freud on this astonishing claim on two accounts. First, I have already suggested that passion and self-love are not opposite emotions, since passion is a form of projection. I asked on my questionnaire whether a woman would rather love or be loved, if there had to be a choice, and the responses were evenly split, with younger women wanting to love, and older women preferring to be loved. Second, I feel that passion, which has as its goal closeness and fusion, is a peculiarly feminine emotion.

The little girl, who shares her mother's gender, would seemingly have to form the deeper and more lasting intense bond, perhaps even fusion, with her mother, while the little boy has to disidentify himself quite early from his mother to establish his male identity (Stoller 1974; Dinnerstein 1976; Chodorow 1978). Indeed, we see many women continue to struggle with this intense attachment to their mother throughout life. Erika Jong's words will resonate with many women:

Of course it all began with my mother. . . . My love for her and my hate for her are so bafflingly intertwined that I can hardly see her. I never know who is who. She is me and I am her and we are all together. The umbilical cord which connects us has never been cut, so it has sickened and rotted and turned black. The very intensity of our needs has made us denounce each other. We want to eat each other up. We want to strangle each other with love. We want to run screaming from each other in panic before either of these things can happen. (1973, p 161)

Even in the poetry that has shaped our Western ideas of romantic love, the infantile origins of passion and intense love are clearly manifest. In the courtly medieval love between knights and revered ladies who were always other men's wives, one finds the basis for our notion of romantic love. Moller (1960) demonstrated convincingly that the knights' love expressed in the minnesongs was similar to the infant's yearnings for his all-powerful, ideal, noble, pure, and unattainable mother. The fantasies expressed in the songs are not at all sexual, but infantlike fantasies for the tender, nurturant ministrations of the mother. Jealousy is not directed at the lady's husband, but at other aspiring knights, the siblings.

The infant is not the only one who experiences passions in the early mother/child relationship. In our study, many applied the emotion of passion to their children. Indeed, some mothers did so spontaneously, before they saw my specific questions on that subject.

Initially it was such an unbelievable experience to be able to love someone so totally and be needed in return. As time passes, I have had to suppress my passion for my son's sake and thus it is no longer a true passion.

I experienced an initial euphoria unlike any previous experience, followed by depression. I was focused solely on my baby for at least six months. Tension was growing between my husband and myself.

One-third of the mothers in my study reacted with this kind of passion, and innumerable women have commented on the unexpected and overwhelming feelings that are suddenly aroused at the very beginning of motherhoood. Bardwick (1971) has used this feeling as a proof of the existence of a maternal instinct, a "philogenetic inheritance" (p. 211), but I think it is simply the act of falling in love.

This overwhelming love for the infant is a passion as total and irrational as any other passion in life. It fits Kremen and Kremen's definition of romantic love very well, with partial knowledge of the love object leading to projections and idealization, during a period of personal transition, for an objectively extremely valued love object. One could even say that the precarious early nature of the mother/infant relationship could be seen as an obstacle to attaining the love object. A postpartum depression can be seen as the suffering that accompanies a passion experience.

In the exclusive passion a mother feels for her infant, other matters and other people lose their former affective value. Displaced by a rival, the young father can often feel betrayed. He may feel the same rejection he felt as a little boy with the arrival of a younger sibling, who stole his mother's attention and the beloved breasts that used to belong to him. We are reminded of Freud's somewhat nostalgic words that "the son receives what the husband had tried to gain for himself. One gets the impression that the love of the man and the love of the woman are always one developmental phase apart" (1933, p. 183). Sigmund Freud himself was replaced by seven younger siblings as a boy, and by six children as a husband.

A man may respond by competing with his wife for the baby's love, or by competing with the baby for the love of the wife, or by withdrawing physically and emotionally, perhaps investing energies in work, hobbies, or other women. The first two solutions lead to the kind of intergenerational alliances and triangles that characterize dysfunctional family patterns. Many marriages never recover from the estrangement created by the third solution, ending up in bitter midlife divorces. Perhaps families in which fathers and mothers equally share the early parenting experience will fare better. This may involve some loss to the mother. Women must be careful not to trade their passions for their infants, the only passions some women may ever know, for a potage of lentils. However, the preservation of a solid marriage and perhaps also the advantage of a less intensely mother-attached child may be a fair exchange for a diluted mother-infant passion.

Passion and Marriage

Marriage counselors tend to feel that romantic love notions undermine the marital relationship by creating excessively unrealistic expectations and therefore inevitable disappointments. Yet, many sociologists suggest quite cynically that few people marry for love, and even fewer for passionate love. An analysis of my questionnaire allowed me to investigate the intriguing questions of how frequently passion tends to precede a marriage and whether a marriage that starts with a passion has a lesser or greater chance of being satisfactory to the woman than a marriage that was contracted without such an initial spark.

I found that of the 474 ever-married women who responded, approximately three-fifths (281 women) had a passion experience with their current or (if divorced) most recent husband at least at some time at the beginning of their relationship. Two-fifths of the ever-married respondents (193 women) did not have such an experience. Some women expressed guilt or shame for having married without passion. Here are the words of a 51-year-old woman in an unhappy marriage:

The love I had for my present husband was not of the same quality as my former passions. I knew it when I married him. Perhaps in some ways I feel guilty about that, but I did love him and wanted to have a good relationship with him.

A 28-year-old woman said:

The fact that I never had a passion for my husband bothers me sometimes, but it alters in no way my love and continued admiration and affection for him.

One young woman, contemplating a potentially passionless marriage, wrote with some misgiving:

I want to get married but I am not in love with my boyfriend. I love him, but I am not in love. I guess I'll end up marrying him; he is dying to marry me.

It seems easy and natural for these women to distinguish between love and passion. Respondents in the older age group (over 45) were more likely to have entered a marriage without a preceding passion experience for the future husband. Curiously enough, this was also true for the most highly educated women (Ph.D., M.D., law degrees). It is comforting to say to such women that they are not a part of a small shameful minority, but that regardless of the romantic aura of our culture, passionless marriages seem almost as frequent as those with passion, according to this sample of women.

I classified the descriptions of all respondents' marriages into six categories, from highly satisfactory to divorced or separated. The level of marital satisfaction was generally high in this group of predominantly middle-class and lower-middle-class educated women, with about half of all the married women fitting either into the "highly satisfactory" or "quite satisfactory" marriage categories. Yet one-quarter of the ever- and/or still-married respondents were living in marriages that ranged from disappointing and devitalized to extremely burdensome.

My data indicate clearly and dramatically that marriages that start with passion are three times as likely to be extremely satisfactory, and twice as likely to be quite satisfactory, as marriages that had not started with passion. "The fires of passion with my husband are now only embers but they do keep burning," said one woman. The marriages without an initial passion were also half-again as likely to be in the "devitalized" category as the other marriages. One 33-year-old woman, who had never experienced passion for her husband, said:

My marriage is quite satisfying—no great passionate romance. I communicate some of my feelings to my husband. He is a good person and a kind person but perhaps not as sensitive as I would like him to be. He seems happy with our relationship. Life is quite fickle and you never can seem to get what your heart most desires.

Yet beginning a marriage with passion does not guarantee against eventual devitalization. This was expressed in the voice of a 43-year-old-woman whose twenty-one-year-long marriage started with passion:

My basic comment would be that I do not seem to have any strong emotional feelings in my marriage. We share many activities together—children and social gatherings—but I feel distant and have no desire to communicate my innermost thoughts.

Moreover, acute conflict was more rampant in marriages that had started with a passion. This may not be surprising. It seems logical that conflict may actually be an integral part of a vital relationship, as the following quote demonstrates:

Each of us has grown almost beyond recognition. We hit a plateau, then have open conflict, even to the point of risking our relationship. Then after much discussion we find ourselves peaceful with each other, more committed to our marriage, yet with new directions and strength. At other times, conflict and struggle may strain a marriage to the breaking point. Marriage is hard work. We're both very intense, our ups and downs are often extreme. Vicissitudes of life have tempered passion. I long for intimacy when life is hard; he retreats and withdraws. "Women's lib" issues have added strain. Still, we are basically committed to each other.

The likelihood of a divorce was about equal in both categories. Divorce may be a passionate enterprise ending a passionate relationship, as in the following example reported in an interview by 34-year-old former student. According to the literature, this marriage seems to typify the union between a successful, hypercritical, obsessional man and an expressive and perhaps hysterical woman (Barnett 1971).

Trudi loved her husband passionately for many years, despite his constant nagging, criticizing, and even occasional rage outbursts that led him, an upper-class lawyer, to batter her. She prized his sexual attractiveness, his incisive wit, his integrity and ambition, and felt terrified that he might abandon her. Their marriage was a series of conflicts starting in the honeymoon. He found any imperfections in her intolerable. While Trudi married with the conviction that her warmth and love was [sic] sufficient for both and that she would teach him how to be tender and loving, she eventually realized that she could not change him. Gradually she gained enough self-confidence to feel more separate and to initiate a separation. In spite of the emotional pain and turmoil, she felt as if a massive weight had been lifted off her shoulder.

For some, it seems clear that marriage preceded by passion can offer the most satisfactory union. Although it does not protect the woman against the possibility of conflict or divorce any more than any other marriage, it seems to hold promise of higher long-term satisfaction. Here is a testimonial from a 46-year-old woman about her twenty-six-year-long marriage, which started with passion:

We consider our marriage a vital marriage—*independent* organisms, yet dependent on each other as best friends. We have thoroughly enjoyed our marriage, are passionately in love, "feel we are one marriage in a million." Like each other. Communicate anything to each other. Sexually, emotionally, socially well suited. We have changed—given each other space, encouraged each other. Yes! We would feel great loss if one of us dies but wouldn't give up what we have now.

Lest we give a false impression, we need to remember that almost one-third of marriages that started without an initial passion were also highly satisfactory. Here are some examples of harmonious marriages that were not preceded by a passion:

We have a strong and stable marriage—much love and respect between the two of us. We respect each other's intellectual pursuits, share child-rearing. There is open and honest dealing with problems, open affection.

Our marriage stands for togetherness, sharing responsibilities and decisions, loving caring and vital.

Yet, of the five women who had their *first* passion *after* their marriage with someone other than their husband, two were unhappily married and three were divorced. It may be these women had married before they had discovered their own potential for deep and intense feelings, and they paid a high price for this.

Still, passions do not guarantee a happy marriage. There is for example the very real danger that passion was blinding a woman's judgment when she got married:

The only problem with the early passion between my husband and myself is that it blinded us both. I am not sure that either of us had a very realistic view of the other.

These vignettes raise the surprising possibility that marital passions can endure for many years. I say surprising, given that idealization, obstacles, and yearning, which are considered intricate aspects of the passion experience, are not likely to occur in a marriage. Philip Slater (1956) has suggested that society is threatened by the dyadic withdrawal into intimacy of two lovers and that marriage has been invented as an antidote to passionate love. It is a creative idea, but I think any dyadic closed relationship is ultimately stagnant and doomed, whether inside or outside of marriage. Even Tristan and Iseult became bored with each other after living for three years alone in the forest and returned voluntarily to court. Intimacy may protect people against emotional isolation but it does not meet their equally urgent needs for social relationships (Weiss 1973).

A substantial number of women (eighty-six) claim that passion has persisted in their marriage. One might suspect that these women have their own independent definitions of passion in mind. Or, it is possible to maintain passion in marriage. I shall let you judge, selecting only marriages that have withstood the test of time.

One 35-year-old woman, married for thirteen years, described her current relationship with her husband as

based on a very strong and continuing friendship developed into love and passion. . . . A relationship that is supportive and still growing, punctuated with differences of opinion and compromising.

One 32-year-old woman, married at age 19, said:

Our marriage has grown through the years as we have become more communicative with each other. We continue to wonder in awe at the continuing interest, love, and freshness of our relationship.

A 51-year-old widow explored her passion for her husband.

My most enduring passion was my husband. I think this has to be explained, as sixteen years of "intense obsessive yearning" may seem exhausting, especially with seven children. My experience was that there were lapses of passion, but eventually I noticed that the passion returned . . . a very difficult marriage. It was our healing passion for one another that made it possible.

And a 45-year-old woman said the following:

All I can say is that twenty-five years ago I fell in love at first sight and I have had a deeply happy relationship with the man ever since. Obviously we know each other well. The passion is a quieter thing certainly after that many years. We have great personal independence and that only seems to have strengthened the relationship.

All but three women who report their marriages as passionate describe it as extremely happy. Yet, there is also a kind of passionate marriage in which the relationship feeds on a confusion of identities, chaos, and uncertainty, all of which create the kind of emotional arousal that can be experienced as intense love. Some alcoholic marriages fit into this category, as do other marriages in which the partners can never take each other for granted because of constant infidelity or even physical brutality. We remember Trudi's marriage as fitting that model. Here are other examples.

One of my respondents, whom I will call Paula, had an alcoholic father with whom she kept up a passionate correspondence and occasional visits until midadolescence. She reported her mother as being cold and harsh. (An Eleanor Roosevelt story in a poverty setting). Paula carried her passion for her father and her low self-esteem into her marriage at age nineteen. She adored her husband and was happy to serve him. He only tolerated her presence. She totally subordinated herself to his whims. He went on drinking binges and philandered but she forgave him because she loved his weakness as well as his brilliance and charm. Paula's husband committed suicide after fifteen years of marriage, and she had not yet recovered eight years later. She wrote: "The passion I bore my husband was the single greatest experience of my life and had the intensity of a religious experience. It gave meaning to my existence and with his death that meaning fell away. The color drained out of all things and the world became ashes in my mouth. I feel that only if I experience another passion will my life cease to be a succession of grey days ticking me to oblivion."

Another example: "My husband repeatedly threatens to leave me but he never does. It always shifts back to love and I seesaw with him. I live on two levels and I hate the insecurity."

It is my impression that even in situations where passions endure in marriage, they do have a very different quality from the exciting, yearning "sufferingship" of a beginning relationship, and that apparent "enduring passion marriages" may in actuality simply be relationships that have maintained their vitality.

The majority of women in my study came to experience too much fusion or closeness in their marriage as oppressive and wanted to become more differentiated and independent, even at the cost of togetherness and perhaps passion. Here is a quote from a 46-year-old woman in a twenty-two-year-long marriage:

I am in a transition stage. Trying to find my own identity, not just husband, children, older family-parents. We are trying to be two individuals, growing—be different and appreciate differences (as I do with my children). It is not going very easily.

Another example comes from a 55-year-old social worker in her second marriage of twenty-two years, one that had not started with passionate feeling.

The relationship has endured because of affection and shared interests. The central problem for me has been an increasing need for independence without relinquishing the marriage.

We have a creative, constantly growing relationship. Have always stressed communication and have found this to be the strength of our relationship. Quality of communication has steadily improved. Took a long time to become honest—fear of hurting the other. Healthiest change when we stopped trying to live off each other's strengths—accepted we were separate personalities—had to develop as separate people—new stage in marriage. Relationship is stronger, more realistic.

In these situations, it appears that the relationship's survival depended on the marriage being secure enough to allow for differentiation and increasing individuation, rather than on ever-growing passion. Togetherness provides a safety measure against loneliness. Yet, when a marital partner expects all his or her emotional satisfactions from a marriage, there is danger of overburdening the relationship. Every frown, bad mood, unkindness, or impatience thus becomes an emotional crisis. When the pain of one becomes the pain of the other, partners can no longer stand by and help each other. Some degree of fusion is perhaps inevitable in intimate relationship. Yet it seems that mature love might require one to love oneself very much and love the other a tiny bit less.

Extramarital Passion

Distance can be created in a marriage with the intrusion of a third party. This can take the form of an extramarital involvement with or without a sexual aspect. Although sexual exclusivity is the official marital ideal, sex without love has become a cheap and widely available commodity in our society. Some studies have indicated that recreational sex can seemingly be incorporated in the marital relationship with no more drastic consequences than playing bridge. It is the passion experience, falling in love with a man or woman outside marriage, that is the real emotional threat. Curiously, an extramarital passion tends not to be taken seriously by the partner unless it is sexually consummated. Mere "head passions" can be relegated to the permissible realm of friendship or fantasy, and there is agreement that no infidelity has taken place.

There are occasional attempts by radical social scientists (Francoeur 1974) to redefine marital fidelity so as to not include sexual exclusivity, but this notion conflicts with women's and men's seemingly instinctive reactions. Such responses might be acquired through cultural prescriptions or through the early model of an at least temporarily intense mother/infant bond, which tends to involve early intense sibling jealousy, as a precursor of later similar adult feelings.

The incidence of extramarital passion in my sample was quite low. Somewhat more than a quarter had such passions, more than half of these were not sexually expressed, and some others occurred during a marital break-up; thus only fifty-nine women (12%) were truly unfaithful, as we understand that concept.

Among my respondents, I found that both sexually consummated and unconsummated passions could occur in every kind of marriage, even the most satisfactory ones, although there were only three sexual infidelities in that category. All three occurred in a time of crisis in the marriage and terminated when the crisis was resolved. Sharing the passion experience with the husband seemed important in these situations and helped to integrate it into the marriage.

The answers to three questions seem especially interesting when we view extramarital passions, and my data give contradictory answers to each of them. The first question is whether passions are necessarily the result of prior marital break-down, and thus merely a symptom of a disrupted marriage, or whether extra-marital passions intrude upon and perhaps disrupt a formerly harmonious marital relationship.

I shall first give an example of an apparently satisfactory marriage that was threatened by a passion. The respondent was a 38-year-old woman, married for sixteen years. Her passion occurred at age 36 and lasted for six months. She grappled with the above question.

I was totally unprepared for this experience. I was at first shocked at having these feelings and overwhelmed by their power. I had had vague feelings of attraction for the several years I had known this man, but the relationship became intense when it became obvious that it was a mutual attraction. My first assumption was that something was drasti-cally wrong with my marriage, even though I had always considered it a good marriage and I put enormous energy into working on that and on my own identity. I became increasingly scared of being out of control with these run-away feelings. I reached a point where I needed to break off the relationship and share all my feelings with my husband. This had an enormous, positive effect on our marriage, making it much closer.

It thus appears possible for passions to occur almost accidentally and fatefully within a marriage viewed as good by both partners. Yet most extramarital passions seem to grow out of some flaw in the marital relationship. We remember the woman whose hus-band kept her on tenterhooks. It seems she eventually found a form of vengeance for his behavior by starting her own sexual love affair:

Although I am emotionally committed to my husband I was totally dom-inated by him. By having a new passion I'm not so dependent on him for satisfaction of my needs, emotionally and physically. I feel stronger when I relate to him and much more independent. Our relationship is better than it was when I didn't have a new passion.

This second example of a passion growing out of marital dissatisfaction also begins to answer my second question: Are extramarital passions always detrimental to a marriage? It does not seem so in the above example, and there were other situations in which an outside passion seems to have sustained rather than damaged a marriage.

I have respect for the institution of marriage and will stay with it, but without outlet, my passions would turn inward and destroy us both.

It took the pressure off my marriage, made lack of communication possible and bearable.

In other less extreme situations, an extramarital nonsexual passion helped a 42-year-old woman to "settle down."

I am glad I had this feeling at that time—looking back it really made my life very lovely for a while. It also made me more realistic in my views about marriage and romance—a more comfortable marriage is a more satisfying life-style in the long haul.

Sexual nonmarital passions may also lead to the eventual growth of the marital relationship:

The experience allowed me to move out of my dependency on my marriage—temporarily very unsettling to the marriage but in the long run very important. It allowed me to see my husband more as a lover, a separate person. It began a process of renegotiating the marriage which is still going on.

One has the feeling here that the spark and revitalization created by this woman's passion was fed back into the marriage and led to a renewal.

Not all extramarital passions were so harmless. Many situations created great anguish or threatened either the woman's own marriage or the marriage of her love object:

My most recent passion is the happiest experience of my life, and also tortuous, as theirs is a really happy marriage. I feel terrible guilt and fear of discovery, yet I am unable to retreat.

The following woman is 31 years old, married since age 19. She describes an extramarital passion that has lasted for almost seven years. It is her first and only passion, and included sexual consummation.

I terminated the relationship for two years because of our marital partners and children, but it began again as intensely. It resulted in a question: Who am I? I entered therapy to evaluate myself. I do feel the relationship has had a profound effect on my future. I am now emerging from a severe identity crisis and I have no idea if the crisis invited the rekindling of the flame or vice versa. My marriage may end because of the ramifications of the last eight months.

The third question I posed myself was whether extramarital passions are compatible with ongoing marital satisfaction. My data give examples of a number of situations in which passions and marriage run side by side without much interference with each other. An example comes from a woman who could combine sexual passions with a relatively satisfactory though devitalized marriage.

Passion is a treasure to savor. I am married to a nice, sweet man with an excellent sense of humor. He is good company, nonthreatening and does not attempt to regulate me in any way. Life is pleasant but not exciting.

A second example comes from a 47-year-old woman who had been married since age 19. She had two sexual passions for women. The first, at age 29, later turned into a lifelong friendship. The second passion at age 38, when she had already four children, was an involvement with a married woman who abruptly terminated the relationship, causing her great despair. This is what she says of her marriage:

We had problems along the way but we have been able to work out most of them. We have mutual respect, have a lot of fun together, and both agree that we have never met anyone else that we would rather be married to.

Telling the husband about the affair seemed beneficial in situations in which the preexisting relationship was basically strong and loving. Others preferred to keep their affairs secret and it remains unclear whether this is more or less of a threat to their marriage.

Passion Between Women

I have so far made little distinction between homosexual and heterosexual passions because my data show very clearly that the feelings evoked are exactly the same. Indeed, if I had not asked my respondents about the gender of their love object, I could never have guessed it from their descriptions. Let us also remember that at least one of the most famous of all passion stories, *Death in Venice* by Thomas Mann (1930), describes the desperate love of an aging man for a boy.

Some of the most passionate statements in my study came from lesbian women, as illustrated by the following: "This passion was so overwhelming I hesitate to call previous ones passion. I had previously thought it did not exist." This respondent, like several others, was so emotionally shaken by her passion that she could no longer tolerate her devitalized marriage and sought a divorce. These women also offered some of the most wrenching statements. A 55-year-old woman told of a baffling relationship to an older woman mentor when she was 27 years old. Others and she herself saw herself as a loving wife and mother, but this new relationship overshadowed all others in her life. Her love for this woman had to remain undeclared, and her anguish and confusion led to a severe depression.

As these examples show, many of my respondents could not be neatly classified as lesbian or straight. Sixty women in my sample reported at least one passion for another woman across a full range from self-defined heterosexual to self-defined lesbian women.

Some were self-defined heterosexual women who had experienced, often in their youth, a sexually unconsummated passion directed toward a woman. About half of these women referred to a teacher, camp counselor, or college roommate. As our culture permits considerable emotional and physical intimacy between women before labeling it as lesbian, these passions could be integrated into a heterosexual identity without arousing too much guilt and conflict, and most women look back with bemused pleasure at these experiences. There were, however, a number of women who expressed considerable turmoil and despair as a consequence of this experience, and several subsequently sought psychiatric help, like the following 33-year-old married mother of two.

We were very good friends and one day I realized how passionately I felt towards this person. Since my love for her was not reciprocated, I had to seek help to end an unrealistic and unrealizable relationship. There was pain and agony but perhaps growth only comes after some painful development. I don't regret experiencing the six months for it was important for me to know that I can feel so intensely for a person. I don't want to go through it again unless the feelings expressed would be mutual.

One 55-year-old woman described her youthful passion for her employer and said, "I concealed my feelings and always felt a secret grief." Many self-defined heterosexual women expressed shame and discomfort when their passion for another woman was sexually expressed. A 28-year-old woman explained that her two-year-long lesbian relationship occurred in college at a time of great loneliness and disintegrated when her life became fuller and happier. She was, at the time of reporting, enthusiastically committed to her current heterosexual relationship. Some other women's sexual passions with women ended in friendship, and they regarded their early involvement as harmless sexual experimentation. These women defined their lesbian sexual involvement as a temporary aberration, while a number of other women defined themselves as bisexual.

I realized my capacity for passion with women is probably greater than with men though I choose to live with a man. I become too dependent on women. The experience of passion with a woman was both the most frightening and in some ways the most fulfilling experience of my life.

A 31-year-old woman wrote of her first heterosexual passion at 22, which made her realize "the height my feelings could reach." She experienced much pain when her lover rejected her after two years, feelings that it "made marriage to someone else hard." Her subsequent passionless marriage lasted two years. At age 30 she experienced a turbulent and ultimately disappointing eight-month-long passion for another woman. She wrote a year later, "My present relationship is with another woman. I think I am finding over the past two years more possibility for real passion between women than between men and women."

I also learned that about half of the twenty-one self-identified lesbian women among my respondents had experienced sexual passions for men, and were or had been married. Some of the other lesbian women also had sexual relations with men, but without major emotional commitment. There were several women who changed orientation once and some even twice during their adult life.

The more we learn about people's true private lives, the less we find that their most intimate personal behavior conforms to conventional societal images. It was not long ago that we were titillated by Eleanor Roosevelt's passionate letters to her friend Lorena Hickok (Faber 1979)—did she or didn't she? Then we were informed that Margaret Mead led a bisexual life (Bateson 1984). As we learn more about people's actual lives, we realize that our textbooks give us outdated or false images of human behavior, that the concept of normalcy needs to be expanded or revised, and that we need to have respect for the great diversity of human behavior and human experience.

The Camelot Dilemma

Passion tends to be a youthful emotion. Among the women who had experienced passions, all but five had their first passion before they were 30 years old, all but eight their second before that age. And most women who had four or more passions had them before the age of 40. There were some exceptions.

Due to my own experience, I was especially interested in women who had encountered passionate love for the first time in midlife, after the age of 40. These passions tend to be dramatic and may precipitate life changes. And I have suggested earlier that first passions that occur after marriage either lead to or are indicators of marital dissatisfaction. In my sample there were only five women who had a *first* passionate love at this later age; two were still married at the time of our interview, one had just separated, and one had never married. This love included sexual consummation for three of these women. Two were freed by this first love experience to terminate a long-time unhappy marriage. Here is what one of them wrote, at the age of 44, about her love for a married man when she was 40 years old, which later led to her divorce:

I had been depressed by feelings of mental and soul stagnation. The experience gave me a will to live. I will be eternally grateful to have known what it is/was to feel—really feel. The person who loved me brought me back to being a whole person—allowed me to be me—gave me back a feeling of worth. I am grateful for my life.

Increased self-esteem was also mentioned by the single woman who had a first passion at the age of 48, and although it was not sexually consummated, it certainly "counted" deeply in her emotional life. As she said, "He made me feel like a person, a woman, a really cherished, and cared about and special person for the first time in my life." One of the striking findings of my study was that marriages that were the result of a later passion rather than the first passion were apt to be happier and less likely to result in divorce. There was not a single woman who had been married after a *fourth* passion who was divorced, and this was not an artifact of age. Here are the words of a 37-year-old woman married for fifteen years, whose husband was her first passion:

My one major passion was for my husband—regret that I had had no others before him. If not for the ingredient of passion, I probably wouldn't have married him. However, having experienced passion, I most likely wouldn't have married anyone for whom I didn't have it. Important to me as a joyous memory, but I was too young and inexperienced to derive full life value from it.

It is not only *first* passions after 40 that are invested with special poignancy, but this is also true of any passion at that age. This reminds us of the plight of Queen Guinevere in Camelot, who was in quite a stable and satisfactory marriage to King Arthur until her passion for a youthful knight tore her life apart. I interviewed a woman scientist who had her first passionate lesbian experience at age 47, a passion that eclipsed all other passion experiences in her life, making her feel that she had been asleep up to that time. It led to her divorce and a permanent shift in her sexual orientation. I interviewed another woman of 54 who, while situated in a stable and apparently enduring marriage, was in the throes of a consuming passion for a man twenty years her junior, a reciprocated passion that was destroying her peace and becoming increasingly unbearable in its intensity. Yet she is addicted to this relationship and cannot bring herself to give it up. And there was yet another woman in my sample, a 49-year-old successful business executive also in a settled marriage, with thriving young adult children, who entertained for months suicidal ideas after her passion for a 29-year-old man was abruptly terminated by the latter's discomfort.

It is interesting how most of these midlife women fall in love with younger men, perhaps because men of their own age would be no match to a passionate midlife woman's zest and vitality. Indeed, the famous stories of such midlife passions, such as Colette's *Cheri* (1951) and *The Black Swan* by Thomas Mann (1956) all pair the aging woman with a younger lover.

Nevertheless, the drive for passion seems to decline as we age. Women seem to want to settle down and lead a calm life, to feel secure and protected. I asked women whether they hoped for another passion experience or wanted to avoid it; the answers were strikingly correlated with age, with the hope for another passion declining as the women grew older. In the age group over 46 years, only 35 percent of the women hoped for another passion, compared to almost twice as many women who were 25 years or younger. Here is what some of these older women wrote:

A 45-year-old. "It is too distracting, too painful."

A 72-year-old widow. "I am too old!"

A 44-year-old. "No, too energy consuming."

A 55-year-old. "I would be surprised at my age. I would rather like to meet someone with whom I could share my interests and be a true friend."

A 56-year-old. "I think to be in the state of emotional arousal in the mid-fifties would be confusing."

A 64-year-old. "Why should I want such an upheaval at this time of my life?"

A 43-year-old. "I plan to avoid it. I disliked the loss of self-control, use of emotion instead of reason. I became too dependent, too vulnerable."

Yet, there are still over a third who hope for another passion.

A 45-year-old in a satisfactory marriage. "More passions please! They enhance enjoyment of life, oneself and other people, even though mine tend to be painful."

In the age group between 25 and 45, the desire for or against having another passion was evenly divided. There are those who yearn for more passions. Here is an example from a lesbian woman:

My one passion was one of the most important experiences of my life. I learned a lot about myself and others. I learned that I was capable of loving and being loved. I think I will always cherish this relationship. I hope for another passion in the future with another person. One I can be certain of.

And others said:

Life is full and richer with another passion. I would like always to have one.

I sincerely hope for another passion, hopefully one which can mellow into a lasting love. To me this is essential for life: to love and be loved. I have a terrible fear of facing a possible passionless future.

But other women state other priorities, such as work or preserving their marriage. One woman artist, who passionately pursued her own work, said:

I used to think passion was something desirable. Now I think any passion lasting more than a few magical hours is a waste of my valuable time.

Right now, at 31, having just in the past year settled into a stable relationship after an incredible passion for the man to whom I am now married, I would just as soon forget about passion for a long time. I've had my share; to hell with it.

Sometimes I think I would like to be courted by another man but I avoid it, as I am happy in my marriage and wouldn't want to jeopardize it. The romance is intriguing, but the reality is not.

Some cannot decide, as this quote illustrates:

I think I fear it like the plague and I say that, all the while knowing that I long for it as well. I blame the movies.

I mentioned earlier that women preferred to be loved, rather than actively to love, as they become older. I have the impression that a marriage in which the man is the more actively loving partner is apt to be a more enduring marriage. Although not ideal, it tends to offer enough satisfaction to both partners. The woman's distance maintains the man's yearning and enhances the woman's sense of self-worth. This kind of emotional equilibrium may equalize the power balance in that the man's greater economic and social power is matched by the woman's greater emotional power. If, however, a woman in such a marriage should gain too much social power herself, the equilibrium becomes unsettled. That may well be the reason why many marriages founder once a woman achieves prominence in her own right.

Generally, in many enduring marriages, the aging man's increasing dependency and the aging woman's increasing autonomy led to a kind of balance in middle life that may be quite different from the initial marital equilibrium. We hear some resignation and compromise in many women's voices. The question about wanting to be loved or loving and the question about hoping for another passion experience vividly brought out women's lifelong conflict between adventure and security, which I call the

Camelot dilemma, and it becomes more pronounced in the later stages of marriage.

The quality of our marriage is very good. I have had many disappointments in my marriage related to my husband's disability to respond to my dissatisfactions. But over the years I have come to trust my husband completely and believe that he cares more about me than anyone or anything else. I think—this is what I want?

It makes me feel safe to sense my husband's total commitment to our marriage.

My husband puts me on a pedestal and I can do no wrong. The relationship is gratifying but not deeply involving.

You can hear the ambivalences in these women's voices.

Passions are a little bit like cake frosting and I seem to need less sugar as I get older—but at times I can be tempted by the high they bring.

I seem to be becoming conservative, for I would not welcome a passion, regarding it now as a type of illusion bound to end. I'd trade a passionate experience for other things I value. But there is no doubt, the high pitch, adventure, and intrigue of passion is tempting.

The dilemma of loving or being loved, adventure versus security, and passion versus creativity is not reserved for married women. Since I have given little space to the passions of young single women, I wish to quote a passage on that subject that my daughter, at the age of 26, left in my typewriter:

To be settled would be not having to worry all the time—will na stop loving you or does na really love you. It would mean the cessation of that constant fear. To be settled would be to accept the role of the *loved*. To take the lover role means you are never settled, never secure. But if you are *lover* in a passion you never stop feeling. It is like a drug, you are high all the time. Even wanting to be dead is being high. If you are loved (or settled) you don't transcend, you make do, you get along. And how could you create when you just go along. But how could you write, live, if you are so miserable that getting from one step to the next is too hard. It's ridiculous to think of a starving person creating a masterpiece. This is what lots of us want as an ideal—to be the *lover*, not the *loved*, but to get enough security, enough returns to be functional. Not necessarily content or happy but to be getting something that's almost enough, enough anyway to be fed some, not to be starving. Just a little hunger, the kind of hunger that activates you. You want to be a wild cat who goes out on her own and roves and plays and can still come home and have some time to be fed and purr in a warm place.

the roving cat

Passions for Better or for Worse

Many feminists have condemned passions as destructive to women, but this stance does not reflect what women are actually feeling, especially not in the long run, not after they have recovered from the pain and turmoil of an upsetting passion experience. Only 10% of these women regretted their passion experience and felt that it left permanent scars.

I feel that the experience of passion was detrimental as it left me feeling hollow and unfulfilled—also isolated.

I developed a kind of shell and bitterness which is probably still with me. The experience still hurts—I fear involving myself totally with anyone. Also a constant battle with feelings of depression and inadequacy.

Almost half the women had found their experience very upsetting in the short run but they did not regret it in the long run. For some, the entire experience was highly positive, and one woman wrote, "it opened a new awareness of the depth of my emotions." Another woman said:

I never thought that the passion and romance could involve me on such a great level—thought it was only found in books. Yet it was real—made me feel beautiful and greatly increased my self-confidence. I had always been shy. I can imagine that it would work the opposite way if it was not reciprocated. It was probably the most important experience of my life. I am grateful it was so positive.

But even many women whose passion involved extreme anguish are happy that they had such intense experiences, no matter what the cost might have been, confirming the old saying that it is better to have loved and lost than never loved.

When the passion ended it plunged me into a deep depression. Two years removed from the experience, I can say that it was good for me; not so much the passion itself, although it made me aware of my intense sexual feelings, but it made me take stock. My close friends tell me that I am ten years more mature since the experience. It was extremely painful when it ended, but growth comes only through pain.

Regardless of the pain, disappointment, and disorientation involved in a passion, I am glad to have experienced such emotional intensity. It was instrumental in bringing about great self-awareness.

No matter that it ends in sadness because for a little while I've been in touch with what feels like the kernel of my soul.

It was beautiful, consuming, incredibly fun, exciting, totally involving while it lasted-ended-resumed-ended-resumed and finally ended. The endings were incredible in the pain and devastation and left permanent scars. But never never have I ever wished it hadn't happened.

Passions in this positive view can be regarded as a major maturational crisis. They seem to lead to psychic growth, deeper self-awareness, greater human compassion, and greater creativity. They can be viewed as forms of regression in the service of the ego.

Passions as a Mental Health Hazard

In viewing the course of passions in women's lives, two main dangers emerge: the danger of permanent loss of identity and the related danger of chronicity, which I have called elsewhere "overloving." (See chapters 11, 14, 15, this volume.) In these instances, the love object becomes a narcissistic extension of oneself, rather than a separate person. Passionate love for a child is creative and life-sustaining while the child is an infant, sustaining in the mother's disregard for the lack of sleep, instant readiness to respond to cries of distress under all circumstances, and generally a devotion rarely expected at any other time in life. Yet should such total devotion persist, it would start to interfere with the young child's need for greater autonomy and differentiation. Whether for a child or for an adult lover, chronic passions can create a destructive prison, especially for the woman herself.

My second passion is still the core of my emotional life. I don't understand it. Why won't it end with him and start with someone else who is near? I haven't seen him for years and I still compare everyone to him. Even as I write this I cry for him. Leaving him was like dying. I died when I left him and I haven't come alive yet.

Simone de Beauvoir (1952) described the dangers of passion in similar terms. She talked about the "Grandes Amoureuses" who surrender themselves to love, devoting themselves entirely to the man, lover, or husband; only he gives joy and meaning to their lives. It is a situation where the potential for disaster is great. The man experiences the woman's ardent love as tyranny and the relationship becomes easily one of oppression and mutual enslavement. A woman who is madly in love becomes possessive, jealous, and vulnerable to deep narcissistic injuries. The following quote is from a 27-year-old woman who had a desperate two-year-long passion for a man she eventually married and divorced.

My love for him was destroying me. There was a gradual loss of identity. At times I thought I was crazy through my despair. I lost all of myself and was ready for the nuthouse. I realized I had to get out. I had to grow up and love me.

While about half of my seven hundred respondents had sought therapy at some point, I was extremely startled to find that in half these cases the reason for seeking help was connected with an upsetting passion experience. Although circumstances surrounding help-seeking for passions were frequently ambiguous and complex, some major constellations of causes emerged. Most frequently mentioned was pain over separation, often aggravated by an acute narcissistic injury caused by feeling rejected, abandoned, or betrayed. Sudden unexplained rejections seem to be particularly hard to accept. This 37-year-old married woman refers to a sexual passion ten years ago when she was single. "He couldn't find a way to live in New York City. One day he moved away without telling me."

Guilt about sexual passion in which either the woman or her lover was married was frequently associated with help-seeking.

I am constantly feeling passionate toward different men in my life, but this is the first passion in which sex is consummated. I love my husband as a person and friend, but don't feel the passion toward him that I feel toward these other men. It is an extremely frustrating situation.

This woman feels that her last sexual passion has damaged her marriage even though she kept it secret from her husband. She is torn with guilt. This theme often overlaps with pain over separation or rejection, for example when a single woman falls in love with a married man.

For some women the violent feelings unleashed by passion were extremely unsettling and they experienced much confusion and anxiety. Many of these examples revolve about change in sexual orientation, which tends to precipitate a major life transition with which women seek help. Following are several examples of such situations. A woman who was a nun reported a year-long sexual passion while she was teaching. The experience was extremely unsettling to her. She describes herself as happily married but with a "sexual hang-up because of my religious background and my first passion experience." A 27-year-old married woman wrote about a four-month passion for a woman when she was 24, still single, and working at her first job. She experienced much confusion and "fuller awareness of self and my bisexual nature," leading to the decision to seek psychiatric help.

Several women sought psychiatric help when a turbulent lesbian affair led to the breakup of a devitalized marriage.

Some women found themselves repeatedly in destructive or disappointing relationships and sought help primarily to understand or combat their self-defeating tendencies. This 25-year-old married woman tells about her first sexual passion, an eighteen-month-long episode during her college years:

I was self-destructive in that I lived with a man who hated women. He rejected me as a woman and as myself. It led to self-doubt and fear of being alone and led me into seeking psychiatric help.

Another illustration comes from a 31-year-old married woman who remembers a two-year-long passion for a married man when she was 25.

He showed little or no interest in me. In therapy I began to examine the myths I attached to some types of men and I began to rid myself of these myths. We examined feelings, wants, desires, needs in regard to men. I began to choose men who did reciprocate my passion and also began to feel more realistic in my expectations of men. Also felt more whole myself, less in need of men.

Finally, there was a small group of women whose lovers committed suicide, had serious accidents, mental or physical illnesses, and who needed help with these reality traumas. Feelings of loss, mourning, and narcissistic injuries were, of course, present in such cases, as in most of the others.

We must also recognize that many women suffer intensely but choose not to seek help, like this 55-year-old woman who remembers her first, sexually unconsummated passion at age 25 while still single.

I became engaged to this person but he started to get indifferent and I left the service to go home. I think I had the symptoms of an emotional illness but did not seek psychiatric help and was able to get through it on my own strength. It was an extremely unhappy time in my life. Wouldn't want to repeat the experience, very painful, but eventually I got over it with considerable effort. I often wonder if I had married my passion, would life have been any different. My present husband has hurt me as well so I feel generally that I have not been lucky in my love experience.

Why do most great lovers in our theater and literature have to be killed? Passions are not tamed, nor are emotions civilized in spite of our society's efforts to channel them into marriage. Denis de Rougemont (1956) pointed out that the most powerful love stories of all times are about passions that break serious social taboos, and he gave *Lolita* (Nabokov 1955) as an example. Tristan and Iseult's was an adulterous passion, a most serious transgression at that time, as was Anna Karenina's. Perhaps society has to protect itself against such transgressions. De Rougemont feels that the goal of true passion is total union, and that can occur only in death. But above all it would appear that the only way a passion can be preserved at its climax in all its glory and beauty is if one or both lovers die.

Passion may become affection or friendship if things are propitious, and we have heard how they may cast a glowing reflection upon many subsequent years of marriage. Since love and hate are close in the emotional continuum, passion may also turn into hatred and injured passion may explode in violent narcissistic rage. Medea's vengeful response to her betrayal may be an awesome example of passion turned into narcissistic rage, while Anna Karenina turned the rage upon herself in suicide. We all understand the nature of crimes of passion. Or else, passion may eventually turn into indifference, which is indeed the opposite of passion.

Conclusion

The early attachment experience in infancy is not just blissful, but full of tumultuous love and hate. Yet it usually offers enough emotional nourishment for people to become humanized for a lifetime. From time to time in life many of us seem to return to this fountain for a form of emotional renewal, reliving in a passion the torments, delights, and the merging with the idealized object of the first year of life. If all goes well, we emerge with a sense of renewed creativity and enhanced ego integration. Passion is thus one form of regression in the service of the ego.

Yet, like all regressions, they have to be time-limited to preserve their creative potential. A prolonged passion, whether for an adult or a child, tends to be a regressive experience into loss of ego boundaries that becomes binding and destructive to the growth of both participants. We can only speculate whether repeated chronic passion experiences mirror an overloving attachment experience.

There are many students of human nature who deplore the excesses of passionate love. Fingarette (1963), for example, in a Taoist spirit, opposed any form of overloving relationships. He believed that "detachment is the essential ground out of which relationships among genuinely autonomous individuals can arise" (p. 272). He called for detachment without indifference; respect without envy or expectations; love without possessiveness; caring without control. Indeed, such mature love would save us the pain, anguish, and turmoil of the passion experiences that my respondents have described to us.

Yet, is there danger that total differentiation in a relationship, such as Fingarette suggested, means the end of deep and intense love? Maybe lack of differentiation is the glue that holds our social fabric together. Will mature detachment extinguish the fire, spark, and life-giving passion nourished by narcissistic needs, and mean the death of creativity?

I have come to the conclusion that significant relationships are forever suspended in the delicate balance that I have called underloving and overloving—detachment that may border on indifference and sterility, or passionate engagement that may become intrusive and destructive. We can embrace this creative act of tightrope walking as a lifelong pursuit.

In order to do justice to both poles I shall end this chapter with two quotes that alternately celebrate the need for distance and the need for passion.

The first quote is from the German poet Rainer Maria Rilke, on the nature of love, taken from Rilke's *Letters on Love* (Mood 1975):

I hold this to be the highest task of a bond between two people: that each should stand guard over the solitude of the other . . . a good marriage is that in which each appoints the other guardian of his solitude. . . . A togetherness between two people is an impossibility, and where it seems nevertheless to exist, it is a narrowing, a reciprocal agreement which robs either one part or both of his fullest freedom and development. But, once the realization is accepted that even between the closest human beings infinite distances continue to exist, a wonderful loving side by side can grow up, if they succeed in loving the distance between them which makes it possible for each to see the other whole and against a wide sky. (pp. 27, 28)

The second is a quote from a love letter written in 1795 by Mary Wollstonecraft (1974), who was a great feminist. Her love letters show her as a heroine of unrequited passion. By ending with her quote, rather than with Rilke's, saving best for last, I am confessing where I put my own weight in this balancing act:

Love is a want of my heart. I have examined myself lately with more care than formerly, and find that to deaden is not to calm the mind.

Aiming at tranquillity, I have almost destroyed all the energy of my soul—almost rooted out what renders it estimable . . . the desire of regaining peace (do you understand me?) has made me forget the respect due to my own emotions—sacred emotions, that are the sure harbingers of the delights I was formed to enjoy. (pp. 127–128)

References

Bak, R. (1973). "Being in love and object loss." *International Journal of Psychoanalysis* 1:22–44.

Bardwick, J. M. (1971). *Psychology of Women*. New York: Harper and Row.

Bateson, M. C. (1984). *With a Daughter's Eye*. New York: Morrow.

de Beauvoir, S. (1952). *The Second Sex*. New York: Knopf.

Barnett, J. (1971). "Narcissism and dependency in obsessional-hysteric marriage." *Family Process* 10 (1):75–83.

Benedek, T. (1976). "Ambivalence, passion and love." *Journal of the American Psychoanalytic Association* 25:53–76.

Carson, R. C. (1969). *Interaction Concepts of Personality*. Chicago: Aldine Press.

Chodorow, N. (1978). *The Reproduction of Mothering*. Berkeley: University of California Press.

Christie, G. (1972). The origins of falling-in-love and infatuation. *American Journal of Psychotherapy* 26:244–56.

Colette, S. G. (1951). *Cheri and the Last of Cheri*. New York: Farrar, Straus and Giroux.

Dinnerstein, D. (1976). *The Mermaid and the Minotaur*. New York: Harper and Row.

Faber, D. (1979). *The Life of Lorena Hickok: E.R.'s Friend*. New York: Morrow.

Fingarette, S. (1963). *The Self in Transformation*. New York: Harper and Row.

Francoeur, A. K., and Francoeur, R. T. (1974). *Hot and Cool Sex*. New York: Harcourt Brace Jovanovich.

Freud, S. (1914). "On narcissism: An introduction." In J. Rickmam (Ed.). *A General Selection from the Works of Sigmund Freud*. New York: Doubleday, Anchor, 1957, pp. 104–23.

—— (1933). "Femininity." *New Introductory Lectures of Psychoanalysis*. New York: Norton, pp. 153–85.

Hunt, M. (1959). *The Natural History of Love*. New York: Minerva Press.

Jong, E. (1973). *Fear of Flying*. New York: Holt, Rinehart and Winston.

Kernberg, O. F. (1976). "Boundaries and structure in love relations." *Journal of the American Psychoanalytic Association* 25 (1):81–114.

Kremen, H., and Kremen, B. (1971). "Romantic love and idealization." *American Journal of Psychoanalysis* 31:143.

Loewenstein, S. F. (1980a). "Passion as a mental health hazard." In C. L. Heckerman (Ed.). *The Evolving Female.* New York: Human Sciences Press.

—— (1980b). "Toward choice and differentiation in the midlife crises of women." In C. L. Heckerman (Ed.). *The Evolving Female.* New York: Human Sciences Press.

—— (1985). "On the diversity of love object orientations among women." *Journal of Social Work and Human Sexuality* 3 (2/3):7–24.

Moller, H. (1960). "The meaning of courtly love." *Journal of American Folklore* 73:39–52.

Mullahy, P. (1952). *The Theories of H. S. Sullivan.* New York: Hermitage House.

Mood, J. L. (1975). *Rilke on Love and Other Difficulties.* New York: Norton.

Nabokov, V. (1955). *Lolita.* New York: Putnam's.

Reich, A. (1953). "Narcissistic object choice in women." *Journal of the American Pyschoanalytic Association* 1:22–44.

Reik, T. (1944). *A Psychologist Looks at Love.* New York: Farrar and Rinehart.

de Rougemont, D. (1956). *Love in the Western World.* New York: Pantheon.

Slater, P. (1956). "On social regression." *American Sociological Review* 26:339–58.

Stoller, R. (1974). *Sex and Gender.* vol. 2. New York: Jason Aronson.

Walster, E., and Walster, G. W. (1978). *A New Look at Love.* Reading, Mass: Addison–Wesley.

Weiss, R. S. (1973). *Loneliness.* Cambridge: MIT Press.

Wollstonecraft, M. (1974). *The Love Letters of Mary Wollstonecraft to Gilbert Imlay* (with a prefatory memoir by Roger Ingpen). Folcroft, Pa.: Folcroft Library Editions.

4 / Silk Yarn*

WE learn that it is important to mourn the death of a person one has loved. I discovered that there may be no opportunity to do so. My aunt Anna Freud died far away, and the people around me had not known her. There was no opportunity to sit with other mourners for the many days I would have needed, to share feelings and cry.

Her memorial services were held abroad, and I was neither included nor could I attend them. I am not a psychoanalyst or a child therapist, neither a student nor a colleague, and not even a well-defined friend. I was after all, only a shadowy figure in her life. Yet I needed a chance to grieve and to bear witness to the relationship between us, and so I wrote down, one year after her death, my memory of our relationship. I shall call my epitaph: Silk Yarn.

"A week is a very long time, you know," she had said at the beginning of that second visit to London in August 1982. "A week is a very *short* time, you know," she said at the end of that visit. Both statements were true. It turned out to be a very long, yet much too short week.

When the telephone call then came in October, in the middle of the night, I fully expected it. For weeks I had panicked each time the telephone rang. I had been sleeping with the bedroom door open so I would not miss its ring from the other room, and yet I had also hoped that no one would inform me. I was in no hurry to hear about her death. "It's all over," said Alice, Tante Anna's friend, who has now become my friend as well. I felt that

*I thank Andrea Fleck Clardy for suggesting this title.

life would now become empty, without love, devoid of meaning.

I visited my aunt twice during that much too short summer of 1982. The first was a much anticipated and carefully planned visit in July, and the second visit in August was my impulsive response to the unbearable prospect of never seeing her again.

I have now finished the intricate sweater I knitted during that summer while sitting next to her. She had encouraged me to knit and watched me with much attention because after her stroke she could not knit any more herself.

She suffered intensely from her enforced idleness. "I am knitting this for both of us," I said. "It is our common project." She nodded approvingly. "I shall think of us sitting on the terrace together whenever I wear this sweater." She smiled. "When I come to see you next Christmas the sweater will be finished and I will be able to show you how beautiful it will look. It is very important that I can show you my sweater next Christmas," I said to her in an urgent voice. "You must wait for me." She lifted her semiparalyzed left hand and counted its fingers with her better right hand. "September," she said and pointed to the ring finger; "October," she said, and pointed to the middle finger; "November," she said, and pointed to the index finger; "December" she said, and pointed to her strangely long thumb. "It's a very long time," she sighed, "and I cannot promise that I shall be there for you." I noticed that she had forgotten to count August, since we were only in the middle of July when this happened; if she had counted August, she would have had to use the little finger and that would have made the wait even longer—indeed too long.

She then rested her hands on her lap and I covered them with mine. "Tante Anna, I love your funny long thumb." She measured our hands against each other. "Look," she said with a pleased smile, "we have similar hands."

I had not planned to spend the whole summer in London because I did not think my presence would have much meaning for her. I had never quite gotten over my fear with Tante Anna of being unwelcome and even a small burden. Tante Anna did not express love freely, and I had not expected that there might be a place in her life, right next to her chair, that she would allow me to fill. I had left her in July with a most heavy heart. Like the other two times when I had left her, there was the dread, even more than before, that we would never meet again. I was moreover doubly sad, beause she had not yet found the right loving words that I could securely hold and remember forever.

After my July departure a letter arrived in the mail. It was of course dictated, but painfully signed by herself. We often wrote to each other in German and I shall translate it for you: "Dear Sophie, it was beautiful that you were here and your departure has left a hole. My thoughts accompany you in your life at home. Do not be sad and I wish you all the best. Your Anna Freud." After crying for a long time, I suddenly realized that I could return to London before school started again. You will not understand the extent of my anguish and joy unless you know that Tante Anna and I had been strangers all our lives and that this had been a source of sadness, disappointment, and rejection for me. She had lived in Cambridge for a year when I also lived in Cambridge, and we had never met. I had gone to the 1971 anniversary conference of the Hampstead Clinic in London, and she had nodded to me in passing. It was only in the winter of 1980 when I had gone for my sabbatical year to London that our relationship had finally started. Such is the price of divided families.

When I called Tante Anna to ask permission to come back, after receiving that letter she sounded happy and invited me for the first time to stay with her in the big house in Maresfield Gardens where she had lived for forty-four years, all her English life.

I could return for only one more week because I could not miss the beginning of classes. I wish I had stayed in London and helped Tante Anna die, but neither she nor I was the kind of person who would ever consider not doing what is expected of us. Now I wish I had stayed in London that fall, but I returned to Boston and taught my classes.

We spent our short weeks together that summer sitting on the terrace of the lovely green garden behind the house, a patch of sanctuary in the midst of London's asphalt. There were two round, colorful flower beds in the middle of the garden, and a gardener was taking care of them. The house had already been signed over to a society that would make a museum out of it, and they were sending over gardeners to keep the garden from going to seed.

"Father used to love sitting on this terrace," she said. "Were you there then?" But I had not been there. The whole family had moved to London in the summer of 1938, after the Austrian Anschluss, but my mother and I had moved to Paris. Tante Anna's question conjured up the vivid dream I had had that spring after hearing of her stroke. I had dreamed that my grandfather was dying in the midst of loving family members while I was far away, living in another city, feeling alone and excluded from the family. I had never fully realized until that dream, how hurtful it had been for me to be separated from my grandfather when he died. Is it possible in life to make up for missed experiences?

Sometimes we moved the rickety chaise longue in which Tante Anna sat all day off the stone terrace and into the grass, for a change of view. Tante Anna did not like to sit in the sun, while I was constantly cold, unprepared for London's chilly temperatures in the middle of summer. "You are shivering," she said, "take one of my hot water bottles." "How good of you to share your warmth with me." "You share your strength with me," she answered. When Tante Anna realized how much I longed to sit in the sun, we struck a bargain: I would place her chair in the patch of shade next to a sunny place, and we would move the chairs with the sun. She wanted both of us to be comfortable. And each time I stood up to move us both, I would kiss her hand, then her arm, her head, and her face. When I first tried to kiss Tante Anna, the summer before, she initially would shrink back, and I would do it more cautiously and tentatively. But this summer, semiparalyzed in her body and her voice and rapidly approaching death, she silently gave me permission to express my love for her in this way. Perhaps she enjoyed being touched with so much tenderness.

Tante Anna was not a woman whom people embraced; they loved her from some distance. Could it be that no one had ever hugged her and caressed her since she was a child? I do not know. "You are the only person who is allowed to love her openly," one of her lifelong women friends said to me with envy. I told

Tante Anna that I had fallen in love with her and she smiled and said, "How inconvenient for you." But I assured her that I considered ours quite a happy love story, as love stories go. And I knew of course that like every other real passion, ours would also end in death.

My mother had died only two years earlier, and as I had sat next to her deathbed, she had asked me to hold her hand during her spasms of pain. It had been an ordeal for me to touch my poor old mother. My heart had been frozen toward her. But those short weeks in the summer of 1982 were long enough to teach me finally, in late midlife, what people felt when they said they loved their mother. I had heard from my friends, students, and sometimes even my children, and had read in books that some people love their mothers very deeply, but I had not known how that might feel. So now I had a bad mother and a good mother. Yet, this winter I dreamed that I took care of a baby that was both Tante Anna and my mother, and after that I knew that I was not only mourning my aunt, but also my mother and that I had finally integrated the good and the bad mother. I think it has taken me much longer than other people to learn about very simple things.

There had been a long-standing rift between these two women, and it would have hurt my mother very much if she had known that Tante Anna had become my good mother. But my mother's death had finally freed me to reclaim this other side of my heritage. Yet it had been a long, slow, and painful struggle of almost three years' persistent wooing, yearning, and not hoping for very much in return. It was not my conscious purpose to go to London to conquer Tante Anna's heart, but somehow that became my main mission during my sabbatical year. She finally granted me an interview that late fall of 1979, and we sat in my grandfather's old office-library and shivered with cold and talked about nothing. "I am tired," she said. "I am sorry to have taken up your time," I replied. It was among the most difficult things I have ever done, but I persisted in calling, writing, reaching out.

Although I had not asked to intern at her clinic, which may have hurt her feelings, I faithfully attended the conferences there that she chaired, and used all my wits to make clever comments.

Later I would learn that she had indeed been pleased and impressed.

I needed Tante Anna's blessing before I could rightfully reclaim the family legacy that I had betrayed, and yet remained faithful to in its core. I needed her blessing to forgive my father, her brother, who had abandoned me in adolescence. I needed her blessing to make sure that I was worthy of being loved by a queen.

In December 1979, Dorothy Burlingham, my aunt's lifelong living and working companion, died. Suddenly and unexpectedly an empty space appeared in Tante Anna's life, and somehow, magically, I was there and took the opportunity to usurp that place. Gradually we fell into a rhythm of my visiting her every evening and staying until I was dismissed. At first the visits lasted only a little while, but as the weeks passed by they got longer and longer, until we would spend many evenings together.

Tante Anna never indulged herself. She was a queen, and she had a poor appetite. She liked strawberries, yet she would never buy strawberries for herself unless they were in season. I understood this sort of thrift because it had been handed down to me as a reaction to my mother's extravagance. But I took a leap from thriftiness to my own extravagance when I went twice to London that summer. I think my love for Tante Anna has helped me to become less thrifty with myself.

When I noticed the parsimony of the household, I would bring Tante Anna fruits out of season and other delicacies. I learned that she enjoyed knitting with expensive yarns, and I foraged the London shops for the nicest yarns that I could find. I never came to her house empty-handed. They were gifts of love, yet I wonder now whether I tried to buy Tante Anna's heart with gifts. Tante Anna, unlike myself, enjoyed "good gifts." The child in her was open to such bribery. Or was she responding to the love behind the gifts? We sat and knitted together. Never before had I been so pleased about my interest and skill in knitting as when I met Tante Anna. It became our shared activity that we both understood and enjoyed.

When I left London after that fateful sabbatical year, she did not yet love me, but her heart was a little more open to me. She wrote: "When you return, if I am still here, you have an invitation to come with me to my country house. I look forward now to show you how beautiful it is here." And later, she wrote: "I shall try to still be here when you return and we shall start our relationship on a higher level, not from scratch, like this time."

Tante Anna had her heart set on knitting with pure silk yarn, but she had not been able to find such yarn anywhere. Upon my return to Boston I searched intensively and was rewarded when I came upon a store that carried the precious silk yarn. Columbus could not have been happier when he first saw land!

I started to send Tante Anna, every few months, large packages of silk yarn. She was already ill that winter of 1981 and spent a great deal of time in bed, knitting silk sweater after silk sweater. Each of my gifts was acknowledged with enthusiasm and gratitude.

"I am overwhelmed by your wonderful gifts," she wrote after the first package. "You are giving me a great deal of pleasure, but should you really do that? I am worried about your generosity for an old Aunt who can do so little for you. After all, not all old Aunts have such expensive hobbies. Many, many thanks and I will let you know how it will get transformed." And later: "This morning with the very first mail arrived your wonderful gift. Once again a sign how generous and extravagant one can be toward an old Aunt. You have rightly guessed that I am in love with silk of every kind. Perhaps not a harmless passion, but better than some others." And later: "You surpass yourself with your last shipment. It is so beautiful that I can only look at it with admiration before I decide what to do with it. Many thanks. I would not be surprised if you become bankrupt some day. Let me know in time so I can help you."

At first I was cautious and selected only beige and white yarns because those were her usual colors. Later, with increasing courage I started to buy silk in bold and daring colors. "You are quite right," she responded, "the blue color is so beautiful that it is irresistible." And when I sent a knitting book, she wrote: "I study the knitting patterns as eagerly as a new psychoanalytic publication. Each new yarn and each new pattern is an adventure."

I could not believe my good fortune. I had fallen in love with an eighty-five-year-old woman to whom I could give pleasure with something I could buy in a store. Moreover, it was luckily something that was expensive enough that it could seem like an extravagant gift.

Tante Anna decided to auction off her large collection of silk sweaters at the occasion of the annual meeting of her clinic, which was attended by people from America who would be happy and honored to buy a silk sweater "handknit by Anna Freud." The money was to establish an annual lecture fund in honor of her father's birthday. By a stroke of genius she had managed to combine the knitting passion of her old age with her lifelong passion for her father.

When I returned to London in the summer of 1981, I was received like an honored visitor, the purveyor of all that silk. We had a fashion show of several hours, during which I admired every silk sweater and shawl she had knit during that long winter in the many months she had spent in bed. The knitting, she explained, had taken the place of all the other things she no longer had the strength to do.

I like to pay my way, in life, in relationships, and yet, I also like to be loved for myself. She had not knit a sweater for me, although I was free to choose one, if I wanted. I did not want to choose one. My love for Tante Anna had developed instantly, but hers needed time to grow.

Tante Anna was now too ill to go to her country house with me, during that summer of 1981. We had missed the right moment. We sat together and knitted, and now and then we had small conversations. The following summer one of her vocal cords would be paralyzed, and making herself understood would become fatiguing and laborious. But even before that, ours had never been a predominantly verbal relationship. I did not use my time with her to ask her many questions. Too many people were eager to ask her too many questions. Mine was not a quest for knowledge but for love.

That endless theme between us: Will you be there next year? —I shall try to wait for you. As we parted that summer, I said to her: "You know, good workers, like you and me, always finish what they start. I will send you so much silk that you will always be in the middle of a knitting project." She seemed very pleased with our pact to fool the fates.

One month later a scarf that she had knitted for me arrived airmail special delivery. I was sad to hear later that it was her knitting friends who had encouraged her to make something for me. She had not thought of it herself. Yet I like to think she was very happy with her gift once she had started it. Of course the giving was not all one-sided. Tante Anna gave me some pieces of family jewelry, but more important to me was the gift of herself.

She often asked me questions about my life, and would express caring concern if all did not go well. "Can you tell me what the things are that hurt you? I want to share them with you," she wrote. She would always recommend work as an antidote to psychic pain.

Yet, my timid inquiries about visiting at Christmas 1981 were rebuked. I now understand that what I took for rebuke was merely a sign of her distress. My visit might actually have been a comfort to her; it certainly would have been to me. How bitterly I regret that misunderstanding. But since my love for Tante Anna was a passion, uncertainty about *her* love for me was forever a problem.

I did not hear directly from Tante Anna from March to May 1982, during the months she spent at the hospital trying bravely to recover from her stroke. I managed my sadness about her illness by sending her a picture postcard every single day during these months. It became my personal therapy to look for beautiful picture postcards. On each postcard I expressed my love and announced my approaching visit in July. Later her nurse would tell me that she decorated her hospital room with the postcards, but I did not know that when I sent them. Now there is no more silk to be sent and no more postcards to be selected.

In May, Tante Anna finally wrote: "I look forward to your coming but you will find a very incapacitated old Aunt," and I changed my plans from a two-week to a three-week stay in London.

The visit in July was much sadder than the subsequent visit in August. She slept a great deal and felt defeated by her physical problems and the ensuing dependency. "I am very miserable," she would say laconically to people who inquired about her health. Conversations became difficult, sometimes tense. On the one hand I did not ever want to ignore her words or assume their meaning. On the other hand I did not want to ask her to repeat the same sentence too many times. But she spoke fluent German and English to the end. Her sharp intelligence was unimpaired, and the core of her personality remained completely intact.

I explained to Tante Anna that she was in no way dependent on others, since she paid with her own savings for a private nurse. She listened carefully and told me the next day that she had considered what I had said, and that I was right. After that she seemed to feel less upset about her physical dependency. Yet Tante Anna found it extremely difficult to ask for something that might be a burden to others. Like all of us, she much preferred that things be offered freely. When I visited her once at the hospital, I found to my dismay that nursing plans had misfired and that she was all alone while receiving a blood transfusion. "What are your plans this afternoon?" she asked casually after an hour's visit. "To stay with you, of course." "Good" she said. Later I slipped out and quietly canceled my afternoon appointments. I don't know if she would have been able to ask me to stay with her.

I read to her a great deal of professional literature during those weeks. She would always fall asleep and wake up when I stopped reading. "Go on, I am listening," she would say, "I love the sound of your voice." I think she was partial to my accent.

Sometimes she would sit alone for hours in the garden. "What do you think about during those hours? Do you think about all you have accomplished in life? I asked her. - "No, I think about all the things I still want to do. And sometimes German poems I learned in childhood go through my head." We would then recite some German poems together and laugh a little.

It was especially hard for her not to be able to knit any more. She had tried desperately for months to regain at least some control of her hands, but they no longer obeyed her. Now and then she would try again, but the stitches would get all mixed up. I would gladly pick them up for her, again and again, but after a while she became too discouraged. "My hands have become too awkward to knit," she said, and gave up. If she tried very hard, she could still make a wool chain with her fingers, and the chain could be rolled up and sewn into something useful like a purse or a bag, if it became long enough. Finally it became too difficult to work on the chain and it lay there in her workbag, useless and abandoned.

I am usually never idle for more than a few minutes, but I was that summer. I sat next to Tante Anna, who slept for many hours, and I just looked at her, day after day, and tried to engrave in my memory her sleeping face, the stone terrace, and the garden around us, so it would stay there forever. From time to time she would wake up and her eyes would fall upon me sitting next to her, and she would smile at me, perhaps in recognition of a familiar face that reminded her of her brother or sister whom she had loved, but who had all died before her because she was the youngest child in her family. One does not forget such moments when a dying queen who is often stern, and sometimes scornful or impatient, and who is one's aunt yet has been a stranger all one's life, gives one an affectionate smile.

Although it might sound exceedingly presumptuous, there is little question that Tante Anna and I were kindred spirits. We presented ourselves in similar ways to the world. Neither Tante Anna nor I had ever thought ourselves beautiful women, but we thought so of each other.

Tante Anna was a beautiful woman at the age of eighty-six. Neither of us had ever worn cosmetics, and we both liked exactly the same kind of loose clothes. Whenever I went to London I took along all my favorite dresses and I would wear a different one every day. Tante Anna would look at me with approving eyes and she would say admiringly, "Your pretty dress matches your beautiful silvery hair." Nobody had ever told me that I had beautiful silvery hair!

Since I have become an academician and work around the clock to fulfill my growing obligations, I no longer have time to sew my own clothes, as Tante Anna did all her life. "You sew all your own clothes by hand?" I asked in great surprise. "Of course," she answered a bit impatiently, "it would after all not be practical to use a sewing machine while I see patients." She was sick in bed when we had this conversation, but she jumped out of bed and showed me with pride and pleasure the many beautiful clothes she had sewn through the years. They were all made of beautiful fabrics, all sewn along the same jumperlike pattern, and all two sizes bigger than necessary.

Both Tante Anna and I were accustomed to speaking in a strong voice and to looking scholarly and serious, but we both remained children in some important ways. I think both of us have been loved and admired by others in similar ways that did not touch us in our core. We both looked at admiration as children might look at colorful balloons at a birthday party, balloons that amuse and entertain for a few minutes, then float away or explode. Tante Anna enjoyed collecting her many doctoral degrees up to the last month of her life, but when she reminisced, she always talked about the children's homes that she had established and administered during the war years in London.

It was in the middle of my July visit that Tante Anna had to go to the hospital for one of her blood transfusions. She suffered from anemia, which eventually could no longer be controlled and killed her. Her medical staff arranged for an ambulance to get her and I was not allowed to come along. Stricken and abandoned, I caught a last glimpse of her ashen, shrunken face as the doors of the ambulance closed and it drove away.

When I came back in August things were very different. I lived in the big house and slept in the room adjoining Tante Anna's and took charge of the household. It seemed so very strange that fate had still given me a chance to live for one week in that house in which I had once felt unwelcome as a guest. The house was full of ghosts of the past. Grandfather had sat on the terrace. Grandmother had sat at the baywindow on the first floor and had been most reluctant to go to the air-raid shelter during the London blitz. There was a ghost of the present as well. Tante Anna's lifelong housekeeper haunted the house day and night with her ravaged body and soul, both consumed over the years by the passionate love and hate that she had felt toward "Miss Freud" all her adult life. She would let no one use the kitchen, yet she could no longer cook properly herself, and many days Tante Anna was served inedible food. The two old women, mistress and servant, were locked in mutual torment that could be broken only by death.

Tante Anna seemed stronger and more lively in August. I believe she had her last burst of strength during that week. She could show some pleasure about my visit. "This is my niece, Martin's daughter, who came all the way from America just to visit me for a week," she would say as she proudly introduced me to visitors. I would greet her at breakfast and stay next to her bed in the evening, until she went to sleep at night. I had never found much pleasure in taking care of sick people, but suddenly I took immense enjoyment in every small way that I could help. Eating and drinking had become increasingly difficult, and she allowed me to ease these daily struggles. One day I found her favorite grapes in the store. We sat together in the garden and I playfully peeled each grape and took out the pit while she ate them with pleasure. "Now you have found a daughter after all; are you glad?" I asked. "Yes," she smiled, "very glad." For the first time in our relationship I felt that she had truly opened her heart toward me and I felt sure that my presence was a joy and comfort to her. I had not been as happy for very many years.

At the end of the year her blood count fell again. This time I was able to take her to the hospital. It was a terrible trip, and she almost died on the way. She had to sit up in an old-fashioned English ambulance that was full of other sick old people, but at least I sat next to her and could hold her in my arms. I had to leave the next day. I wrote her daily of course, but we never talked again, because the nurse said she had become too weak to telephone. Tante Anna was old and sick and deserved to die in peace, but our love had lasted for too short a time.

I have often wondered how my life would have gone if Tante Anna and I had found each other earlier. I bitterly regret all those years of unnecessary estrangement. I had meant to ask her what they were about, but in the end I forgot to do that. I think my life would have been different in important ways. I have the fantasy that her emotional presence could have added much happiness and richness to my life. Yet Tante Anna was a powerful woman, and it is quite possible that this great love that I had for her could have resulted in my intellectual or emotional bondage at an earlier time. After all, such loving bondage is also a part of the family legacy. We met at the only time when theoretical differences were irrelevant to both of us.

I also wonder whether Tante Anna could have loved me so generously earlier in her life. She was not a woman who opened her heart easily to other people. Life was not always easy for the men and women who had sought her out to be their mother. Perhaps our relationship could not have been other than brief.

Tante Anna loved my father, her older brother, very much. Through our relationship I have finally been able to make peace with my father. Not only have I learned through Tante Anna what it means to love a mother, but also how it feels to lose a mother whom one has loved. I also learned from her how to face death with fortitude. I learned a great deal from my Aunt in a very short time.

Although I loved Tante Anna as a substitute mother, my father's sister, my grandfather's daughter, and as a woman of distinction and fame, I loved her above all as a human being, for herself and her willingness to open her guarded heart to me. I must accept life and death as they are. I have come to the end of this journey.

5 / The Visit

THE woman had long ago decided never to stand in line for movies or restaurants, and even for toilets only in an emergency. She now made the decision to add telephone calls to the list of unacceptable waiting activities. There she found herself, Sunday after Sunday afternoon, reluctant to go out for a walk, to visit a friend, to leave the house, lest she miss an opportunity to hear his enchanting British voice from across the ocean.

But the lack of a call today had yet another dimension. She had absolutely counted on his calling her on this particular day. She had carefully mentioned her breast biopsy during their last meeting, and he had dutifully noted it in his diary. She had assumed that he would call her, certainly not on the day of the operation, but the subsequent Sunday, since that was his customary calling day and he was not a man given to rash impulsive actions.

He had either forgotten to call—one does not check one's appointment book on Sunday after all—or he had not forgiven her for writing her story about him. She knew she should never have told him about it during that last meeting when they had said good-bye to each other for yet another year. The story was unlikely to see the light of day in any case, and if it ever did, he was unlikely to encounter it. As a don, forever pressed with academic pursuits he certainly had no time to read short stories. But she had not been able to resist sharing the happy news with him, since she gave him credit for sparking her creativity. Writing her awkward little stories was her greatest pleasure in life. Wanting to include him in her celebration, she had brushed aside her certainty that this private man would hate and dread the idea of a story in which he was the main character. Soon after she had told him about the story, she had to leave Cambridge for the train to London and the airport back to Boston. They had tried to cover up the breach created by her story but parting was never easy for them, and it seemed just one more version of the last minute quarrels that they tended to produce. She had felt quite bad about having originated this particular fight.

Yet she had assumed that it was just more of the same, and she had started to wait, as in other years, for her Sunday calls. It had been a month now since her return, but he had not called and he had not written. That, however, had not been unusual. It was her style to need extra contact quickly after having seen someone she loved, and his style to take a vacation from the relationship after a period of face-to-face closeness. Still, his not calling her after her operation, however minor and routine she had made it appear, must be a signal that he was now ready to terminate the relationship. She did not really think he was that angry about the story. More likely he had forgotten or was otherwise occupied.

Her memory went back to how the past summer's visit had started. "I shall take you to a gallery," he had said to her on the telephone, when she announced her annual summer visit during his late spring call. She could hear hesitation in his voice, betraying his momentary panic that she would expect more things from him, more time, more love, more attention, than he could possibly give her. It also irritated her that his tone sounded like that of a man who suggested a daring trip to the South Sea Islands. Besides, she did not like the typical masculine wording "take you" of his invitation. She was not a woman who liked to be *taken* most anywhere. But she was also longing to connect with him on any level he could accept. So, instead of correcting his language, she had written him a short note every single day, starting two weeks before they met, in the hope that they would not have to meet as strangers once again, as in the past, but instead could simply continue to weave the web of their relatedness.

They managed to meet in his lovely office, up on the fourth floor in some antique tower, on the very day of her arrival, a novel idea that she had suggested to him and that he had taken on as his own. What a relief it had been not to wait for hours until he finally called her. Sitting together once again in his office, where they had first met some years ago, they were both cautious. He had once been her tutor during a sabbatical year six years ago, when she had realized a lifelong dream to study history at Trinity College, in Cambridge. She was a psychologist, but history was a field she had always regretted not having pursued. She had lived in London and worked at a clinic, but almost surreptitiously she had taken the train at Kings Cross to Cambridge every Tuesday morning for her weekly tutorial and to spend the two days in the library.

Initially they had some fierce disagreements and he scoffed at her idea that the role of industrialists in bringing Hitler to power was not clear-cut. He was not used to tutoring students who disagreed with him and her being so much older and a "professor" in her own land, albeit in a different field, had been a challenge for him. She had wanted to please him very badly but not at the expense of her intellectual integrity. They had each done extensive research to convince the other of their own viewpoint. It was with relief and triumph that they finally integrated their ideas and even wrote a paper together at the very last moment. He had seemed very pleased and proud when he called her with the news that their paper had been accepted in a prestigious British journal. By the time the glorious year was over, she had fallen in love with him, while he, on his part, was cautiously interested in starting a correspondence.

On this last summer's first encounter, in order to bridge the strangeness between them, she quickly spoke of the letter she had received from him just before leaving home. She had experienced it as a despairing letter. But he raised his eyebrows in semisurprise; he could not quite remember what he might have written to her, things were going well enough. Yet mysteriously and magically, he had had a change of heart and made new plans since they talked on the telephone. Perhaps he needed some support and sensed her readiness to help him in any way that might be useful and acceptable to him. He asked her to read the unfinished first draft of his book, which he wanted to write so badly and yet had not found a way to finish, given his multiple competing obligations. So, instead of planning their annual trip to a museum, he set up a series of common meetings for them, almost one a day over the week she would spend in Cambridge. She was stunned that he wanted to spend that much time with her. She had always known him as a man who anxiously looked at his watch, all through the day, every fifteen minutes. She attributed his being haunted by the passing of time to a minor stroke he had had half a year before they met. It seemed to have left him keenly appreciative of the shortness of life and preoccupied with his mortality and immortality. It had also left him with a slightly impaired left arm and left leg, inevitably slowing him down in many ways and no doubt adding to his feeling pressed and fatigued. She had broken her hand the winter before and had experienced how much more complicated and wearisome life became with only one useful hand. It had helped her understand more deeply the constant burden his handicap imposed on him.

He did not want to meet in his home, where his anorectic daughter might possibly decide to cook for them, and he did not want to meet at his school office, where he felt haunted by constant demands. Instead, they met in the small flat where she stayed whenever she came to visit this town. The people who owned the flat were her friends, coming and going, tactfully remaining in the background. He was willing to climb the steep one flight of stairs, which was laborious and tiring for him. It was hard for her to watch his stressful climb. She found one chair in this modest little flat that would support his back well enough. And he arrived every morning, exactly on time, and sat in the one good chair as if he had found a place of comfort and inner peace.

She read all hundred and fifty pages of his manuscript on the day of her arrival, reading late into the night, forgetting her jet lag, and feeling enormous pleasure and perhaps relief that he had written a fine book. His book focused on the betrayal aspects of the Versailles Treaty; he was interested in using psychological concepts in his historical analyses, something that was often frowned upon by serious scholars. He had been especially anxious to get her assurance that his psychological interpretations were valid and meaningful, since this was a new area for him. He was anxious about the reception that his novel ideas would have among his colleagues while hoping to receive the equivalent of a historian's Nobel Prize.

They sat together in their island, day after day, and while she made concrete suggestions, she hoped above all to encourage him and to contain his grandiose fantasies and discouragements, which got in his way. As they spent more time together, he shared his worries, concerns, and fears with her, all of which impeded his progress with his book. Sharing his feelings was part of the work they did together. She was most happy to become his teacher and therapist, because these were life roles in which she felt valued and secure. Now and then, she would have liked to get up to kiss him, or walking by the back of his chair, she was tempted to put her arms around his neck, but she restrained herself, knowing that it was against his rules.

She bought food for them, and she knew enough about his habits to prepare him a cup of coffee at 11:00 A.M. and to serve lunch at 1:00 P.M.; she was enchanted that she could feed him so well in their island home. Then he would leave at 2:00, yet magically return the next day. Over lunch there was room to talk about their difficult relationship. "Whenever I write a paper," she told him, "my first impulse is to send it to you. My second thought is bitterness that you will not make the effort to read it, and I decide to withhold my paper from you. Then finally, I want to be generous and loving toward you, and I end up sending you the paper which you then don't acknowledge. It is as if you don't value my thoughts. And yet, in asking me to help you with your book, you suggest to me that I might be able to teach you things." She also felt free to tell him that she viewed her feelings for him like an alien addiction, a foreign body in an otherwise well-disciplined life. She told him that she thought his own feelings for her were merely based on being flattered that a woman of her caliber would love him so much. She took both of his hands in hers as she told him these hard and painful thoughts, and she was grateful that he could listen to her feelings and that he might even later reach out to her in some slightly different way, to convey that he had heard her. It was also true that all her bad feelings became less toxic in the telling.

His fragility evoked a special generosity of spirit in her. As much as she had resented the role of unloving wife, which she had assumed and in which she had been cast by her former husband for so many years, that much more she treasured by contrast the feelings of openness and the wish to help him, which he generated in her. She knew from the beginning that he was a well-married man who loved his wife, but this did not matter that much. She thought she was a woman who would rather love than be loved.

They met on Saturday, Monday, Tuesday, and Wednesday, and she gladly put aside whatever other plans she had made for her vacation, hardly remembering what they might have been. He also came by on Thursday, but that was not a good day any longer, because by then her anguish about another year's interval before they would meet again had taken hold of her. He brought her a hugh bunch of red gladiolas and tiger lillies, which was a strange experience for her, because giving gifts was her role in the relationship, not his. "Oh, how many beautiful flowers," she said, and he laughed in his embarrassed small boy way. "I wanted to be generous for once," he replied.

She also had a gift for him. She had bought him a package of his favorite candies and enclosed directions explaining that he should eat a piece of chocolate whenever he felt particularly discouraged. They were "magic" candies, that would instantly remind him that he had a right and even a duty to enjoy life.

She thought that he sensed her distress about this being their last meeting, but he did not know how to comfort her. Her own husband had also always been helpless when faced with her grief. Perhaps she was the kind of person whom nobody could comfort. Or perhaps he could not comfort her because he did not share her distress. She had told him how hard it was for her always to carry alone the sadness of their parting. It confused her how he could turn to her for solace, warmth, and affirmation, and let her go again without a word of regret.

While she went out for an errand she gave him a letter she had written him the evening before. At the end of that letter, as a postscript, she gave voice to her fantastic proposition that he should take her along on Saturday to the planned visit to his mother about which he had told her. He had told her that his eighty-year-old mother had moved after her husband's death to a stately country mansion that had been transformed into a retirement home for aristocratic ladies and gentlemen. She had written this request for a common visit with much trepidation, feeling too anxious to voice it directly. When she returned, he thanked her for the letter, but made no other comment, and they continued to work on the organization of his book. She could even think of a title for his book that he really liked. How would he dedicate his book? "To my wife, without whom this book could never have been written," which was true of course, since his wife was a devoted and caretaking steady companion, while she was only an occasional apparition in his life.

As the time to part came nearer and nearer and he did not even once refer to the visit to his mother, she imagined that her request had been too outrageous even to refuse. Yet once again she gathered her courage and referred to her question, and it turned out that he had neglected to read her postscript. He considered the matter with some astonishment and informed her that he would be going with his troubled daughter, at his mother's request. She then became quite bold, assured him that she would behave very well in front of his mother, and announced that she would wait for his call, in case his daughter changed her mind. He seemed afraid that she would be disappointed and warned her not to count on him. The opportunity to spend time with his daughter had priority over anything else. But when she came home on Friday evening a message awaited her that the trip was taking place and that she was invited to come along.

The rain had stopped long enough to allow them a glorious ride through the English countryside. They were both in a holiday mood, and she was intent on savoring every minute of that precious day; she was the kind of woman who tried to store moments of great happiness that came to her as other people might store potatoes in a cellar to protect themselves against possible future starvation. She tried to tell the man beside her how much these meadows reminded her of pictures from a favorite childhood book about a man who could talk animal language. She remembered the pictures of old horses peacefully grazing on meadows in a farm for retired horses that Dr. Doolittle had purchased for them. He seldom asked her questions about herself, apparently preferring to tell her incidents from his own life, which was alright with her. But sometimes she did not wait for questions and simply told him about things that were important to her, and that seemed alright for him as well. She had longed for years to take a trip with him. "This is our practice for the trip to Paris we shall take some day," she said to him, referring to her playful fantasy.

From time to time she put her hand on his hand on the steering wheel. He had lovely fingers and delicate hands. He neither winced nor smiled as she did this. It was hard for her never to know whether he enjoyed being touched in these ways, or whether he simply submitted to her as the price he felt he had to pay for her friendship. She could sense that it was the latter.

She had explained to him how daring it had felt to ask him to meet his mother, not only once by letter, but then again in person. He quite agreed that she had taken an enormous risk. She was initially worried that she had perhaps coerced him into doing something he basically had not wanted to do, a common theme for both of them in their relationship; but she had comforted herself, remembering how easy it would have been for him to tell her that his daughter was coming along. Then she asked him what had been hard for him in this whole matter. He explained that he had for once given his daughter a choice between coming and not coming on this visit, and the daughter had chosen not to come. She wondered whether the father had conveyed to his daughter that he would rather go with someone else, but she did not share that thought with him. The hard parts were, he explained after further questions, blushing like a schoolboy, that he was ashamed to introduce a foreign Jew to his genteel upper-class mother. He spoke of an episode in which his mother had made an anti-Semitic comment, and it became uncertain whether he was ashamed of her or ashamed of his mother, since it was a mixture of both feelings that he shared with her. What would she think of his mother and what would his mother think of her?

She was amused and touched by his embarrassment and honesty. She had taken it for granted that his mother as a British aristocrat would have feelings about Jews. Yet she also knew quite certainly that she could win his mother's heart, especially since she had a natural affection for old ladies, and she forbade him to instruct her on the subjects she was allowed to discuss with his mother. "You will interrogate her in your usual way," he said in a fretful voice, "and she might not like your questions."

The old mother, who was still a beautiful woman with sparkling blue eyes and facial expressions like her son's, received her most graciously yet with formality. She had asked his permission to bring along the flowers he had given her, since she was leaving town the next day in any case. She reminded him that the flowers would be her gift, since they were her flowers, and the mother loved them and arranged them most carefully in one of her antique vases. She admired all the beautiful objects, relics from her past life, that filled the mother's single room, and she loved the stunning embroidery that the mother still designed and executed. She also enjoyed doing embroidery, and soon she and the mother were engrossed in a conversation about a common interest.

They had lunch in an elegant dining room at a reserved guest table with a white table cloth. The mother introduced them with some pride to some of the other very old guests. During lunch she teased the old woman gently, talking to her about feminist ideas, and they started to joke and laugh together. Later they went back upstairs to have their coffee and the mother invited her son to have his usual nap on her bed. They sat on either side of the bed, quietly reading and watching together over his well-being. From time to time they smiled at each other and she thought the older woman was giving her permission to enter their charmed circle.

The afternoon grew much longer than anticipated, since the son's enjoyment at seeing his mother so lively and stimulated had grown hour by hour. He almost forgot to look at his watch. When she had noticed that the mother read mostly historical diaries, she suggested to her that she should write her own biography for her grandchildren, and the mother took her seriously and started to remember her love of writing when she had been a schoolgirl. When they finally left, the mother embraced her with spontaneity, warmth, and a little sadness that the visit had ended.

He told her on the way home that he had not seen his mother

in such a lively mood for many years. Perhaps she had finally recovered from the loss of her husband, three years ago. He seemed most pleased that he had asked her to come along, and he thanked her for being a person who took risks, thus teaching him that this was also possible. There was closeness and happiness between them for having shared this afternoon. He talked with pride about having gotten up at six in the morning during the last two days to write his two new chapters. It was the first writing he had done after many months of silence. Since she was a greedy woman who needed to be told things rather than have them implied, she asked him whether she had inspired him. He could affirm her when she asked such direct questions, yet it was not in him to tell her spontaneously in words that she could hear and feel, how much their time together had meant to him. This was sad for her because she was a woman who needed words, even though she had also learned to hear his nonverbal signals, even across the ocean. She had read his new chapters while he was dozing on his mother's bed, and noticed that he had used her ideas and suggestions. They would, after all, give birth to something together.

He then announced that his wife felt they should reward her for helping him with his book by taking her out to dinner. Would she go along with that? She remained silent for a long time, hating the thought that something she disliked doing was framed as a reward for her. He tolerated her very long silence in his respectful way, yet did not acknowledge her obvious distress. She finally suggested that she would drop over after dinner to have a cup of tea with them. But he called her within the hour to tell her that his wife wanted to go out for dinner and he hoped that she would come along. She did not want to make his life more difficult and accepted the invitation. It was not as if she disliked his wife; on the contrary, she liked her very well, and besides she was glad that he had someone who took such good care of him. The wife was most pleasant, apparently appreciative of the help she had given her husband with his book, and eager to talk about their visit to her mother-in-law. Her simpler social class background had always been a problem for her in his aristocratic family. Listening to the wife's mixed feelings, she remembered how she had always felt disapproved by her own mother-in-law. It was much easier to appreciate the mother of a friend.

Husband and wife were about to go on vacation, and as the evening wore on the issue of the day was debated before her: should he be allowed to take his book writing on vacation or not. He promised that he would write only in the early morning hours, but she did not believe him. "I'm in a no-win position," the wife said to her. "If he takes his book, he will not be available to me on our holiday, and if he does not take his book he will resent it." She recognized their dilemma as a loving marital dispute, since it affirmed the wife's wish for his company, and she knew that they would find some compromise solution. She reflected how gratifying it must be for this man to sit between two women who loved him and who both wanted to spend more time with him. After dinner, husband and wife walked down the street, arm in arm, which seemed to ease his walking. But the wife suddenly seemed to feel uneasy about her husband's friend walking alone behind them. She disengaged herself and offered her the front seat of the car. As she left the car, he bent over to kiss her good-bye on her cheek, but she withdrew her head, turned away from him, and quickly closing the car door, she wished the wife a good vacation.

It had been after his return from their vacation that she had gone down to Cambridge for a short last-minute visit, to say good-bye, and to have one last quarrel about her story.

It was now seven o'clock, the usual deadline after which a call from England became most unlikely. The woman settled down at her word processor. She needed to change the end of her story. Twenty minutes later the telephone started to ring; it rang for quite a long time. Was it one of her daughters inquiring about her health? Or could he have changed his mind and called un-characteristically late? The telephone stopped ringing.

6 / Reunion

AT first, the professor refused instantly when asked to be the keynote speaker at yet another annual conference. Even the promise of a special award did not tempt her. It had been too exhausting a year. Later, she felt a nagging sense she'd made the wrong decision. The request to speak had come from her professional association in Lincoln, Nebraska. Someone whom she had once loved very deeply taught at the university there. She thought he would undoubtedly attend the annual state convention of his own field, in his own town. Here was her opportunity to see him again, to see whether he had grown fat or remained slim in the fifteen years since she had seen him last, and to see whether her heart would still beat faster when she saw him. Why had she never quite finished her emotional business with anyone she had encountered throughout life? She was forever going back in time, returning to live in the city where she was born, seeking out people who had once been meaningful to her. Did she hope to recover some childhood happiness or maybe simply some form of love that had escaped her, and that would surely continue to evade her?

She called the committee back, and said she had changed her mind and that she would be happy to deliver a paper for their convention.

The man she had loved had a French name, Pierre. His mother had grown up in France and perhaps expressed her homesickness in the name she had given her son. This was the story he told to explain his name to her, along with describing the many ways in which the mother's ongoing homesickness had cast a shadow over his whole childhood. It had not been clear to her whether his mother's apparent chronic depression had been simply related to missing her homeland, or whether marrying an elegant American sergeant during the war who had never become more than an underpaid bookkeeper in a hardware store had contributed to her unhappiness.

Pierre and she had started their first academic job at the same school, he as a young man in his first job, and she as a woman in midlife who was starting an academic career in the field in which she had been a practitioner. Pierre's house, where he lived with his wife and children, was located halfway between her home and school. Since she drove to work, while he took the streetcar, it had been a natural development for her to offer him rides home, which he eagerly accepted. She loved to gossip about their department and they had laughed a great deal together. Had he noticed the subtle poisoned arrows that a certain assistant professor had aimed at a senior professor in the faculty meeting? Did she think his contribution to the curriculum committee had been properly appreciated? Yes, she agreed that it was probably true that their department head used her English accent to emphasize her upper class lineage, but she thought that his own slight hint of a French accent was equally elegant. No, she was sure that their dean had not meant to undermine him since he had just recently referred to Pierre as a "diamond in the rough."

They also shared strong interest in their common field and both loved books. With time they began to dream of opening a bookstore together. While she was a seasoned teacher, he had never taught before, and she felt pleased when he turned to her for practical advice. They found so much to talk about that their half-hour ride became too short. As the months rolled by, he would continue talking, with the car parked in front of his house, telling one last interesting story, and later two or three more stories, before he left. Her husband and son at home were waiting for her for dinner, no doubt with hungry impatience, but work was work, and she was entitled to work late, if that was required. Before she met Pierre her emotional life had revolved around her adolescent son, who was in his last year of high school and she had struggled to spend as much time with him as he would reluctantly allow. Suddenly that whole relationship lost its urgency and she knew for the first time that she could let him grow up and go his own way without too much sorrow.

Thinking back, she could see how much Pierre had loved words, especially his own, and she imagined that he had never had such an attentive audience. She in turn had lived in a silent marriage for many years, and being talked to in the intimate setting of a car became with time an intoxicating experience. She had luxuriated in the flowing river of his words. She could no longer recall how long it had taken her to fall in love with him, but it must have been in early spring, perhaps soon after he began to recount the struggles and traumatic experiences of his childhood and adolescence. He told her he was convinced that the arid intellectual atmosphere of his years at home had been responsible for his enormous difficulty in finishing his dissertation. He would now be expected to produce scholarly articles to further his academic career and was consumed with anxiety that his endless procrastination would interfere. "It's easy for you," he often said to her, "you were born with a silver spoon in your mouth." Yet during that winter, he had begun writing an article and with her almost daily questions and encouragement, had been able to finish it. They had celebrated by stopping for an ice cream soda on the way home. In retrospect, it was the peak moment of their relationship.

Her realization that she had fallen desperately in love had been a major life crisis. Until that time, she had considered herself quite content in her marriage. But suddenly her whole marriage and with it her whole life structure had come into question. How could a well married woman of fifty-one years, just starting an academic career, passionately fall in love with a married man young enough to be her son? It was not what she had learned from her many textbooks; she was not prepared for such an event. The beautiful friendship had become a tormenting passion which invaded her life.

In late spring, her son decided to move in with some friends who invited him to share an apartment they had found near their high school. She had opposed his move, feeling sure that it would interfere with his studies, but since her husband promoted the plan, she had lost the battle.

She would have liked to talk to Pierre about that life crisis, but found no way to bring it up. He was preoccupied with the renewal of his academic contract and needed a great deal of reassurance. Yet, it was the very day after her son had moved out that her self-control had broken down. "Do you know that I have fallen in love with you?" she had said to him, as he stopped his car in front of his house. Then she had tried to stroke his curly dark brown hair and burst into tears. Pierre had never left the car with so much haste. The next day he had valiently tried to return to their old rules but she had lost interest in his agenda. "It's not about sex," she finally said to him, "it's about the intimacy of exchanging thoughts and feelings." This time he stayed in the car long enough to disavow their relationship with haste, anxiety and urgency. It was a therapist he had sought in her, surely not a lover!

For some weeks, she had continued to drive him home with bitter exchanges too painful to recall after all these years. While she continued to teach—perhaps work somehow kept her afloat—she found it harder and harder to teach a whole class without crying. Luckily the subjects of the end of the year dealt with death and separation and other life sorrows, and so it seemed quite natural if during discussions, tears occasionally welled up in her eyes. Mercifully, the school year finally ended and he had received a much better paid academic position in his home town, Lincoln, Nebraska.

She mourned the relationship for two years, but then new projects and other relationships had taken over in healing ways. Yet, this entire interlude, invisible to most people who knew her, had changed her self-concept and had been a fatal blow to her marriage.

In this trip to the convention, she would be going as a divorced woman. Perhaps she would have a chance to explain to him how it had all happened. And it pleased her that Pierre would witness her receiving a special professional award.

Her paper, for the convention which she called "Learning to

Heal," was written in many ways for him—to tell him about her professional growth and about herself, a subject matter about which he had always been curiously disinterested. He had rarely asked her any personal questions.

The committee served coffee and pastries before her talk began, and people approached her for friendly exchanges. She kept her eyes on the door of the auditorium. There were several people from Pierre's department at the university, and they mentioned that he had urged them to attend her talk since she was bound to offer interesting ideas. He too, she was told, was planning to come.

The proceedings began with the award which outlined her scholarly accomplishments, and continued with her lecture. She enjoyed the award, and she enjoyed reading her new paper, and her disappointment that he had not come did not interfere with her ability to present her ideas with enough elegance to please her audience.

The talk was followed by a short reception and people lined up to thank her, to shake her hand, and to ask for her autograph. At that moment Pierre walked in, and she gasped with recognition. What a pity he had not grown a paunch! It would have made things easier. She had since become an elderly woman, while time seemed to have passed him by. Pierre aggressively cut into the front of the line and instantly continued the conversation that they had interrupted fifteen years ago. "Let's be careful," he said in an intimate tone, "that woman behind me has sharp ears and besides she is a gossip." And then he added with a grimace, "I could tell you things about her, she teaches in my department and the students keep complaining about her." He quickly guided her into a corner and they both laughed, hiding from that nosy faculty colleague.

"Why didn't you answer the letter I wrote you eight years ago?" he asked.

"I hadn't forgiven you, and I waited for a second try but you gave up very quickly," she replied.

"I felt very rejected when you didn't answer my letter" he continued. "I wrote to you after my analyst died and I desperately needed some comfort."

"You didn't explain that in your letter. You went into analysis?"

"Yes, you know, I wasn't doing that well, the way I felt about myself and I couldn't get myself to write those damn articles."

"Well, did you get to feel better?" she asked.

"No, not much has changed with me, he died before we could make enough progress, and his death was a terrible blow."

"I'm sorry to hear that" she said.

"I see you have done well for yourself," he then said with an edge to his voice. "Every time I open a journal I find an article of yours. I think I shall become assistant dean before too long and as an administrator they won't expect me to write articles; that will be a relief."

People had found her in the corner, and were claiming their right to her presence by crowding around them. "My marriage continues to limp along," he quickly added in a low voice, "I had a short love affair, but it ended very unhappily. I guess I'll be running along, it was good to see you again."—"Why didn't you come to my talk?" she called after him as he turned away. "So sorry, I was busy," he called back to her, already at the door, as she dutifully started to autograph programs.

Within the week, she received a chatty letter from Pierre, talking about the politics of becoming assistant dean and expressing satisfaction about their short meeting. "Dear Pierre," she replied, "I too enjoyed meeting you again after all these years and you looked as handsome as ever. I was glad to hear your important news. I would have liked to start a new friendship with you, because my heart is still open to you. I wrote my talk for you, as a gift of a piece of my life that I wanted to share with you. You could not spare the hour it would have taken to come and hear my presentation and now I cannot spare the time to exchange letters with you." And then she sent him her best wishes for his future and quickly posted the letter.

7 / Learning to Heal

*T*HE title of this essay may appear to be presumptuous, and I ask your indulgence. Learning has certainly been at the core of my life—from books, from relationships, and from every experience that I have ever had. Healing myself and healing others has been another primary ongoing lifegoal.

Those of you who think that I was born with a therapeutic silver spoon in my mouth are quite in error. On the contrary, it took me an inordinately long time to develop the qualities of openness, empathy, acceptance, and self-love that healing involves. I do not think that healing can ever be a technical skill. I see it as interacting with people in such a way that some mutual healing, however modest, may take place. Helping others, I believe, can only occur simultaneously with helping oneself, with one activity sustaining the other. Learning to heal refers to my continuing, not always successful, efforts to heal myself and to interact in a healing way with my students, my clients, my friends, and even with members of my family.

Although fortunate in my adult life, I had a difficult childhood and adolescence. I have regularly opened myself to pain, mostly by loving too much, sometimes too little, the wrong people, or in the wrong way. I tend to embrace suffering at regular intervals, which makes life more problematic, but I think having experienced pain is an absolutely prerequisite apprenticeship for psychotherapy.

Many of my students have a maturity and wisdom that took me half a lifetime to acquire, and I am constantly surprised when they seem to understand what they are doing as therapists. I had to acquaint myself personally with many of the passionate emotions and anguish that human beings experience before I could connect with people in pain.

As a very young woman in social work school I kept asking my teachers and supervisors what casework or therapy was all about. They seemed to guard their answers like precious secrets. Perhaps they tried to give explanations that I could not hear. Although considered a most promising student, I was in reality blindly groping with no idea of what helping people might involve. After thirty-five years I am ready to share some reflections on the question that I so urgently asked as a young woman.

I had been in the United States only four years, barely emerging from dark years of wars and danger, when I entered social work school. I had little knowledge of the profession. I knew that I did not want to change or even necessarily help others, but I was endlessly curious about the human condition. I wanted to interact with, understand, and learn from other people. Social work appeared to be a fruitful and accessible avenue for doing this, and miraculously enough, it has kept its promise. Like Allen Wheelis in his youthful *Quest for Identity* (1958), I too might have been searching for one-sided intimacy that would connect me with people without demanding openness on my part. Openness seemed a very dangerous business in those days.

In my first year of training in a child welfare agency I was assigned eleven-year-old Naomi. Her mother had died some years earlier, and she and her older siblings lived with a father whose health had deteriorated to such a degree that he could no longer be responsible for his youngest child. Naomi had to be placed in a children's home, and I was the worker who had to break the news to her, prepare her for the move, and accompany her to her new home. I had not been involved in the decision to move her, and I could only give her second-hand official explanations. Naomi did not wish to leave her father and her siblings. She was enraged and decided not to talk to me. She did not utter a single word during our visits, our agonizing shopping trips, endless medical check-ups in various clinics, and all the follow-up visits. Only now can I admire the incredible strength and fighting spirit she mustered. But at the age of twenty-two I felt like a desperate and helpless little girl myself. I started to have crying spells and nightmares, which I kept secret from everyone. The child's hatred felt personal and devastating; I felt as if Naomi and I were locked in a silent struggle and she had defeated me. Yet I stayed with her through the year. In retrospect, perhaps her victory over me had given her a feeling of power at a time when she otherwise would have felt totally impotent. I sometimes still wonder how I might have coped with this situation.

As a beginning therapist I was not prepared for my client's hostility. A pleasant and well-behaved girl/woman, I had not ever examined my own hatreds. Anxious to be loved and appreciated by my clients, I learned quickly to appease them with my warm and winning ways. But some seemed unappeasable.

Two years after my experience with Naomi, I was working in my first job, which was in a family service agency. I was assigned to work with Mrs. LaFarge, an elderly widow whom I was supposed to help become emotionally and financially self-sufficient. Mrs. LaFarge, however, apparently saw the purpose of my weekly home visits to her as a long-awaited opportunity to discharge on me the accumulated venom of her victimized life time. I dreaded my visits like some infernal punishment, and had I had any somatizing skills, I would certainly have become violently sick every Wednesday afternoon. I felt I owed it to Mrs. LaFarge, whose life was so much worse than mine, to bear her rage with outward equanimity, and I was so busy not retaliating that I became quite paralyzed in her presence. Eventually Mrs. LaFarge's son was involved in some criminal activity and she responded with a heart attack, which permitted her to become an invalid and receive full-time care. My services were no longer needed and my penance was terminated.

I am relieved to report that I gradually made some progress in dealing with angry clients. Some twelve years later, acting as a consultant to a public school system, I saw a client, Mrs. Oswald, whose twelve-year-old son was behaving so aggressively that he had to be transferred to a class for emotionally disturbed children. When I first went to see her, Mrs. Oswald almost did not let me enter her dilapidated house. She received me with a barrage of insults against the school system, last year's teacher, the current teacher, the guidance counselor, the principal, and nosy, officious social workers who forced themselves into her house to make trouble. In this case I tried to understand what parts of Mrs. Oswald's rage were justified. As a mother, I knew perfectly well that schools play a big part in messing up our children. I had fought with enough teachers to know that I might have similar feelings in her situation, even though I had learned to express such feelings in educated and psychologically sophisticated language. I listened to Mrs. Oswald's bitter complaints and agreed that her contacts with the school system sounded extremely frustrating. Suddenly she started to cry in despair and declared that she could no longer control her boy. Her husband was in prison; one of the younger children had medical needs that she could not meet; she herself was working long hours, and she was at the end of her rope. We were then able to plan to ease her burdens to some small extent.

It was of course relatively easy to deal with anger that was clearly projective and undeserved, in a relationship of limited emotional investment. Yet it was a first step, and I was able to learn from Mrs. Oswald that rage can simply be a bastion against hopelessness and despair.

I think I used to overlove my clients, making it difficult for them to get angry at me. Perhaps I still do. I feel caught between wanting to be open and accepting of criticism without being defensive, yet not wanting to placate my clients by apologizing. "I can't stand it when you use Rogerian techniques on me to cover up your confusion. You did that during the entire session," says my superintellectual client to me. "Did I really do that? I am so sorry," I reply. Later I wonder why this client has such trouble getting angry at me.

After living for forty years in a marriage in which confrontations were too difficult and angry feelings silently accumulated until they choked the relationship, I almost desperately try to engage in and be open to honest confrontations. It has been very difficult, and yet increasingly I find that acknowledging and discussing hurts and misunderstandings is a major way of being and remaining loving in a relationship. "Whenever you apologize so profusely for not being able to come and see me," I say to my friend, "it makes me feel as if you come to see me for my sake, rather than for your own." He appears surprised and then explains that he transforms his own feelings of regret into apologies. I love my friend for not calling me crazy when I say such things.

It helped me to deal with angry feelings when I could shift my attention from the content of a message to its intended or unintended interpersonal significance. I have a contract with a client for six meetings. She is shy and subdued and wants to become more outgoing and assertive. She is most pleasant and full of admiration for me and I give her lots of good advice. One week she takes a deep breath and tells me that she realizes that she is wasting her money and that all this talk was not very useful and that I had not said anything that she had not already known. Yes, it did hurt for a moment, but I realized almost as quickly that she had finally reached the goal of becoming assertive toward a rather awesome authority, her therapist. I chose not to defeat her by becoming interpretative, patronizing, or benevolent. I take her accusation seriously and we discuss its merit.

My second-year student placement was in a guidance clinic for preschool autistic children and their parents. It provided the background for raising my first child. In my next life I shall choose some other less anxiety-arousing apprenticeship. This internship steered me toward working with parents and children for many years, and it started my ambivalent and very personal struggle regarding "who is to blame" for disturbed children. Married but still childless at the time, I learned with great interest that mothers were to blame for their children's emotional problems. I was assigned to work only with parents: in those days the child was defined as the patient and was, therefore, assigned to the psychiatrist, the high-status member of the child guidance team. Social workers were assigned to parents, who seemed to be the real cause of the problem, since they were held responsible for having messed up their children. I wondered for years what a curious division of labor this was, until it occurred to me that it simply mirrored in its confusion Freud's double legacy: first, the biologistic legacy that ascribes mysterious biological urges to children; and second, the interpersonal legacy that blames parents for not loving their children enough. In my own preparental days my sympathy and empathy rested with the poor, emotionally exploited children, and my learning consisted in forgiving parents for their sins and errors.

I had been deeply alienated from both of my parents and had no appreciation of the nature of motherhood and perhaps even fatherhood. After I became a mother I suddenly realized the passionate nature of parenthood, experiencing with my children the entire range of emotions from selfless, passionate love to murderous hate. "I will kill him" I thought in a moment of rage against my son. "I will kill my husband," I thought a few seconds later—it was a slightly safer thought. In another few seconds I settled on killing myself.

If I had to decide what life experience prepared me best for my two life roles of counselor and teacher, I would choose motherhood. Indeed, when I returned to this same clinic some years later, with my own three variously problematic children at home, my perspective had totally changed. This time I identified profoundly with the parents. Their pain, guilt, and anxiety were mine as well. Often parents did not even need to tell me all about their worries—I could anticipate and feel them without words. I did a lot of reassuring in those days.

Yet, there is also no need for me to repudiate totally my younger therapeutic self. Even in my preparental days I could not believe the clinic's philosophy that childhood autism was caused by a particular kind of cold and distant mothering, and I wrote my master's thesis to disprove this. I was always convinced that mothers of autistic children were waging a heroic fight to rear and rescue constitutionally damaged children. Parents of autistic and schizophrenic children have now written about this devastating experience and also about the mental health professionals who misunderstood them in various ways. I believe their accusations are fair. The staff of this clinic was well-meaning and eager to help, and yet their theoretical framework led them to make foolish and malevolent interpretations. When I discussed with my supervisor a mother's desperate inability to toilet train her four-year-old nonverbal autistic son, she said to me, "You have to find out why this mother has a need to have feces smeared all over the house." During a conference, a psychiatrist once said after watching home movies of another autistic child, "This father seems to have had a need to keep a camera between himself and his son."

It is important to me to record these events, because the struggle to maintain and validate my own perceptions, which were often different from those of the people around me, has been a major life theme. I am very relieved that I did not completely succumb to the spirit of that mental health system, which I now view as destructive. I was on these mothers' side and I refused to blame them or even their unconscious for their fearsome fate. I hope my belief in their innocence sustained them to some degree. They were the first clients who taught me the meaning of "standing by."

However, I did not win all my battles. Mr. Morgan was a prominent and successful business man whose life goal was to rescue his three-year-old autistic boy. We worked together for one whole year, and I had great respect and compassion for his efforts. He fell ill with a virulent form of cancer and the psychiatric decision was that I was not to visit him at the hospital. I never understood the reason for this decision, but I lacked the self-confidence to fight it. Who was I to insist on my opinion? To a large extent I was still an obedient little girl in those days. Not visiting Mr. Morgan at the hospital and allowing such a sudden cut-off of our relationship felt like a betrayal on my part, which troubled me for many years.

Eventually doubts about my therapeutic effectiveness became too insistent, and I took a five-year respite from child guidance work. I did not yet know that a person who stands by, reliably, caringly, and nonjudgmentally can mean a great deal to another human being. Moreover, I did not yet have enough self-confidence to think that my presence in someone else's life could make much difference. It would take the experience of my own psychotherapy before I could begin to appreciate such interpersonal holding.

I took a job as an adoption worker. The opportunity of joining a baby who needed a family with a family that wanted a baby seemed exhilarating at the time. In the 1950s the now popular search of adoptees for their biological parents still lay in the future. We were also not yet aware that relinquishing a baby may precipitate lifelong unresolved grief reactions in the birth mother. In the early fifties we still tried to play God. We tested our babies to make sure they were "adoptable," inflicting upon them an interim foster home placement and potentially traumatic early separation experience, all for the sake of matching our children to the intellectual expectations of our adoptive parents. We also tried to match our babies' ethnic coloring to those of their adoptive parents. None of the matchings ever made sense to me, but they were agency policy. Moreover, my much-loved and respected supervisor stood for them, and I had not yet learned to challenge a loved authority figure. Now and then, of course, I tried to transgress the rules, but not with impunity.

I had chosen a beautiful olive-skinned, dark-eyed baby of Italian descent for a Nordic-looking couple. They were highly educated mental health professionals, and through my identification with them I felt that they deserved an especially well-developing child. To my surprise they saw the child as alien and preferred to wait for a fair one. A few months later the mental health grapevine brought me a story of a nameless social worker, myself of course, who was totally insensitive to adoptive parents' feelings. I can hear in my mind's ear the laughing of social workers who are now placing for adoption severely handicapped children, older children with traumatic life histories, or biracial children. I thought it would be thought-provoking to illustrate the dramatic changes in child welfare practices within one short professional lifetime.

After five years, and an additional year in a state children's mental hospital, the lure of further intensive therapeutic training drew me back, for the third time, to the clinic in which I had received my student training.

This clinic believed in the value of long-term work with clients, a luxury of the 1950s and early 1960s mental health services. I don't know whether it was a justified expense, but I am enormously grateful for the experience. Clients whom I saw over three or four years have left a permanent imprint on my life.

Mrs. Kramer, for example, the mother of a very frightened, obsessional little boy named Paul, was a bad caricature of a Jewish mother. She kvetched and kvetched and kvetched uninterrupt-edly for three solid years, and I bore it with quite good graces. She was my client and I cared about her. Members of the Kramer family received their major support and nurturance from each other during periods of illness. Therefore they all took careful turns being ill, each member respectfully limiting the extent of his turn in order not to overload the family sympathy resources. Since Paul had so much anxiety about defecating, I suggested to Mrs. Kramer not to take his temperature anally so very often. She wanted to oblige; she decided to take the child's temperature orally from then on, but then found she needed to check it anally to make sure it was accurate. Mrs. Kramer taught me patience and tol-erance. No other complaining has ever seemed excessive since then. Perhaps it was just as well that I was not yet familiar with paradoxical techniques that would have cut through her com-plaining. Little Paul, I hear, has developed quite well, and Mrs. Kramer and I remember each other with affection.

All the parents of disturbed children I ever saw during those and later days had troubled marriages. I still feel unsure whether the children's problems were the result of parental conflicts, as is suggested by psychodynamic and even family system theory, or whether having problematic children perhaps creates parental conflicts. Do children's problems drive parents to quarreling, or are conflicted marriages, along with troubled children, simply a byproduct of the organization of the nuclear family? Are children driven crazy by schizophrenogenic families, or is schizophrenia a contagious disease in which a child can contaminate his or her parents? I have never known a family without at least one *Sor-genkind* (worry child). Perhaps social systems simply need to dis-charge their tensions upon at least one member. Whatever the answer, I believe that family therapy would have been a more effective approach to helping these troubled young children.

Mr. Minos was another parent whom I saw for over three years. He facilitated a crucial breakthrough in my development as a therapist and as a person. I saw him in connection with a re-search project on the effects of the death of a parent on a young child. Mr. Minos' wife had died of cancer, and he experienced in his body all of his wife's symptoms. He could not be reassured by doctors because he assumed that they were lying to him and always would lie, just as they and he himself had always lied to his wife. He was a shy and inarticulate blue-collar worker for whom conversations about his feelings were a startling but expanding new experience. Brought up to be a lady, I had been hampered in my work with clients by my reticence to ask indiscreet or intrusive questions. Mr. Minos, however, seemed to experience my questions as keys that unlocked his capacity to communicate. I suddenly came to understand that asking good questions could have a liberating effect. In turn, I also like to be asked interesting questions. Sometimes I am even sad if people don't care enough about me to ask me good questions. I have become a person who views "good questions," in both therapeutic and social situations, as gifts rather than intrusive assaults. This insight changed my style of interacting with people and has enriched my human encounters.

Of course, not everyone is receptive to actual or symbolic gifts. During my stay in England, that land of reticence, people viewed my style with a mixture of horror, envy, and admiration. Asking real questions means that one might get real answers. Real answers are often upsetting, disturbing, or painful. One needs to learn to bear the answers.

Being passionately loved, as a therapist and later as a teacher, was as difficult to accept and get used to as being passionately hated; sometimes these two emotions proved interrelated.

One client, Mrs. Washington, was a deprived single mother with an autistic little girl. We worked together for three years, confronting many difficult issues—her blackness and my whiteness, her poverty, rage, and aspirations for a better future. We worked on termination for half a year, and a new worker was replacing me. But when I left, she made a suicidal attempt.

Mrs. Austin was a mother I met with weekly for eight months in relation to her son's persistent wish to dress and play like a girl. She had grown up emotionally deprived, a poor little rich girl with a neglectful glamorous father, who eventually left the family, and a floridly paranoid mother who continued to upset her life. She was brought up by maids. Meeting me, a woman of her age who was empathic and caring, was intolerable to Mrs.

Austin, evoking frightening yearnings for a good mother she had never known. Had we met under other circumstances, Mrs. Austin and I might have become friends. But we were worker and client, confined to a professionally circumscribed relationship. For months Mrs. Austin bitterly attacked me for being a tight-lipped, straight-skirted professional robot. Eventually she could no longer tolerate sitting with me in the same room, although she called me at home for many years. I was heartbroken, since I had such a special liking for her.

Had I been responsible for Mrs. Washington's and Mrs. Austin's "therapeutic passions," or in our more common lingo, excessive transference reactions? Could it be that less warmth, less caring, and a more neutral attitude would have protected them? After my own therapeutic experience I began to be able to grasp the intensity, seriousness, and peculiar reality of transference love. Suddenly I could understand Mrs. Austin's violent love-hate reactions and Mrs. Washington's suicide attempt.

I had suffered for years from periods of depression. Although they had never interfered with my functioning in my various roles, nor did they "show" on the surface, they appeared severe to me. Eventually I sought psychotherapeutic help from a male psychoanalyst. I remained in psychotherapy for two years, at which point he left town. As a mental health professional I had been surrounded by friends and colleagues who either were, or had been for years, in psychoanalysis or psychotherapy. I had resisted any kind of therapy until then, dreading and anticipating endless tearful hours of unhappy childhood reminiscences. It was a relief and disappointment when this fantasy did not come true.

The psychiatrist I had chosen was extremely gentle, and I grew to love him deeply. No one else had ever listened to my obsessive ruminations with such patience, without becoming in turn contaminated with worry and anxiety. His sensitive attempt to meet my yearning to be understood was most satisfying while it lasted, but it created an addictive dependency that I dreaded. During the two years I saw him I cried only once, about my grandfather's death. We never touched my passionate, loving, and hating self. I don't know whether it was not yet available to me. He and I thought that my reticence was due to my defensive armor, which he respected with the utmost care. Today I suspect that he could no more bear violent feelings than I could at that time, and that we were both intent on protecting each other. His leaving town (and leaving me), interrupting treatment, recapitulated my father's abandoning me in early adolescence, an unmourned event in my life. We might have compared these two events, and I even made some attempts to do so, but I gave up when I sensed his resistance. I felt that it would have made him too guilty and uncomfortable.

I later learned that many women are similarly selective about what they tell their male therapists. In spite of appearances we women have learned that it is our function to protect men, especially from our strong emotions. We do not want to hurt our male therapists' feelings, and especially not their self-esteem, nor upset them, nor feel too much shame ourselves, in front of a man. I experienced the enormous pain of ending an important relationship. The "working through" phase of the termination had been a meaningless ritual. I finally fully understood the power of the treatment relationship and the awesome responsibility it creates for the therapist. It took me a whole year of silent mourning to recover from the loss. I resolved that this would be my last formal healing attempt. The dependency it had created was too frightening. Clearly, I have not forgiven my therapist for abandoning me and for having been able to tolerate neither my love nor my anger. Abandonment, initiated by myself or others, continues to be a life theme for me.

I have suggested all along that healing myself and healing others had to go together in my life. Did I turn to teaching instead of continuing as a clinician because I found the process of healing myself too difficult?

My children were growing up and I dared for the first time to plan for my own future, instead of drifting from one job to the next. I had become a faculty field supervisor in a psychiatric clinic in a prestigious hospital. With greater self-confidence, I became increasingly intolerant of the hierarchical hospital arrangements that placed all social workers at the lower end of the professional totem pole. My much-respected faculty supervisor explained to me that we social workers were to use our casework skills to enable and support the professional growth of young and mostly male psychiatric residents. Although I must admit a weakness for young men, at that point in my life I had just become weary of mothering children and even wearier of mothering young men of a different profession. I then realized that my part-time teaching had given me great satisfaction and that teaching was my most natural medium of self-expression. After much soul-searching agony I returned to school for an advanced academic degree, which opened the way to academia, a setting where I receive a great deal of deference and respect.

My casework background was not valued by the professional school to which I applied. Rumors reached me that they accepted me in the hope of converting Freud's granddaughter. They succeeded. It was actually not my heritage, but my social work training and practice that had consigned me for years to a psychoanalytically-colored world. No other system had ever acquired any reality for me.

My conversion experience centered around reading *Stigma* by Erving Goffman (1963), a microsociological, symbolic interactionist perspective on human behavior. Goffman ignored people's inner space, he ignored sexual and aggressive instincts, the Oedipus complex, and even the effects of an inadequate attachment experience. His people are social actors who play to various audiences, who engage in power struggles and in other survival games in which self-esteem is at stake. I started my theoretical voyage from inner space to outer space. Everything I had ever observed started to shift. All my accumulating doubts had been justified; new solutions were presenting themselves to years of puzzling questions: How can people with loving mothers and internalized superegos have participated in the Holocaust, I had asked myself. Because most people do what others expect them to do, answered Goffman (1963), Milgram (1974), and Asch (1955). The walls came tumbling down. The books had lied to me. They had also lied about penis envy, the vaginal orgasm, female narcissism, menopause, motherhood, and about how to rear children and lead a good life. Later I started to write papers on many of these subjects, trying to sort out systematically the lies and the truths. These new ideas eventually led me to cybernetic theory and to an entirely new world view. Through thinking, feeling, and living I acquired the conviction that life was round and that opposites belong together.

When other people change theoretical frameworks it may be an important professional life event. My change was simultaneously an act of betrayal to my family as well as a declaration of cognitive emancipation. I would from now on be able to raise my own theoretical voice among colleagues in my field. I had made one more step in my struggle against the double burden of conformity and obedience that constricts women's lives.

My new theoretical views led me to an interest in working with groups in both therapeutic and didactic contexts, allowing me to integrate my old role as a therapist and my new role as an educator. I started to lead psychosocial transition groups that provide time-limited, nonstigmatizing counseling during a life transition. Such transitions may be loss of a marital partner, the birth of a child, or a change in status following an illness. Such counseling is truly preventive, reaches people in a period of vulnerability, and aims "to facilitate change in (people's) assumptive world" (Parkes 1971, p. 110). These groups promote healing through guidance on the new life space, information on the probable stages of this transition and its various aspects, group support, mutual problem solving, and intimate sharing of difficult common experiences in a peer setting.

I believe some of the healing power of these groups rests in bearing witness to one's own suffering among a group of peers who form at least a temporary community. Bearing witness in speaking or writing, in public or just to one significant other (who could be a therapist), is a powerful human urge. In doing so we need to be heard, nonjudgmentally accepted, and above all, believed. Bearing witness should not be confused with catharsis, an emptying of inner space. It is a social act of sharing. I believe that creative forms of "bearing witness" account for the healing that goes on in consciousness-raising groups, self-help groups, psychodrama, gestalt, or psychodynamic groups as well as in individual counseling. Different people may need to find different communities to which they want to bear witness. Family therapists have observed the healing effect that a parent's open grieving and bearing witness to his childhood pain may have upon mate and children. The survivors of concentration camps drew strength from their wish to bear witness to the entire world. My way of bearing witness is to write papers that I share with my professional community. It is my way of being seen and heard. Women need to speak up, "to break some of the silence and isolation which reinforces the personlessness of women" (Metzger 1976, p. 408). The private voice in the public sphere confirms our common experience through which we begin to assert ourselves" (Metzger 1976, p. 406).

I believe in the power of education as a medium of change. It has been, for example, my experience that information that is guilt-reducing can have dramatic effects: I had a student who had been raped before the beginning of school and had been extremely upset for many weeks, always on the verge of dropping out. I managed to squeeze in a special lecture about people's guilt about their misfortunes, be it the death of a spouse, the birth of a retarded child, or rape. I explained to the students that this sense of guilt has the function of preserving the illusion of a just world and of control over one's life. If one is responsible for one's misfortunes, then one can perhaps avert them in the future. I mentioned rape just as an example, with no special emphasis, but the lecture had its desired effect. The student who had been raped felt much better and was able to stop her constant agonizing about her own guilt in the rape.

After teaching for many years I have become keenly conscious of my students' anxiety about, and preoccupation with, autonomy and self-esteem issues. Moreover, I do not think my students are different in these ways from any other groups of human beings. I take the interpersonal meaning of any class comment as seriously as I take its content. I hear a student affirming his or her right to disagree with me; a student's willingness to support me, perhaps in the hope of being especially loved; a student's need to demonstrate competence or simply to become visible; a student's fear to appear foolish. Sometimes I answer on that level, with some care: Marilyn, who struggles with class participation, has a comment. "Of course I am not an expert in this area," she begins, "but it seems to me . . . " "Yes," I say, "always disqualify yourself first before you mention a good idea. It is what women are supposed to do." Marilyn has three more interesting comments before the end of class. I give an assignment that is so interesting that the students cannot resist it, yet they want to change it in various ways. They would like to do it in groups, rather than individually. I am in total disagreement, but I give in, not, I hope, because I want to be liked as a teacher (which I do) or because I don't have enough energy to argue with them, but because I believe the issue is a struggle for control, and I don't have to win them all.

I would also hope that the content of my teaching generally has sometimes been therapeutic, and many women have assured me that this has been true for them. Actually, betrayal of expectations, which is such a prominent aspect of women's lives (see my discussion in Chapter 16), is among the most shattering of life experiences. It may take women many years to rebuild a new assumptive world (Parkes 1971) after their old one has been shattered through social or personal betrayal experiences. I believe teaching women about societal myths and thus challenging some of their expectations, at least on a cognitive level, may itself be a powerful preventive mental health intervention.

My women's classes tend to generate a strong spirit of commonality, becoming forms of consciousness-raising sessions. Women seem to realize, either through my teaching or their readings, that their personal anxieties are shared by many other women. Through the support of other women they find the courage to change their lives. Some women have started a career after they have studied with me; they have left an abusive husband, gone back to school, started to set limits with their adolescent children, given up long-standing depressions. Some husbands feel ambivalent about their wives' taking my courses. They are glad because their wives may become more exciting and enterprising, and they are sorry because their wives become more assertive and confronting. One woman decided to stop cooking for her husband; another merely decided to stop sorting out his socks. I believe good therapy involves a great deal of learning, and good teaching ought to be therapeutic.

It gives me deep satisfaction that many of my formal and informal classes tend to become places where intimate sharing and healing of wounds (including sometimes my own wounds) take place. I believe the world is grey and it is up to us to paint it anew each day with colors. There are days when my ability to paint fails me; I am overcome with a sense of futility and loss of meaning. Yet magically, whenever that happens, my students restore my spirits and renew my belief in the purpose and goodness of life. I think it is my own openness toward them, a stance that I have reached in late midlife, that makes this mutual healing possible.

Maintaining reserve and privacy and allowing few people into one's life-space can be a strong and admirable position. It was a stand taken by my mother in mistrust and bitterness and by my aunt in some self-protectiveness and pride. I had at one point contemplated a similar life-stance, but I have changed my mind. I think it was the passions of my life that led me to a position of openness. It was through these intense love experiences and the pain that accompanied them that I learned to enter the emotional world of other human beings with empathy, compassion, understanding, and acceptance, and without judgment. I would rather lead a rich and exciting life than a proud one. And I would rather take great interpersonal risks than play it safe. If I were to give an answer today to my initial questions about the essence of individual therapy, it would lead me to this openness.

I have described in this essay how hard it has been for me to grow up. The voyage from young adulthood to late midlife seems such a crowded one. Have I become a different person over time? After describing how much I have changed, I want to claim some core to my identity. Even as a timid young social worker, devastated by clients' silences and attacks, I had a measure of self-confidence and toughness. Even as an academician, respected, admired, and loved by many people, I often feel like an unlovable, worthless, orphaned little girl.

Although I was a private and closed young woman, I always had some very deep relationships. Now that I am stressing my open stance, I am simultaneously too busy with work, unavailable, preoccupied, and ultimately closed to many people, much of the time. I can feel loving and I have made myself vulnerable, yet I eliminate some people who hurt me and treat them as if they were dead. I try to engage in confrontations, but just as often I am a coward, or I am not even in touch with my feelings until days, weeks, or years later. Perhaps all through my life I have been both "queen" (or at least princess) and "beggargirl," hateful and loving, optimistic and depressed, tender and harsh, forgiving and unforgiving. Perhaps all of us carry all these polarities and turn to one or the other pole, as situations and circumstances demand, with some hope that with increasing age and wisdom, we may turn more often toward our more creative possibilities.

References

Asch, S. (1955). "Opinions and social pressure." *Scientific American* 31–5.

Goffman, E. (1963). *Stigma*. Englewood, N.J.: Prentice-Hall.

Metzger, D. (1976). "It is always the woman who is raped." *American Journal of Psychiatry* 133 :405–12.

Milgram, S. (1974). *Obedience to Authority*. New York: Harper and Row.

Parkes, C. M. (1971). "Psycho-social transitions: A field for study." *Journal of Social Science and Medicine* 5:101–15.

Wheelis, A. (1958). *Quest for Identity*. New York: Norton.

8 / The Passion and Challenge of Teaching

"*A* SENSE of knowing where one is going" is how Erikson de-fined identity (1959, p. 118), and it describes precisely how I felt when I found my identity as an educator. My discovery of teaching was delayed until midlife, which gave me a compelling urge to make up for lost years. My identity was greatly enriched by earlier experiences that I had brought to teaching, or that had brought me to it. My forty years of apprenticeship as a social worker, therapist, friend to other women, wife, and mother would become an integral part of the perspective that orders the passion and power, the doubts and challenges of my role as a teacher.

Looking at my life, I find many contradictions. Perhaps para-dox characterizes a woman's life. I view myself as quite auton-omous, yet I depend on the approval of my students and the recognition of my colleagues. Despite a family background of great accomplishment, it took me a long time to find my true profes-sional calling. Personality characteristics that were strengths in work situations added to my failings as a mother. Work was an emotional necessity for me, but I long denied its significance in my life. My ambitions require solitude, yet I am sustained by my relationships with a community of women and men. Thus, my life has been neither orderly nor rational.

At the age of forty-two, I suddenly took some initiative in a way that was unusual for me. While I had had interesting and challenging jobs before then, they had essentially been ready-made. This time I pursued my personal vision, designing a course on the parent-teacher relationship for teachers-in-training, drawing not only on my experience as a parent but on years of clinical work with troubled families. I wanted to help young teachers deal with the anxieties of equally young parents, to help promote a partnership, to replace the secret competition and apprehension that often exists between them. My purpose was to train teachers in interviewing skills and to help them increase their understanding and tolerance for the parents' viewpoint and circumstances. Since this goal grew directly out of my own fearful relationships with teachers, designing this course was my characteristic way of mastering life's difficulties through an intellectual project.

I sent my handwritten course outline—a labor of love—to the director of a teachers' training college. As I anxiously waited for a reply, the fantasy that I might be allowed to teach such a course filled me with incredible happiness. Can impossible dreams become reality? The director expressed interest in the outline but offered me only the opportunity to conduct one session as a guest lecturer. I indignantly refused her offer. It was a crushing defeat. In retrospect I can see how naïve and presumptuous I was. Then, one week before the fall semester began, the person who taught a somewhat similar course fell ill—no, I did not practice voodoo—and I was called upon to teach my course.

My background as a psychiatric social worker proved to be an ideal preparation for dealing with students in a classroom. Many encounters with troubled parents had given me enough practical experience to give flesh and meaning to theoretical content. But even more important were the interpersonal skills that I had learned as a caseworker, such as attentiveness to the individual expressed or unexpressed needs of each student.

I approached this first teaching job without anxiety or hesitation, replacing such normally expected feelings in a new venture with enormous zest and enthusiasm. I hope and believe that my students loved this course as much as I did. I had always loved going to school. I belonged in a classroom, and it suddenly became clear that I had always meant to be a teacher. Even when I raised my children, I had most enjoyed the teaching aspects of child rearing. I had finally progressed to the head of the class. I had finally come home.

Teaching that first course was a glorious experience that united all the meaningful aspects of my life. I began to develop other courses, and eventually my career was steered in new directions. Would my life have taken very different shape if the regular teacher had not become ill at that crucial moment?

People sometimes perceive me as a determined and goal-oriented career woman. I may have ended up with this identity, but I certainly did not start out that way. Levinson's (1978) men entered adulthood with a dream of adult accomplishment that guided them in the decisions that shaped their lives. It was quite the opposite with me. I think my career shaped my ambitions.

I also believe that my own efforts played only a small part in bringing me to my present and extremely fortunate position as educator, in which I am respected for work that also gives meaning to my life. In many ways I have drifted through life, taking on opportunities that seemed to present themselves. Although striving to take charge of my own life has been a lifelong goal, deep-down I agree with Amelie Rorty (1977):

> In truth, the real agents of my life have been, as I believe they are in every life, Time and Chance. Most of the events that were formative were coincidences. . . . Everything crucial might easily have been totally different. The good things that have happened to me—and there have been many—seem to have been largely a matter of good fortune. I am less convinced that damaging things might have gone otherwise. I do not have the sense of having been at the center of my life, directing its course. (p. 41)

My love of teaching finally led me to seek entrance into the academic world through the official sanction of a Ph.D. degree. It astonished me to realize that successful competition with high-status male students of my own age was as significant in raising my belief in my abilities as the degree itself.

When I first began working, I had no sense of building a career, dreams of glory, particular sense of personal competence, or definite professional goals. This seems surprising, since I come from a background that had provided unusually strong models and professional expectations.

In contrast to other ambitious women, who according to research studies and autobiographies (Addams 1910; Roosevelt 1939; Hellman 1969; Chisholm 1970; Deutsch 1973; Lozoff 1973; Henning 1973) were somewhat distant from their mothers and had especially strong bonds with their fathers, my primary model, both positively and negatively, has been my mother. My mother was an ambitious professional woman. She reached the age of eighty-four before she retired from full-time practice as a speech therapist, and her work sustained her admirably through a rather lonely old age. As I grow older I strive to accept my identification with my mother's strengths and I wage a losing battle against my identification with her shadows. I know this is a familiar battle for many women and a difficult one to win. Family legend has it—and you may guess who spread this legend—that my father said about me to my mother, "Look at her bad grades, and you always claim she is so intelligent." My mother defended me. She believed in me and wanted me to do well. It is very fortunate to have a mother who wishes one well. She took it completely for granted that I would become a professional woman, and I grew up with this basic assumption. I suspect that she even hoped that I might receive some of the fame and glory that she missed and that would have meant so much to her. She worked throughout my childhood, and I always assumed that this is what women are meant to do.

As a child, my first ambition was to become "das bravste Kind von Wien" (the best behaved child in Vienna). I cannot decide whether this meant that I was being socialized to be a good little girl or whether I sought the competition and self-abnegation involved in such a goal. In either case, this early ambition contained both a sense of specialness and an obligation to meet high standards.

Even with this compelling script for achievement, conflicting societal expectations interfered with a clear pursuit of professional goals. My latent ambition found destructive expression through projection, first on my husband, and then on each of my three children, of the unfair and absurd expectation that they would fill my needs for intellectual achievement and public recognition. I have thus burdened my children with a legacy of excessive ambition. In recent years, working around the clock seven days a week, I have become more consistently confident that life had meaning and can be managed. Controlling my own life, I have less need to control the life of others and can now take responsibility for only my own successes and failures, which is a big relief.

I am more satisfied with my life now than I was during my active motherhood years. Would I have had a more productive and fulfilling life if, instead of raising children, I had discovered and used my talents as an educator in earlier years?

I did not decide to become a mother because I yearned for a child or had a special love for babies. On the contrary, I had been working at a child guidance clinic where I had seen everything that could go wrong with young children. I simply had a child because it never occurred to me that there was a choice. Life was easier in those days.

Motherhood swamped me with an array of intense and new emotions. Staying at home made me restless and depressed. My one full-time year at home was unsuccessful. My need to excel and to be in full control of situations, along with my high energy level—all assets in working situations—interfered with being a relaxed and accepting young mother. I poured all my vitality and passion into one little baby.

I started to work part-time when my daughter was one year old and continued to do so while nursing and rearing two more children, gradually increasing my working hours as the family grew older. Splitting my life into the two roles of social worker and mother raised problems of organization but no major emotional conflicts. Although I had the luxury of household help during working hours, I remained my children's primary caretaker and in full charge of the household. I had been reared primarily by Fraeuleins and was quite determined to be the emotional anchor for my own children. My husband was certainly ready to help, but he was pursuing his own career in a more goal-directed way than I, working long hours and supporting our family financially. We had an unspoken agreement that all major decisions regarding our children would be in my hands. I admire and wonder how some of today's young mothers are eager to share child rearing with their husbands. I don't know whether I could have been that generous. Although I do not know whether my husband could or would have arranged his working life differently, I wish I had had the wisdom and generosity of spirit to move in that direction.

I want to bear witness loudly and clearly to the fact that none of my jobs ever approached in difficulty the emotional and intellectual demands of rearing children in our society. Even today, my heart beats faster when I remember the stress and anxiety of dealing with delayed developmental milestones, prolonged bedwetting, eczemas that must not be scratched, difficulties in reading and spelling, homesickness at summer camp, drug experimentation, refusal to get out of bed in the morning, Valentine's Day without valentines, getting into college, and once there, making it to graduation.

As a psychoanalytically trained mental health professional, I was convinced that early development, especially the early mother-child interaction, irreversibly sets the stage for later personality formation. I saw each passing developmental problem as a threatening portent, and now I sometimes wonder whether my theoretical background poisoned my child-rearing years with needless excessive anxiety. I am now careful to alert my students to newer, less deterministic research in child development (Clark and Clark 1977) and to literature that questions some of the expert advice offered to mothers (Wortis 1971; Ehrenreich and English 1978).

Researchers have been exploring the still unanswered question of why women are more vulnerable to depression than men (Weissman and Klerman 1977). My own depressions were often related to child-rearing anxieties. The myth of blissful motherhood has only recently and mercifully been exploded (McBride 1973; Radl 1973; Rich 1976; Cohler 1984). Recent research suggests that rearing young children can be a mental health hazard for some women and that employment can be an important mitigator of this stress (Belle 1982). Most men have two major roles, which increases their chances of finding satisfaction in at least one of them (Gove and Tudor 1973). It was certainly important for me that I did not put all my self-esteem eggs into that one motherhood basket. Having both roles eased rather than increased the strain of rearing children for me.

I avoided role conflicts by establishing clear priorities that I seldom transgressed. For example, I organized matters so that I would not need to stay home if the children were sick, even quite sick. I wanted to be a completely dependable working mother, the best behaved child in Boston. Yet I was always home for dinner and refused to accept either work or social engagements that would take me away from home in the evening. My children have confronted me with my shortcomings as a mother, but unavailability was not one of their complaints. I believe my role conflicts were more manageable because my part-time social work job had well-defined hours. Unlike some of my friends, I could never have managed to be in a job without time boundaries such as academic pursuits while raising three children.

It is also true that being a working mother helped me with, but did not wholly protect me against, overinvolvement with my children. I continued to feel their pains and failures more keenly than my own. As I differentiate myself from my children I try to remember that they have to lead their own lives, bear their own pain, and make their own mistakes.

I have come to the conclusion that both my emotional and professional life would have been impoverished had I chosen to remain childless. My deepest intellectual insights ultimately come from my own life experiences. Without feeling the anguish and joys of motherhood, I could never have fully grasped its meaning or intensity. I thus could not have fully found my way into many other women's hearts and minds. I could not have become a student and teacher of issues relating to women's lives.

My children were my first students, and like all students, they taught me at least as much as I taught them; indeed they have been my most compelling teachers. They helped me first to grow up and then to stay young. They have introduced me to new perspectives and life-styles and have helped me to become more tolerant. They taught me wisdom, compassion, and humility. Although I was a most imperfect mother, they have forgiven me and now treat me with respect and affection, an unexpected bonanza in midlife.

The choice of working or not working, or working part-time or full-time, was a luxury that was granted to middle-class women of my generation. On the one hand, the idea that I worked for pleasure rather than for money was reassuring. Work was less of a compelling duty, which left me free to leave a job when it offered no new challenge. On the other hand, it made work almost a form of self-indulgence, even a luxury, since it propelled us into a higher tax bracket while all my earnings were actually spent on child care. Although for me work was an emotional necessity, it brought no visible benefit to my family except insofar as it protected my children, to some small extent, from an overcontrolling mother.

I remember the eagerness and energy with which I approached my part-time work in the child welfare field. Like many part-time workers, I seemed to be carrying a full-time load, especially since there was always time to do some extra work at home after the children were asleep. I have the impression that such full-time performance at part-time pay is a very good deal for employers.

Work provided me with much satisfaction, and yet I long denied its significance in my life. My self-esteem was not derived from competence at work but from my children's well-being. It took me about fifteen years to stop thinking of work as recreation, and even now I have difficulty with our society's strict distinction between work and leisure. I continue to find my greatest pleasure in work. My peak experiences come after teaching an especially good class or finishing a paper. People have called me a workaholic because I am better at working than at playing, but I think I am lucky to have found work that I love.

I have always used work to modulate emotional crises in my life, because the discipline demanded by work has protected me from excessive absorption with the crisis at hand. In addition, I have converted many of these crises into intellectual problems to be studied and objectified through theoretical formulations. Thus, I have used work as the highest form of play and as a way of mastering the problems of living. Perhaps this is why I am known as a person who is usually cheerful while working.

As my job activities expanded, other pursuits such as entertaining, hobbies, or housekeeping had to be curtailed. While this did not affect my children, it caused hardship to my husband, and I felt guilty for neglecting my role as a wife. My working life had gained its own momentum and had become an irrepressible necessity.

My early days as a working mother taught me to protect my time cold bloodedly. I now hoard my time as a miser hoards money, carefully accounting for every moment but splurging now and then to spend a whole afternoon with a friend. Hoarding time is unwomanly, often greeted with consternation and resentment. Only a time-hoarder understands another time-hoarder; others consider one unfriendly, selfish, or arrogant. It often means that one cannot be helpful to all the people who would like one's help. Many women turn to me for information, advice, and support; once again, as with rearing children, difficult choices must be made. I have had to set priorities as to what claims people will have on my time. Anyone who has ever been my student has very high priority for me. I take seriously the bond established between us and I have a sense of lifelong commitment to students. To some extent I think about them as I do about my children. I have educated them to the best of my ability and sent them out into the world, but this does not end my responsibility to them or my interest in their growth.

Although my good friends assure me that I am there for them when they need me, the time problem nevertheless interferes with my wish and need to be closely connected to many other people.

Keeping up with the new books and articles in my field of human behavior and feminist studies is of course an impossible task, making me feel forever behind, poorly informed, and derelict in my duties. But I love teaching precisely because it allows me to live in a world of books. There was a time in my adolescence when I felt that books made life worth living. I now have an official mandate to do what I enjoy doing most: to read books and then to share my thoughts, perceptions, and feelings with my students. I now read everything with that focus, which makes my reading more enriching. I make innumerable notes in the margins of my books, in case I decide to use that book for teaching. I sometimes feel I don't just read my books, I devour them. I start many classes with a warm-up period, seizing the captive audience to make impromptu books reviews. I have an endless list of books to read in retirement, but I wonder whether I shall enjoy them as much without the opportunity to share my reactions.

Creativity poses another challenge. Nothing demands more inner discipline than self-imposed work. It is done at the expense of seeing friends, going to a movie, reading a novel, sewing, baking a cake, or doing all those other things that are inviting and relaxing. Tillie Olsen (1965) has become the spokesperson for mothers who cannot find the energy or time for creative efforts. At least these mothers have a good excuse; the rest of us have only ourselves to blame for frittering our lives away. It is most difficult to find the solitude needed for creative effort. Miller (1976) pointed out that "affiliation is both a fundamental strength, and at the same time the inevitable source of many of women's current problems" (p. 89). Some of my women colleagues who are more talented than I have never been able to write scholarly papers because of their inability to work alone. I have been able to master this necessary discipline, but only in spurts. I get up every ten minutes to eat or drink something. Writing papers is both exhilerating and excruciating for me.

For many years I felt myself a prisoner of the values and assumptions of psychoanalytic theory. I had not planned it that way, but I realize in retrospect that each of my papers tries to come to grips, after many months of reading and research, with some aspect of that theory. Rejecting the destructive aspects of this framework, which had such intense personal meaning for me, became my own declaration of independence. My theoretical papers are therefore highly personal documents.

Both the creative process of writing and the process of recuperating from rejection and failure when papers are not accepted have been tests of endurance for me. When I first started to submit papers for publication, they tended to be rejected. It would then take me months to revise them or to send them to another journal, to say nothing of writing another paper. When my husband also started to worry about finding manila envelopes in the mailbox, I gained a sense of proportion. As I reassured him that I could survive the disappointment, I to some extent reassured myself. With time I learned to write publishable papers and to become more resilient to setbacks. The opportunity to exchange ideas in writing with an international community of scholars is deeply satisfying. My first published paper was as important to my identity as an educator as the first course that I taught.

I have never been attuned to the "fear of success" syndrome (Horner 1972; Condry and Dyer 1976). I personally feel torn between wanting public recognition and whatever modest fame comes my way, and despising the empty publicity that sometimes goes with it, fearing the world will encroach upon my life and swallow me up. I am, however, very alive to the fear of failure that success entails (which some have claimed is the same as fear of success), and I suspect that the real source of fear of success is the haunting possibility that it cannot be maintained. May Sarton (1978), for example, told us how difficult it is for an author to have every new book measured against all her other books.

With every new class, there is the fear of establishing new criteria against which one will be measured in the future. I fear that a successful class will not be matched next week, and I sometimes warn my students that the next class will be less interesting. In the same vein, I receive compliments about a good class uneasily, perceiving them as subtle criticisms of prior classes.

I am especially vulnerable to criticism from my students. One critical comment, especially from a respected student, used to undermine my confidence for days. With increasing self-confidence, I find myself more open to criticism these days, especially after I understood that being open to criticism is much more crucial to the teaching and learning process than teaching perfect classes. Students need a respectful and acknowledging teacher, rather than one who never makes mistakes. I am now more able to learn from criticism, more ready to see it in perspective, less devastated, and more philosophical about not being liked and appreciated by every student. It is rewarding to realize that the process of being more open and vulnerable has actually made me stronger. I no longer interpret criticism as a total invalidation of my worth, but rather as an issue to be examined.

I fail my students in many ways that interfere with their learning and they disappoint me in important ways as well. We take time out, in the middle of the course to talk about this. "You are too opinionated," they say. "You subtly ridicule different viewpoints." "You tell us stories instead of going over the readings." "You get angry when we are sick." "You expect too much from us." "Yes," I say to some of their comments, while I dispute others, in what I hope is a nonpunitive and nondefensive spirit. And then I share my own frustrations as well. "My teaching is inhibited when I notice that some of you come to class without having done your readings," I tell them. "I am disappointed when some of you are not willing to take any personal risks in our classroom discussions." We experience safety and trust in this exchange. My students and I will make an effort to meet our expectations more fully.

As a woman, I have been brought up to please others (Miller 1976, p. 110). It was a major triumph for me when I first managed to write book reviews that contained some critical thoughts. In a similar spirit, it is hard for me to displease my students or to feel in disharmony with them. Students are not usually aware to what extent teaching involves interaction. The mere presence of one or two silently or openly hostile students in a small class inhibits my ability to enjoy the class or to give fully of myself. Or sometimes it is my own anger, for example if students arrive late, that interferes with my teaching. I am even sensitive to the quality of the response of an audience in a large lecture hall: if positive "vibes" are missing or I cannot elicit them, I am drained of energy and can no longer communicate. I suspect that my characteristic sensitivity to the moods of others (Miller 1976, p. 61) is both an asset and a liability in my professional life.

I find it difficult to weigh the value of my own goals against the opinions of students when the two clash. There are so many of them and only one of me—how can I be sure I am right? Although teaching is a lonely enterprise most of the time, I feel that autonomy is one of an educator's most enviable privileges. Ultimately I can find the key to good teaching within myself. I can use my own power.

Powerful women are still a novel and unwelcome presence in our society. It has been suggested that a woman's power is awesome and aversive to both men and women since it is a traumatic throwback to the absolute power of the mother in early life (Lerner 1974; Dinnerstein 1976). In my early years of teaching some of my students were intimidated and resentful of my "overbearing" style. I do not know whether my students, for the most part in the last stages of emancipation from their mothers, were justified in their complaints or not. My own self-image as a nurturing and caring teacher who had little sense of personal power clashed with my students' perceptions. It took several years for their reactions to become credible to me. Perhaps, in the process of gaining assertiveness and self-confidence, I confused the use of power as personal strength with the use of power as the exercise of influence (Miller 1976, p. 117). I think I was carried away with the hope of convincing students of my particular viewpoint. Once I fully understood their feelings of vulnerability and powerlessness, I became more cautious about the use of power in the classroom, without, however, relinquishing leadership. Untutored in the use of power (Miller 1976, p. 116–124), women teachers have to monitor it carefully.

Eventually I learned to become authoritative rather than authoritarian. This coincided with starting a large adult education class and with giving frequent lectures. I would not have been able to project myself to large audiences, to present myself with assurance, to field friendly and hostile questions with, I hope, skill and humor, if I had not learned to think of myself, at least in some ways, as a woman of power.

Although coming into my own power has sustained me in my midlife years, I continue to question to what extent this power is an integral part of my identity. I have recently, while away from home, become aware of its shifting nature and of its dependence on my social context. I hope that I own some of my power, but I suspect most of it is merely loaned to me by my affirming human community. (See Chapter 2, this volume.)

I have been particularly fortunate in the many relationships that have fostered my emotional and intellectual growth and helped me attain my goals. My husband's respect and belief in my abilities was an important source of self-confidence in early adulthood. He also offered me financial security, which allowed me to take risks in choosing work situations. Later I found that becoming a workaholic and a woman of power was not conducive to maintaining the marriage of my younger, more dependent and submissive years, and we have drifted apart. He remains the man I married, but I have become a different woman.

I have been supported by women and men in teaching, supervisory, and collegial roles. One of my social work mentors became my close and lifelong friend, a good mother who wishes me well. She is an invalid and I have the privilege of sustaining her in her old age. All through life I have had close and loving friends. We applaud each other's victories and support each other in times of defeat. In recent times I have found a large community of women and men who sustain me through their belief in me and their interest in my writing and teaching. I think of many of them as daughters and sons; perhaps they will visit me when I am old. Mothers and children take turns in their care-taking roles.

For a while I was so enchanted with teaching as interpersonal communication that I drifted away from my clinical training. Then I realized that education is a powerful therapeutic tool. I took on opportunities to teach mature adult women who use theoretical knowledge to lead more self-aware and self-fulfilled lives. Women who take my courses seem to come into their own power. They learn to conquer the world. It is exciting when different strands of one's life come together.

Before I knew what teaching was all about, I was afraid that it would lose its challenge after a few years and that I would become arid and stale. I did not yet quite realize that similar course content becomes quite different with different groups of students and thus stays forever fresh. Yet, to avoid even the possibility of stagnation, I change the content of my old courses every year, and I am forever designing new ones. Teaching a new course is an exciting adventure, full of hardship, risk, and uncertainty. There are days when I am afraid that I cannot keep up with the dramas and challenges that I manage to impose on my life. I have come to realize that I shall never fully master the kind of teaching that I envision, but the effort forces me to use and stretch all my talents and abilities. The frontiers of teaching and learning are infinitely broad and receding.

Teachers are in an exposed position, their performance forever open to scrutiny and judgment. There are days when I grow weary of performing, entertaining, and filling up others' emptiness. There are days when I tire of offering stimulation, encouragement, and comfort, and of being the target of my students' unresolved parental loves and hatreds.

A student reproaches me that I looked at the clock while she was talking. She never talks again, that whole semester. Another student feels that I have favorites and she is not one of them. Another student feels bitter because I did not recognize her when we met in the street. Another student admits to having stolen a special pencil from my desk, as a memento. Another student cries, because I, of all people have written a critical comment on her paper. "I saw you in the grocery store," a student says to me in surprise. "Yes, did you think I only eat books?" "No, I did not know demi-Gods need food," she replies.

But curiously, as the years go by, I am not as easily defeated, perhaps because along with being more open I have also grown more detached. I used to get angry at students who did not meet my standards; I positively disliked and scorned them. With greater wisdom I have become less narcissistically engaged, both in my praise and criticism. I had to relearn the same lesson that motherhood had taught me. Students, like children, must learn and achieve for themselves, not for their teachers. I must beware that my care and concern for my students, like motherly love and concern, does not become a prison. Sarton (1761) made this dilemma the subject of one of her early novels; it is one familiar to women teachers. The teacher role demands not only warmth and nurturance, but also distance, authority, and evaluation.

I have grown from a passive, eager learner and teacher whose talent was to abstract and explain others' concepts, into a person able to evaluate ideas and to choose and build my own concepts and values. As an educator I am forced continually to examine my values and ideas because I must state them clearly and defend them well. My acts and words are both very visible. As a model to my students I must live by the values that I teach. Above all, teaching is a way of sharing myself, of making an impact on the world, of making my intellectual and political contribution to society.

Finding my identity as educator has given my life new meaning and new drama. It involves my keen and caring interest in people and my enjoyment of reading, writing, and talking. It sanctions my wish to be a lifelong learner. It nurtures my creativity. This identity has helped me overcome my narcissism and its accompanying depression. The public performances in which I often take pleasure, and the recognition that I have received, are both an indulgence and a sublimation of that narcissism. The sheer enjoyment of my work helps to protect me against depression. My work with adult women has forced me to attend to my own maturation and differentiation.

My identity as an educator was neither forged in adolescence nor consolidated through marriage. For me—and I think this is true for many women—the sequential stages of identity, intimacy, and generativity, regardless of the order in which they are proposed (Erikson 1959; Goethals 1976), do not describe the order of my life. Self-definition came first through motherhood and later, more autonomously, through work and competence. I had to proceed simultaneously on all fronts to master the complexities of many roles.

I have grown from a sweet and obedient little girl to a woman of passion and power. But the standard of being "the best behaved little girl in Vienna" has remained a core aspect of my identity. I used to long to be really bad—just once in my life not to live up to everyone's expectations, especially my own. Someday I plan to become a "shameless old lady" (Brecht 1949).

Although I have led a privileged life and may not be considered a traditional woman, I still expect that many women will recognize themselves in me. I have never spoken to another woman, regardless of how different our life circumstances, without feeling profound kinship with her struggles. A striking feature of my development, one that I share with many other women, has been my late intellectual awakening. Although I have worked all my life, it was only in my forties that work became emotionally significant and a source of self-esteem, and only in my fifties that my latent ambition found self-expression.

Thus I find myself in midlife with a passion for my work. Like any other passion, it is addictive and enslaving. Although a passion for work makes one less dependent on other people than passion for a person, it does not assure invulnerability. I still rely on students, institutions, health, and other circumstances for the opportunity to continue teaching. The thought of retirement fills me with black dread.

I am beginning to understand that the paradoxes of my life are related to being a student and teacher of topics that intimately touch my own and other people's lives. Such a field demands total devotion to its subject matter as well as rich life experiences. It demands both tight self-discipline and a loosening of creativity. It demands openness to people and absorption with ideas; protection of time and energy, as well as endless commitment to students; it demands both solitude and many human encounters. It demands skills of objectivity and observation as well as involvement, distance as well as intimacy. It demands self-assurance, power, and humility.

References

Addams, J. (1910). *Twenty Years at Hull House.* New York: Macmillan, 1966.

Belle, D. (Ed). (1982). *Lives in Stress.* Beverly Hills: Sage Publications.

Brecht, B. (1949). *Kalendergeschichten* (Stories of the Calendar). Berlin: Gebrueder Weiss.

Chisholm, S. (1970). *Unbought and Unbossed.* Boston: Houghton Mifflin.

Clarke, A., and Clarke, A. D. (1977). *Early Experience: Myth and Evidence.* New York: Free Press.

Condry, J., and Dyer, S. (1976). "Fear of success: Attribution of cause to the victim." *Journal of Social Issues* 32: 63–83.

Cohler, B. J. (1984). "Parenthood, psychopathology and childcare." In R. Cohen, B. J. Cohler, and S. H. Weissman (Eds.). *Parenthood.* New York: Guilford Press.

Deutsch, H. (1973). *Confrontations with Myself.* New York: Norton

Dinnerstein, D. (1976). *The Mermaid and the Minotaur.* New York: Harper and Row.

Ehrenreich, B. and English, D. (1978). *For Her Own Good: 150 Years of the Experts' Advice to Women.* New York: Anchor Press/Doubleday.

Erikson, E. (1959). "The problem of ego identity." *Psychological Issues* 1(1): 101–64.

Goethals, G. W. (1976). "The evolution of sexual and genital intimacy: A comparison of Erik Erikson and Harry Stack Sullivan." *Journal of the American Academy of Psychoanalysis* 4(4):1–16.

Gove, W. R., and Tudor, J. F. (1973). "Adult sex roles and mental illness." *American Journal of Sociology* 78:812–35.

Hellman, L. (1969). *An Unfinished Woman.* Boston: Little Brown.

Henning, M. (1973). "Family dynamics for developing positive achievement motivation in women: The successful woman executive." *Annals of the New York Academy of Sciences* 208:77–81.

Horner, M. (1972). "The motive to avoid success and changing aspirations of college women." In J. Bardwick (Ed.). *Readings on the Psychology of Women.* New York: Harper and Row.

Lazarre, J. (1976). *The Mother Knot.* New York: McGraw-Hill.

Lerner, H. (1974). "Early origins of envy and devaluation of women: Implications for sex role stereotypes." *Bulletin of the Menninger Clinic* 36(6):538–53.

Levinson, D. J., et al. (1978). *The Seasons of a Man's Life.* New York: Knopf.

Lozoff, M. (1973). "Fathers and autonomy in women." *Annals of the New York Academy of Sciences* 208:91–97.

McBride, A. B. (1973). *The Growth and Development of Mothers.* New York: Harper and Row.

Miller, J. B. (1976). *Toward a New Psychology of Women.* Boston: Beacon Press.

Olsen, T. (1965). "Silences." *Harper's Magazine.* October, pp. 153–61.

Radl, S. (1973). *Mother's Day Is Over.* New York: Charterhouse.

Rich, A. (1976). *Of Women Born.* New York: Norton.

Roosevelt, E. (1939). *This Is My Story.* New York: Harper and Row.

Rorty, A. O. (1977). "Dependency, individuality, and work." In S. Ruddick and P. Daniels (Eds.). *Working It Out.* New York: Pantheon.

Sarton, M. (1961). *The Small Room.* New York: Norton.

——. (1978). Comment made during a Radcliffe open forum, April 4.

Weissman, M. M., and Klerman, G. (1977). "Sex differences and the epidemiology of depression." *Archives of General Psychiatry* 34:98–111.

Wortis, R. (1971). "The acceptance of the concept of the maternal role by behavioral scientists: Its effect on women." *American Journal of Orthopsychiatry* 41:733–46.

9 / Silences

*A*s soon as the Teacher woke up she knew that something was wrong. An acute malaise pervaded her body. It was not that she hadn't slept enough hours, especially since it was Saturday and she had not needed to set her alarm clock. No, neither was it the aura of a migraine attack; she recognized those instantly, they had quite a different feeling. The Teacher got up and took her bath. "Will you take a long or short bath?" her husband called from the kitchen. His voice sounded curiously distant, but there was no need to attend to his words since for years he had asked her the same question every morning. The Teacher would have preferred to take her morning bath without having to premeditate its length. But she did not know how to convey that wish to her well-meaning and solicitous husband, who wanted to prepare a four-minute soft-boiled egg for her every morning.

"Something is wrong with me," the Teacher said to her husband after having taken only a short bath. "Perhaps you are coming down with a cold," her husband replied. "Take some extra vitamin C pills, it might ward it off. Don't expect me for dinner tonight, we're having an office crisis about that government contract. God knows what might happen to us if we don't get it," he added in his usual doomful voice. The Teacher quickly turned on the morning news to drown out her husband's chronic business worries. As a young mother she used to be terrified by the constant threat that her husband would lose his job, but she had finally protected herself against this sword of Damocles by earning enough money to maintain the household no matter what happened to him, his firm, and his government contracts. Why had she bothered to mention her malaise to him, she wondered, when she had resolved over and over not to expect comfort from him. At the same time she reflected that his voice had been different, as if coming from a distance. And now the same was true for the voice on the radio. After her husband left for work, the Teacher started to test her ears while listening to the radio. It became apparent to her that she had become deaf in her left ear. She was at a loss as to what to do in this situation.

The telephone rang and her seventh best friend called to say hello. "I think I am deaf in one ear," the Teacher said in panic. "Don't worry," her friend replied," one can always learn to lip read." She referred to her husband, who was partially deaf and said that he managed very well. The Teacher knew that the husband's work was in the catacombs of library stacks and his identity, unlike hers, did not depend on talking with and listening to people. "I too have not been feeling well," her friend added. "I frequently have stomach cramps after I eat." In that moment the Teacher relegated her seventh best friend to the thirty-fourth rank, and she got off the phone as soon as possible.

The Teacher then called her daughter, the only one of her three children who had already finished college and had settled in the area. She explained the situation, and her daughter did not let her down. She expressed extreme concern and offered to visit her instantly. But the Teacher had set the weekend aside to read her students' examinations. She wanted to return them on Monday, to spare her students another day of anxious waiting. Besides, she knew that her daughter had just broken off with her lover and was herself in acute distress. If her daughter visited she would have to listen to her sad stories, and in her present condition she could not face any suffering except her own.

The Teacher had misgivings about calling her best friend, since her friend had the irritating but unswerving conviction that all accidents and illnesses were self-created and thus under one's own control. She called her nevertheless, and her friend also instantly offered to come over and help her exorcise the hostile forces that she had allowed to take hold of her body. Perhaps they could meditate together. Or perhaps the Teacher would finally allow her friend to lead her into a state of trance from which she would find the strength to resist the illness. The Teacher felt quite unready to take responsibility for the calamity that had befallen her. This would have to be her last telephone call.

Instead of starting to read the examinations, the Teacher sat down and wrote a letter to a man across the ocean whom she had met during her sabbatical three years ago, and whom she had unilaterally loved since that time. Since this man seemed quite impervious to whatever anxieties she chose to share with him, she could safely pour some of her terror into her letter. She also had learned that she could count on his friendly response, probably within a month or six weeks, in which he would either express hope that her hearing had improved, or would more likely have forgotten the matter and write about other things. Writing her letter took most of the morning and gave her some comfort.

The rest of the weekend was duly devoted to correcting exams. The Teacher was pleased that her students had learned so much and that she did not need to fail anyone. She took refuge in reading those exams as others might escape into listening to music or perhaps drinking.

The Teacher had her first class on Monday afternoon and decided to see a doctor on that morning. She got an emergency appointment at a big training hospital where many of her students had their internships, and indeed she met several of them in the hallways. After an audiogram and various tests it was established that she had some mysterious nerve deafness. The doctor thought that it might be Ménière's Syndrome and that it might well spread to the other ear. He could not suggest any particular treatment. He asked her whether she needed some tranquilizers and briefly debated whether hospitalization was indicated to undertake a series of diagnostic tests, but looking at the Teacher, he quickly gave up on both ideas.

The Teacher emerged from the doctors office and started to look for the medical library. The friendly librarian, who knew her from a distance, entreated her not to look up her alleged disease. The Teacher reflected that had this woman been her student, she would have learned that certain people gain strength from knowledge. After finding the name of her diagnosis in a medical dictionary, she felt some certainty that the doctor was wrong but drew little comfort from that thought, since she had no alternative explanation. She drove to the school from the hospital and found some students in tears in the entrance hallway. Rumor had spread that the Teacher had been seen emerging from the neurology section of the hospital and that she probably had a brain tumor. The Teacher embraced her students and reassured them. She taught her class as well as usually, although she was confused about the direction from which the students' voices originated. It was a very active and engaged class, which the Teacher interpreted as her students' way of showing caring and affection for her. If her deafness were to confine itself to one ear, she could manage it.

"I am deaf in one ear," she told her husband during the evening meal, "and the doctor said that the deafness might spread to the other ear." Her husband looked at her sadly and helplessly. The Teacher thought that he probably knew that the end of her work might mean the end of her meaningful life, and that he felt deeply for her. She wondered whether he remained silent because he feared his words of comfort would be the wrong words. She had taken away his power to comfort her, and perhaps there was indeed no way in which he could find the right words.

The Teacher spent the next days trying to decide what she should do with her life if she were to become deaf. Without teaching she would lose her identity, her community, and the only way she could make a useful difference in the world. Suicide was of course the right answer, but the Teacher knew she was a coward and she did not think she could manage that.

Some of her friends tried to reassure her and told her that one could remain a teacher even if one were deaf. She had, after all, a talent for teaching very large lecture classes, which might be taught without any discussion. Her voice, she was told, would not deteriorate until a few years hence. Her friends were foolish to imagine that she would undertake things that she could no longer do well. She would definitely stop teaching. Well, for years she had wanted to do library research and write books and articles for which her teaching left her no time. This was her chance, but it no longer seemed inviting.

The Teacher loved to play tennis, and here again, she had never had the time to practice enough to become an expert player. If she threw herself into playing tennis every day, she could perhaps become the best tennis player in her age group. She wondered whether one needed to hear the bouncing of the ball to become a first-class tennis player. But she was fifty-two years old, and at best, she would be an old woman who played remarkably well for her age.

The Teacher had always imagined that she would become a guru in her old age. People might come from all over the world to ask her advice about leading a good enough life. She might now have to change this image of how to grow old. She was also unsure how to keep up her friendships. How could she maintain friends if she could not exchange thoughts and feelings with them. She was relieved that she loved many people in foreign lands, with whom she could continue to exchange letters. Yet, without people around her she might become hollow and empty, and finally inner silence might match her deafness. The silent death of her marriage would invade the rest of her life.

On the ninth day of her partial deafness, it occurred to the Teacher that she could learn sign language and teach social sciences to deaf students. The thought cheered her enormously. It would be a great challenge to translate psychological concepts into sign language. She remembered how difficult that had been for the interpreters of deaf students in her classes. She would become an expert in sign language at the age of fifty-three, just as she had mastered the English language at the age of eighteen. It could well be that she would become the same kind of outstanding and inspiring teacher, sparking a love of ideas in her deaf students, as she was for her hearing ones.

On the tenth day, the Teacher turned on the car radio and heard it with both ears. She finally started to cry.

10 / Work and Love: The Divided Self

For men must work and women must weep.

THE THREE FISHERS, CHARLES KINGSLEY

ONCE upon a time there was a miller's daughter who was over-heard boasting that she could spin straw into gold. This is a modern fairy tale, and the miller's daughter was neither young nor beautiful, she was neither a wicked stepmother nor a gnarled witch, she was simply a presumptuous woman. And since there were relatively few women in her village who knew that skill, although it was not uncommon among men, she was challenged to realize her boast that she could do things as well as those men.

It was in the month of May, fortunately during a very rainy year, that the miller's daughter was locked up in her house for long periods of time, expected to spin gold out of straw. It so happened that the village had one gold festival after another, in that rainy month of May.

The miller's daughter sat in her house and looked at the rain. She wrung her hands and waited for Rumpelstiltskin, but he did not come to her rescue. She was left all alone with mountains of straw. She was very, very tired and longed to play with her friends. She thought she had earned that privilege. She had been spinning cloth all year, and most of the young women in the village were already wearing garments made of the cloth she had spun. But spinning garments was not a very honorable activity in that village; spinning gold was all that counted.

If she did not produce gold by the time the cock had crowed for three mornings in a row, she would be exposed in the marketplace, and the villagers would point at her shamefulness and call her an imposter.

If she were to succeed, however, she would have a short moment of glory. And since she was the miller's daughter and not his son, she wanted not only such glory, she wanted to be loved as well. Besides, she yearned not for the love of those who were ready to love her, but to have the power of choosing whom she wanted to love. She also wanted to be loved for herself and not merely for the skill of spinning straw into gold. And yet she also hoped that people would love her more because she knew how to spin gold, rather than become envious or fearful of her skills. You can see that she was a preposterously greedy woman, with contradictory wishes, and so she was bound to be disappointed and hurt, somewhere along the way.

Let us think about this miller's daughter, her excessive narcissism, dependency, tenuous self-esteem, and vulnerability to depression. What are the consequences for her being a woman with special skills? Perhaps we should quickly refer her to the nearest mental health center. We can see that she is overwhelmed by her struggle to compete with men of distinction while she also wishes to be loved by them, or at least by those whom she chooses. She is exhausted by her struggle to spin garments for the village women while knowing that spinning gold is more valued. She is torn by wishing to spend time with her friends while having to work around the clock. She is conflicted by her wish to boast about her accomplishments, while also thinking them exceedingly modest. She wants to raise her voice, to be heard, seen, understood, and admired, while yearning for tranquility. At any minute she might become depressed.

It is true her inner turmoil is well-contained; she is a most competent spinner; the presentation of her public self is most reassuring, and she never causes trouble to anyone—yet think of what her Rohrschach might look like—after all, she clearly has a divided self.

Now that many women have entered the arena of achievement and competition in the world of work, it is time that we address

their struggles. There are many miller's daughters in the world today, and our situation deserves a serious analysis.

Self-Regard

Let us begin by examining the miller's daughter's narcissism.

We can probably agree on a definition of narcissism that includes
preoccupation with and absorption in the self. Most theorists would
agree that narcissistic persons are plagued by self-doubts and thus
constantly need others to confirm their worth as human beings.
They are excessively dependent on "external sources of admiration,
love, and confirmation" (Kernberg 1975, p. 319). Such doubts are
sometimes covered by fantasies of grandiosity and specialness (Bursten 1977).

If Sigmund Freud invented the Oedipus complex to normalize his
own love, hatred, and loyalty conflicts toward his parents, and if
Erik Erikson could seize on the issue of adolescent identity to come
to grips with his own struggle regarding his family origins, and if
Rollo May can generalize his conflict between living and dying into
a universal existential dilemma, then I can insist that my own self-
doubts, need for outside confirmation and, of course, grandiosity,
as I am just demonstrating, are also universal features.

Sigmund Freud declared that women are more narcissistic than
men. It was a strange assertion by a man who was intensely narcissistic by most definitions, if we consider that psychoanalysis was
an integral part of his identity. I have never met anyone who was
not intensely narcissistic in the sense defined above. My altruistic
social work students cry or get angry or depressed when they are
criticized, although some students maintain a veneer of self-control.
In our small learning groups, where students express their greatest
fear of what might happen in the group, they write: "I might be
rejected; I might make a fool of myself; I might be ignored." Despite
their outward show of confidence, their need to be seen, validated,
recognized, and appreciated is intense. The issue in most therapy
groups, and I think in other kinds of groups as well, and maybe
even in life is: who gets air time. All other issues are quite second-
ary. Most people, we have discovered in these groups, are alert to
minute nonverbal signals when they appraise others' reactions to

themselves. I sometimes wonder whether paranoid people are simply extremely well-attuned to the slightest signs of hostility, which most of us have learned to ignore, but which might well be there, in many interactions. Guntrip (1969) also affirmed the near universal self-doubts in our society:

'What are people most afraid of?' . . . The one omnipresent fear is the fear of being and appearing weak, inadequate, less of a person than others or less than equal to the demands of the situation, a failure: the fear of letting oneself down and looking a fool in face of an unsupportive and even hostile world. (1969, p. 175)

The literature actually leaves it somewhat uncertain whether narcissism involves excessive or insufficient self-love. It is easy to love oneself too much or too little or for the wrong reasons. We are supposed to love ourselves so well that we can sustain all manner of narcissistic injuries without despairing and losing our self-esteem. It is a big order to love oneself so well, and nobody (certainly not our parents) has prepared us to do so. Indeed, preoccupation with self-esteem issues might be inevitable in a society in which children are generally used for narcissistic ornaments by their mothers and fathers. Most children are loved conditionally, for being obedient, good, smart, attractive, and generally a source of pride for their parents. Thus, children (who grow into adults) also learn to love themselves for their talents, or their looks, or their achievements, all of which can be lacking, unappreciated, and above all ephemeral. It makes for a very shaky life.

Yet it is also not useful to blame parents who are preparing their children for survival in our society. Perhaps it is necessary for socialization into a competitive and junglelike society such as ours, that children be loved conditionally. Thus we have few adults who take their self-worth for granted as an integral aspect of the self.

While men and women are surely equally occupied with self-regard issues, these issues may take different forms. I think men and women sometimes look different because they may play for different audiences and thus need different kinds of applause. I was alerted to this by a scientist friend who gently laughed at what he calls my "need for mirroring." He denies any such needs for himself because he has his own internal standards, which he calls more stringent than any that others could impose upon him. Perhaps my scientist friend could be called egocentric rather than narcissistic, but it highlighted the two opposite ways of expressing self-absorption. My scientist friend is inner-directed and certainly absorbed in his own ideas, if not with himself. He plays for select audiences, a few chosen living and dead persons. He easily forgets what people tell him and envies my good memory. I believe the notoriously failing memory of middle-aged men is due to this kind of self-absorption. He feels extreme distress if he cannot meet his own excessive standards, reacting with shame, self-devaluation, and obsessional ruminations.

I feel that I join other women in being more outer-directed. Far from being self-absorbed, we are intensely outer-directed, engaged in love and hate with the world out there, from which we seek admiration. I don't know who could be called the greater narcissist. Yet, these categories seem very artificial. Most people do need a great deal of affirmation from others, but men have been trained to hide this need from themselves and from others. Perhaps men tend to need more affirmation in the area of work and women in the area of love—but I am writing after all about our miller's daughters, androgynous women who have become vulnerable in both realms of work *and* love.

People vary in their ability to hide their self-concerns and self-doubts; they vary in their values, standards, life goals, and their capacity to meet them. Fortunate are those whose talents, skills, and opportunities match their aspirations. But above all, people vary in the way they define their self-interests. The personal construction of self-interest can stop, short-sightedly, with one's immediate person, family, and short-term goals, or it can include a realization of one's own interconnectedness with the well-being of one's students, one's clients, the organization for which one works, justice among people, the cessation of the arms race, and even the survival of seals. Once we recognize that we live in a hopelessly interconnected and interdependent world, all of these issues can become intensely narcissistic concerns. Bateson (1972) has defined wisdom as awareness of the whole circuitry rather than focus on a narrow arc. So perhaps it is a measure of wisdom that distinguishes people, rather than their degree of narcissism.

It could be argued that women's greater inclination to become depressed is a measure of their greater narcissistic vulnerability. Women's almost universal tendency to depression is indeed dramatic. It has been demonstrated through numerous research reports, with much speculation on causes. (Weissman and Klerman 1977). I have repeatedly asked groups of several hundred women in classrooms or audiences if anyone did *not* have at least one moderately severe depression in her life. Nobody ever raises her hand. Perhaps, however, it might look embarrassing in such a context not to have been depressed. I do not know how male audiences would respond to such a question, but research suggests that the answer might be different. Some differences might simply arise from men's not being in touch with their own feelings, but there may be true differences as well. We can search for the reasons, but I do not agree that they lie in women's greater narcissism.

First, we need to eliminate all reasons for realistic depressions related to lack of resources, violence, lack of control over one's life, isolation, bad health, troublesome children, and overwhelming multiple problems, all of which assault women, such as single mothers, who live in poverty (Belle 1982) more than men.

Second, we need to consider that depression might be one way of going on strike and yet remaining a dutiful, conscientious, and self-sacrificing woman. From being utterly other-directed and selfless, a woman may become totally preoccupied with herself, a dramatic reversal. But depression is so painful that it punishes the person who goes on strike, ensuring a rebellion without pleasure.

In a marriage in which both partners may potentially be depressed, it is the wife who may obligingly carry the depression, especially since she is culturally more entitled to do so. Husbands are allowed to be alcoholic and violent rather than depressed. I wonder what might happen if women refused to carry their husbands' depression.

If we think of depression as related to self-esteem issues

(Bibring 1953), there could actually be multiple explanations for women's apparent greater self-doubts. Self-esteem has been connected by four different theoretical schools to four major conditions:

1) The secure establishment of an autonomous self (Laing 1965; Shapiro 1981; Kohut 1977);
2) Early and ongoing experiences of mastery (White 1963);
3) Early experiences of being prized by significant others (Erikson 1959; Guntrip 1969);
4) Ongoing esteem supplied by significant others and significant members of society (Kernberg 1975).

I believe that women are somewhat disadvantaged in each of these categories. First, regarding the establishment of an autonomous self, it has been suggested that it is more difficult to separate from a primary caretaker of the same gender (Stoller 1972; Chodorow 1978). Establishment of a girl's core gender identity does not demand the little boy's early, painful, yet autonomy-inducing identification withdrawal from his mother.

Second, while both genders probably have an equal opportunity for early competence experiences, traditional sex roles favor men for later life opportunities in this area.

Most important, in my eyes, are points three and four. Girls look to their fathers, the family member with most power and status, for self-affirmation. Yet fathers, judging from my students' papers and from famous women's biographies, not to mention my own father (see Chapter 17), are very unreliable sources of esteem for their daughters, especially during the adolescent phase. In adult life many women continue to look to men for supporting their self-regard. I think women as a whole are more generous in supporting men's self-esteem than vice-versa, although admittedly, there are notable exceptions of famous women whose mentors were men. Yet while strong, competent men attract women's love and admiration, the reverse does not seem to be true. Strong, competent women seem to make men feel threatened, useless (Weiss 1985), and inadequate, and it appears they remind men of their all-powerful, controlling mother of early childhood (Lerner 1974; Dinnerstein 1976). It also seems true that mothers turn more often to their sons, rather than to their daughters, for narcissistic gratification, redressing the balance once again.

I would like to argue, however, that women are exposed to repeated experiences of betrayal in their lives, all of them related to narcissistic injuries, and that these experiences could well account for the high incidence of depression among women.

Love

I shall define as betrayal any experience that undermines the implicit or explicit assumptions that govern people's lives, and I will focus on three such typical events. I shall dramatize them by focusing on certain negative identities that women tend to assume in the course of life, borrowing from our literary heritage.

Hans Christian Andersen's "Little Mermaid" can be the figure for the first betrayal experience of romantic love in adolescence. The little mermaid yearns to gain the love of the prince and an immortal human soul. Seeking the advice to the all-knowing mer-witch (perhaps an early psychotherapist), she is told that she can gain the prince and a soul only by giving up her mermaid tail and her beautiful singing voice. I suggest to you that the tail represents her "masculine aggressive strivings" and her voice symbolizes her identity. She makes these sacrifices, but in vain. The prince loves her, but only as a child; mute, she has become an incompetent child/bride. His true love goes to another woman, presumably one who has kept her own identity. Helene Deutsch (1945, p. 251) wrote that women are taught to give up their aggression for the sake of being loved and that the aggression turns inward, as feminine masochism, or I presume as depression. The little mermaid has extreme pain and suffering when she turns human. Every step taken with her new feet feels like a knife driven into her body. In my study of passionate love, I looked at experiences in the lives of seven hundred women. Half of these women had sought emotional help at some point in their lives, and half of these 350 women who had sought help had done so for passionate love-related reasons. There had been some kind of rejection, hurt, humiliation, or disconfirmation that had left them devastated (see Chapter 3).

The Andersen fairy tale actually does not hold out false promises. On the contrary, it warns the adolescent girl of the possible dangerous consequences of sacrificing her identity for the love of a prince. It is in the Grimm's fairy tales that the image of the fair maiden who patiently waits for the prince is exalted. Sleeping Beauty, Cinderella, and Snow White grow up expecting to be rescued by the prince from experiences of drudgery, pain, evil, and even death. Perhaps even in this brave new generation some young women still get married to escape an unpleasant home situation, just as Cinderella did. Often they enter marriage with excessively unrealistic expectations, the source of which is both tenacious cultural myths and the yearning to find the truly loving parents whom they may never have had. Fairy tales with their "happily ever after" endings symbolize these yearnings, but they also perpetuate them, arousing unrealistic expectations that can lead to a bitter betrayal experience. Although I have placed the crisis of romantic love in adolescence, it is not confined to that period. We know from such heroines as Guinevere, wife of King Arthur, or Anna Karenina, that romantic passion can occur at any stage in a woman's life with a vehemence equal to or surpassing adolescent love, often expressing the pent-up emotions of many loveless years.

The second major crisis of betrayal can be placed in middle life and may be dramatized by Medea, as told in the beautiful play by Euripides. Jason and his companions, the Argonauts, come to Medea's far-off land to steal her father's golden fleece. They are young men in search of ego-boosting adventures. Medea falls in love with Jason and helps him attain his goals by putting her famous skills and wits at his disposition. In the process of gaining glory and success for her husband, she alienates her own family and friends in successive adventures. When Jason eventually betrays her for another younger, more powerful woman, she explodes in extreme violence and vengefulness, killing her rival as well as her own children. These are symbolic acts that we do not need to take literally. Many women in a crisis of betrayal abandon their children physically or emotionally or destructively use them as tools of vengeance. Women tend to forgive Medea or at least to feel empathic with her. We all recognize some aspect of Medea's violence in ourselves.

That divorce has become a widespread phenomenon in our society should not blind us to the fact that it nevertheless remains a poignant drama of love, hate, and shattered hopes for each individual. It is especially bitter for women in midlife, at a time when a man is still considered in his desirable prime, while she herself has very diminished opportunities for finding a suitable partner.

The fact that a woman's worth is often measured by her youth and beauty cannot be considered a betrayal, in the sense of an unexpected event. A girl learns in early childhood that her fate is mysteriously tied up with being beautiful, or at least pretty.

If we accept the definition of betrayal as the disappointment of assumptions that guided one's life, then a traditional woman who expected care taking, loyalty, and safety in her marriage will feel betrayed not only by sexual infidelity, but by any circumstances that undermine these expectations, be it the husband's incompetence, alcoholism, or even death. Perhaps the intense anger that is described in autobiographical novels (Caine 1974) as well as in social science literature, which is true only of widows and not of widowers, (Glick, Weiss, and Parkes 1974), is at least partly a response to the broken promises of life expectations.

It is true, of course, that many women do not experience betrayal by their spouses or lovers. However, I suggest that women are becoming increasingly more aware of this possibility and are adopting various strategies.

Some women protect themselves by remaining aloof and never surrendering their inner selves. Perhaps Freud's famous or infamous claim that women never truly love men, supposedly because of their excessive narcissism, refers to women who use that kind of armoring. Other women deal with the constant possibility of betrayal by living in daily dread and never expressing their true needs in their relationships to a man, lest he abandon them. It is this dread that prevents women from using the power they usually have in their marriages to negotiate changes they desperately want. It is also to this dread that advertising media appeal when selling the innumerable devices that claim to secure a man, from the right brand of coffee to vaginal deodorants.

There is a third, growing group of women who ward off the trauma of betrayal by carefully preserving a separate identity, starting in adolescence, and by attaining a measure of emotional and financial independence, probably at some cost to devotion and togetherness.

The third negative identity for which I have fortunately found a splendid heroine is that of Portnoy's mother (Roth 1969). She is a caricature of the loved and hated Jewish mother, but Jewish mothers have become the American middle-class model. Such a mother has read in all the books, or at least has heard through word of mouth, that if she is tender, loving, and understanding, and ever ready to make every personal sacrifice, then her child will grow up to be successful and will bring her boundless joy and pride. It used to be the son rather than the daughter who was more vulnerable to the mother's semipurposeful strategy of binding him into a powerful love relationship when he is very young, and then controlling him through guilt-arousing techniques and threats of love withdrawal. The mother's continued, passionate, and narcissistic involvement creates a sense of great specialness, entitlement, and perhaps grandiosity in the son. He internalizes his mother's high expectations, yet also senses that he is being used and exploited by his mother. He feels intense ambivalence, with ensuing guilt, and sometimes it is only through repudiation with distance and coldness that the son can gain an illusory sense of autonomy.

From the mother's side there is not only the attempt to delegate to the son her own thwarted ambitions, but also a determination to live up to the cultural ideal of perfect motherhood. Yet such universal feelings of motherhood as frustration, anxiety, resentment, and boredom tend to emerge in rather subtle ways, and they need to be split off as socially unacceptable. In addition to these individual feelings, there is the need to socialize the child into the behavioral norms of a particular society, with all the coercion, restrictions, and frustrations that this involves for both mother and child.

In an amusing book review, Bruno Bettelheim (1970) pronounced Portnoy a perfect narcissist, and we presume that this was the result of his mother's overlove. After all, Narcissus himself was a child "with whom one could have fallen in love even in his cradle" (Hamilton 1982, p. 21). The problem is not simple, because the boundary between loving, encouraging, and setting high standards, and "overloving" a child, is a thin one. Moreover, the outcome is uncertain. While history describes tragic examples of the potential megalomanic destructiveness of narcissistic men, such as Hitler, whom Stierlin (1977) considered his mother's "bound delegate" son, we also have other "overowned" sons, such as Winston Churchill, Sigmund Freud, or Franklin Roosevelt, who have made unique contributions to our society (Loewenstein 1977).

Portnoy's mother, along with other mothers, is prepared to face neither her own negative feelings nor those of her child, and her son's guilt-ridden antagonism strikes her as deeply undeserved ingratitude. She has probably read about Freud's Oedipus complex and knows that little boys tend to fall in love with their mothers. She has long ago come to terms with the concept of Oedipal love; love is after all a positive, life-enhancing emotion, even when directed towards an incestuous object. Freud, however, did not explore the darker side of the mother/son relationship as illustrated by Orestes, who murders his mother in the Greek myth. Motherhood involves love and hate by both mother *and* child, and Portnoy's mother is not prepared for that.

The physical and emotional loss of the child hits the mother in her middle life. Portnoy's mother, who has little investment in her own personal development or even in the relationship to her husband or friends, is left in bitterness and isolation. Unlike Medea, she turns her rage over the betrayal of motherhood against herself and becomes depressed (Bart 1971).

There are mothers who are even more deeply betrayed than Mrs. Portnoy, whose son, however self-absorbed or unloving, had made it in the world to some degree. I am thinking of women whose children are killed in wars, or even worse, commit suicide or become mentally ill, adding incomprehending guilt to inconsolable grief. I have sought very long for a suitable heroine of that kind of betrayal; I have considered Mother Courage (Brecht

1941), who lost her children to war and "good causes." Or perhaps we should consider Gertrude, the mother of Hamlet, who was bitterly punished for whatever transgressions may have been hers. Perhaps Mrs. Alving in Ibsen's *Ghosts* (1881), who must take care of her syphilitic son for the rest of her life, is an even better heroine. I don't know why it was so hard to find just the right heroine, since this kind of devastating betrayal is not at all uncommon.

I don't know whether it is possible to be armed against life betrayals by changing one's expectations. I have tried (in Chapter 16) to warn women against the fairy tale myths of ever-lasting love and blissful motherhood, but it is hard to heed such warnings. We need, after all, a great deal of unreasonable optimism to approach the road of life.

I have outlined the possible life course of a traditional woman born in the pre-World War II era. It is possible that women who can currently express their healthy or unhealthy narcissistic needs in their own careers will no longer need to use their children to the same extent. Another change is the greater possibility that not only sons but also daughters can be delegated to carry their mothers' or fathers' disappointed aspirations. Perhaps the miller's daughter is such a delegated child. Here again, it is above all the demystification of totally blissful motherhood that will protect current and future mothers against false expectations. In addition, a supermother is being redefined as one who not only can give her child unstinting devotion, but who also promotes her child's autonomy while she attends simultaneously to her own development.

Work

Considering the many hurdles in the realm of love, work presents itself as both a welcome alternative and second source of satisfaction for women (Fiske 1980; Smelser 1980). Working mothers may thus be viewed as leading potentially the fullest and most satisfying of all lives, since they can rely on either work or love, or perhaps even on both, for meaning and fulfillment in their lives. This is especially true of professional women with challenging jobs, but research suggests that employment may also protect less educated women who live in poverty against depression. Yet after demystifying the realm of love, we must also cast a cautionary glance at the realm of work.

A young friend of mine, mother of three children under the age of five, is starting a full-time social work job while maintaining her singing career in the evening. She says, "I want to write a book about having your cake and eating it too." Presumably writing a book will be her fourth job. We are all very greedy and dazzled by the new opportunities for self-expression and participation in the world of work without giving up any traditional roles. The situation leads to overload and exhaustion, but that is not even the whole picture.

I suggested earlier that most people need an ongoing effort to maintain their self-regard. They tend to attach their sense of worth to success in the area either of work or of love. I would argue that failure in the area of priority is devastating, even if substitute satisfaction in the other area may be available.

When I was a young and overloving mother, work was for me a welcome distraction, a steadying influence, play, and recreation, but I staked my self-esteem on the welfare of my children. Success at work did not protect me against depression when my children had difficulties. Disaster in one's area of priority, be it love or work, can invade the other area and render it meaningless. One friend was a successful academician until her child became schizophrenic in adolescence. At that point her career lost the meaning she had formerly been able to invest in it, and she resigned from her tenured position to devote herself to her child.

The miller's daughter loved to spin, and the activity gave meaning to her life, yet she spun so hard making garments and even gold that she had no time for anything else. Her work started to feel like a treadmill, as if she were merely fulfilling a series of obligations, as I try to express in the following poem.

Work and Love

They say that work
makes up for love
when love is bad.

Perhaps they're right?
When I awake
at crack of dawn
not with your image
in my heart
which beats instead
for book reviews
reading lists
papers, reports
urgent, waiting.
Perhaps it's safe
to forget love.
Yet work sans love
is drudgery
joyless
meaningless
futile
unsustaining
of life on earth.

The self-esteem of professional men is usually organized around the world of work. Leventman's research (1981) on the effects of the 1970 unemployment crisis among engineers complements earlier research on black street corner men (Liebow 1967). With the loss of work, neither of these two groups of men could maintain their ability to love themselves or their families. "My data reveal," wrote Leventman, "that the ties that bind the American new middle-class family are so tenuous that in the space of several months, unemployment can tear the fabric of affection and respect" (1981, p. 166).

I brought in men's vulnerability to stress the point that men are just as vulnerable as women, although the causes of distress and their responses to it may vary. While women become depressed, men tend to respond to stress more often with alcoholism and violence. Rather than ask why women have greater self-esteem issues, we should inquire into the different sources of narcissistic vulnerability for either gender. Moreover, total investment in the world of work is not limited to men. Some professional women approach work with quite the same passion that other women reserve for their love relationships.

Virginia Woolf is a compelling example of a brilliant woman who has deeply vulnerable self-doubts in her work. Her biographers suggest that "It is difficult not to conclude that the headaches, sleeplessness, and suicidal depression of 1913, together with the episodes of 1915, were primarily the result of a single cause: the publication of *Voyage Out*, and that they represented the hysterias of a highly sensitive writer, always close to the edge of sanity, fearful that she would be 'found out' and adjudged mad by insensitive critics. . . . " (Spater and Parsons 1977, p. 68).

Here was yet another woman, although admittedly a mad one, who was afraid to be found out, just like the miller's daughter. We might believe that Virginia's doubts about her work also invaded her ability to love, similar to unemployed men. "The principal feature of Virginia's ravings during her mad spells was criticism of others—of men in general, of Leonard [her husband] in particular . . . " (p. 68). An alternate view is that Virginia was doubly vulnerable in both "love" (which encompasses hate) and work. Her first suicide attempt took place a year after her marriage. Blessed with a husband who was totally devoted to her, she could not express her hatred in any other way; she had to become mad. Laing (1965) reported a case history in which a daughter became defeated by her inability to express her rage against her overdevoted selfless mother. "Julie's shreds of sanity . . . depended on the possibility of being able to lodge some bad in her actual mother. The impossibility of doing this, in a sane way, was one of the factors that contributed to a schizophrenic psychosis" (p. 194). It is my idiosyncratic hypothesis that Virginia Woolf had a similar dilemma. Eventually she felt so oppressed by Leonard that she had to commit suicide, since she saw no other way of disentangling herself from his unceasing intrusive devotion. It is not only women who are guilty of overloving. Given the right circumstances, men can do so quite as well.

Thus women as well as men can have a priority commitment and ensuing vulnerability to either love *or* work, but I think most typical of professional women is an equal double commitment, or a blending of the two, with ensuing double vulnerability. Professional women not only enjoy a doubly enriched life, they also face a double jeopardy regarding narcissistic hurts.

I think the diary of Anna Vorontosov, the semiautobiographical heroine created by Sylvia Ashton-Warner in *Spinster* (1959), describes in exceptional depth and unsentimental compassion the fate of many professional women. Anna is a wonderfully creative teacher who has found very original methods to teach reading and writing to the culturally disadvantaged Maori children of New Zealand. She is, however, utterly dependent on her male inspector's approval of her unconventional teaching methods. Like the miller's daughter, Anna does not manage to keep love and work in neat compartments. They get quite uncomfortably mixed up.

Anna! You make the mistake of living by love! All your rules of behaviour and of morals and of work are confused with it. Love is not wholly respectable, you know. . . . For one thing it clogs organization and for another it's no good in thinking. Passion too: there's no place for it in a schoolroom. . . . (p. 230)

Although she loves the inspector silently and passionately in fantasy, all she ultimately wants from him is recognition and admiration for her work. He is blind to her love and talents and does not give her the affirmation for which she craves. Profoundly disconfirmed, Anna Vorontosov buries the two beautiful textbooks she had written for her Maori children and resigns from her job in total defeat. In womanly fashion she concludes that it is not others who have failed her, but she who has failed them.

The sum total of my efforts have just not added up enough to justify grading. And I do not blame him for my own many unwieldy and solitary mistakes. One does not blame another for your misfortunes. You carry the capacity within yourself. One must not blame another. (p. 238)

Alma Mahler, Gustav's Mahler's wife, also buried her songs in the earth when they received no recognition from her husband. Would a talented young man ever be totally defeated by a woman's lack of approval or recognition?

The tendency of many women to be oversensitive to personally motivated and unjustified criticism or to feel responsible for other people's unkindness is a primary example of the earlier mentioned outer-directed narcissism. It demonstrates a basic lack of self-confidence and a distorted sense of one's own power, but it is also caused by taking others very seriously. Even if only a few of my students do not appreciate my teaching, I must take their criticism seriously, since I cannot imagine that anyone's response is totally invalid. One of the most competent women I have ever known went into psychotherapy because of the self-doubts that her angry ex-husband's insults aroused in her. Women's capacity to internalize unfair criticism is boundless and endless.

In my experience, professional women are the first truly androgynous people in our society. Some of us still remember how to love and weep—how could we ever forget that—and we are learning to work and stand on our own feet. Socialized to care about love and attachment, to be obedient and selfless, to be gentle and nurturant, we enter a world of work in which we may meet values of personal achievement, competition, and self-assertiveness. It is hard to combine such contradictory inclinations and expectations. Yet social systems cannot remain the same when they absorb new members. I believe women's full participation cannot but change the world of work.

Strong women feel that no one in the world, especially not their husbands, male lovers, or male therapists, can tolerate their love, rage, or despair. It is easier to become mad when one's emotions become explosive. Being a strong woman is still a lonely position, because we miller's daughters feel neither as powerful nor as independent as others assume us to be.

The Divided Self

A strong woman wants to be allowed to express both strength *and* weakness, autonomy *and* dependency, and to be accepted and loved rather than punished for the contradictory aspects of her *divided self*.

In his book on Eleanor Roosevelt's correspondence (1982), Joseph Lash commented on the startling discrepancies between

people's public and private selves. "As the private papers of respectable Victorians—Americans as well as British—become
available, it is often a shock to discover the gap between obei-
sance to public mores and private lives" (p. xii).

Eleanor Roosevelt, Virginia Woolf, Anna Vorontosov, Simone
de Beauvoir, Anna Freud, these are my models and my heroines,
yet none of them represents the societal ideals of femininity, social conformity, or so-called normality. Simone de Beauvoir found
an intellectual soul-mate, yet her sexual passions went to other
men; Anna Vorontosov and Virginia Woolf had creative fire, yet
both were also immature. Virginia was mad and depressed, and
Anna drank too much and had absurd and unrealistic fantasies
of passion. Anna Freud's overriding life passion was her father.
Eleanor Roosevelt was married and bore five children, yet emotionally she remained a celibate woman and her passions went
to women and men friends, excluding her own family. She ro-
mantically kissed the photograph of a woman friend before going
out to fight poverty and unemployment.

Women are not the only ones who have a divided self. Whenever we look at anyone's life beyond the surface, we find the
most startling contradictions. We recently learned (Carotenuto 1982)
that Carl Jung, that great humanistic psychologist, enjoyed sexual
relations with some of his women patients and rationalized it
as a possible form of payment for his services. Of course, Jung
is not admirable in some other respects as well; I am using him as
an example only because he is dead and fortunately not related
to me.

Guntrip (1969) wrote about the weak, infantile ego around which
is formed the adapted shell of the false self. He gave us an image
of an onion with a festering, rotten core. My metaphor of the self
is different, because I believe that opposites belong together. I
see the narcissistic self and the altruistic self, the private self and
the public self, the dependent self and the autonomous self, and
all our other multiple selves side by side, each equally valid. At
times we manage to integrate those many selves and then we feel
whole, and at other moments of stress we feel torn in many directions, with the sense of a divided self.

There is no reason why our primitive selves should necessarily be considered more valid than our socialized selves. I have even wondered whether "reaction formation," which is based on the image of a *layered* self in which the deepest layer represents the highest truth, is a useful concept. If we substitute the metaphor of a *divided* self, we imply that people have conflicting, simultaneous positive and negative emotions that may be equally authentic. I used to think that my self-assurance was a mere cover-up for my self-doubts, until I felt comfortable owning both polarities.

While descriptions of developmental stages in human growth have offered critical theoretical steps, some observers have recently focused increased attention on the simultaneous or rapidly alternating acquisition and expression of different capacities and needs. We have noticed, for example, that both attachment *and* separation, trust *and* autonomy characterize the first year of life (Stern 1985), while generativity and intimacy (Erikson 1959) go hand in hand, especially in women's lives. While Erikson seemed to relegate having children to the stage of generativity rather than intimacy it is hard to imagine a more intimate relationship than that between a mother and her children.

In a similar vein, Piaget's vision of a relentless march toward ever greater rationality is being questioned. Riegel (1973), for example, pointed to Hegel's theory that contradictions "are the most basic property of nature and mind . . . [and a] . . . necessary condition of thought" (p. 351). Most people, Riegel suggested, "operate simultaneously at different levels of cognition, perhaps switching back and forth between them or choosing one for one area of activity and another for another area" (p. 364). Cognitive dissonance theory notwithstanding, most of us live with a great deal of ambiguity and contradictions in our reasoning and thoughts. Certainly, stress will cause many people to regress to magical and egocentric thought. The same process appears to be habitual for emotional development. Most people are simultaneously wise and foolish, mature and immature, active and passive, cowardly and courageous, obedient and rebellious, stingy and generous.

Daniel Levinson (1978) has emphasized the balance of a number of basic dichotomies in middle life, but I think such precarious balancing goes on all through life. Struggles around particular dichotomies might characterize some age periods more than others. We often observe the pull between the search for adventure and security in young adulthood, while a conflict between activity versus passivity, or generosity versus stinginess, might concern older people. Yet, as the life cycle has become more fluid, new choices open up in middle life, raising once again the issue of risk versus safety. Relative sanity seems to depend on some ability to integrate or balance these internal contradictions. People who have very pronounced obsessional or hysterical styles seem to have lost that balance.

At times when I have felt torn between strong contradictory pulls, such as my wish to reach out to people, yet also to ward them off, or my desire to forgive and yet to remain unforgiving, I have experienced my mother's ghost inside me, pulling me in directions that I had decided to avoid. Such acute struggles may be the price of living in opposition to an internalized parent. Exposure to conflicting parental missions may be yet another element of the divided self, and women have been consistently exposed to contradictory messages, as illustrated in this old nursery rhyme.

Mother may I go out to swim?
Yes my darling daughter
Hang your clothes on a hickory limb
And don't go near the water.

Men and women have divided some of these polarities among themselves. Unlike some theorists, I do *not* think that such divisions are primarily due to different childhood socialization and early learning, because I have seen too many people switch rapidly and quite easily from playing out one polarity to its opposite, should circumstances demand it. We have seen passive, dependent women become strong and self-reliant after they lose their husbands. The distribution of polarities seems to be dictated by social customs, role prescriptions, and life circumstances. Perhaps the ability to move between polarities as required by life circumstances is another sign of relative mental health.

Intimacy, for example, is difficult for most couples. Traditionally the woman is in charge of seeking closeness while the man preserves distance, carefully limiting the possibility for intimacy. In a marriage like that of Virginia and Leonard Woolf, however, where the woman takes on the distancing role, the man will readily become the pursuer. Systems generally tend to represent both polarities, and it becomes relatively arbitrary who carries the complementary attributes. Trouble seems to arise in projective identification when one partner completely disowns and hands over some aspect of the divided self to the other partner.

I have attempted to argue that the discrepancy between "normal" in the utopian sense and "normal" in the statistically most prevalent sense has become so wide that our concepts of normality and pathology need to be revised. I must therefore leave the decision as to the psychiatric referral of the miller's daughter to you. Perhaps a last piece of this case history might be useful to you. It is a poem she and I wrote in a retrospective mood about the plight of the miller's daughter. We wrote it in a moment of disenchantment in her life. We also wrote it to answer Sigmund Freud's famous question: What do women want? Freud meant to ask what do women want from men? It is a question forever repeated by other men.

Dear
long-forbearing husband
son
brother
men friends
around the world

Thank you for
having been
in my life
assuring me
that I was
good enough
to nurture
a male child
to be loved

or admired
or respected
by some men
since I could not
have learned
to love myself
without
your male approval.

But now
we are all
growing up
growing old
and I find
that I am
too strong
too independent
too powerful
too weak
too childish
greedy and demanding
to keep up
with you.

Now we can go
our separate paths
hoping they might
intersect
for moments
in the years
to come.

References

Ashton-Warner, S. (1959). *Spinster*. New York: Simon and Schuster.
Bart, P. B. (1971). "Depression in middle-aged women." In V. Gornick
    and B. K. Moran (Eds.). *Woman in Sexist Society*. New York: Basic Books.
Bateson, G. (1972). *Steps to an Ecology of Mind*. New York: Ballentine.
Belle, D. (Ed.). (1982). *Lives in Stress*. Beverly Hills: Sage

Bettelheim, B. (1970). "Portnoy psychoanalyzed." *Psychiatry and Social Science Review* 4: 2–9.

Bibring, E. (1953). "The mechanism of depression." In P. Greenacre (Ed.). *Affective Disorders.* New York: International Universities Press.

Brecht, B. (1941). "Mother Courage and Her Children." In R. Manheim and T. Willett (Eds.) *Collected Plays. Vol. 5.* New York: Pantheon.

Bursten, B. (1977). "The narcissistic course." In M. C. Nelson (Ed.). *The Narcissistic Condition.* New York: Human Sciences Press.

Caine, L. (1974). *Widow.* New York: Morrow.

Carotenuto, A. (1982). *A Secret Symmetry.* New York: Pantheon.

Chodorow, N. (1978). *The Reproduction of Mothering.* Berkeley: University of California Press.

Deutsch, H. (1944). *The Psychology of Women,* vol. 1. New York: Grune and Stratton.

———. (1945). *The Psychology of Women,* vol. 2. New York: Grune and Stratton.

Dinnerstein, D. (1976). *The Mermaid and the Minotaur.* New York: Harper and Row.

Erikson, E. (1959). "Growth and crises of the healthy personality." *Psychological Issues* 1(1): 50–100.

Fiske, M. (1980). "Changing hierarchies of commitment in adulthood." In N. J. Smelser and E. H. Erikson (Eds.). *Themes of Work and Love in Adulthood.* Cambridge: Harvard University Press.

Freud, S. (1914). "On narcissism." In J. Rickman (Ed.). *A General Selection from the Works of Sigmund Freud.* Garden City, N.Y.: Doubleday Anchor, 1957, pp. 104–23.

Glick, I. O., Weiss, R. S., and Parkes, C. M. (1974). *The First Year of Bereavement.* New York: Wiley.

Guntrip, H. (1969). *Schizoid Phenomena, Object Relations, and the Self.* New York: International Universities Press.

Hamilton, V. (1982). *Narcissus and Oedipus.* London: Routledge and Kegan Paul.

Ibsen, H. (1881). "Ghosts." In *Complete Major Prose Plays.* New York: Farrar, Strauss and Giroux, 1978.

Kernberg, O. (1975). *Borderline Conditions and Pathological Narcissism.* New York: Jason Aronson.

Kingsley, C. (1878). *Poems.* London: Macmillan.

Kohut, H. (1977). *The Restoration of the Self.* New York: International Universities Press.

Laing, R. D. (1965). *The Divided Self.* New York: Penguin Books.

Lash, J. P. (1982). *Love, Eleanor.* Garden City, N.Y.: Doubleday.

Lerner, H. (1974). "Early origins of envy and devaluation of women: Implications for sex role stereotypes." *Bulletin of the Menninger Clinic* 36: 538–53.

Leventman, P. (1981). *Professionals Out of Work*. New York: Free Press.

Levinson, D., et al. (1978). *The Seasons of a Man's Life*. New York: Knopf.

Liebow, E. (1967). *Tally's Corner*. Boston: Little, Brown.

Loewenstein, S. (1977). "An overview of the concept of narcissism." *Social Casework* 58(3): 136–42.

Loewenstein, S. F. (1980). "Passion as a mental health hazard." In C. L. Heckerman (Ed.). *The Evolving Female*. New York: Human Sciences Press.

Riegel, K. F. (1973). "Dialectic operations: The final period of cognitive development." *Human Development* 16: 346–70.

Roth, P. (1967). *Portnoy's Complaint*. New York: Random House.

Shapiro, D. (1981). *Autonomy and Rigid Character*. New York: Basic Books.

Smelser, N. J. (1980). "Vicissitudes of work and love in Anglo-American society." In N. J. Smelser and E. H. Erikson (Eds.). *Themes of Work and Love in Adulthood*. Cambridge: Harvard University Press.

Spater, F., and Parsons, I. (1977). *A Marriage of True Minds*. New York: Harcourt, Brace, Jovanovich.

Stern, D. (1985). *The Interpersonal World of the Infant*. New York: Basic Books.

Stierlin, H. (1977). *Adolf Hitler. A Family Perspective*. New York: Psychohistory Press.

Stoller, R. (1972). "The 'bedrock' of masculinity and femininity: Bisexuality." *Archives of General Psychiatry* 26: 207–12.

Weiss, R. S. (1985). "Men and the family." *Family Process* 24(1): 49–58.

Weissman, M. M., and Klerman, G. (1977). "Sex differences and the epidemiology of depression." *Archives of General Psychiatry* 34(1); 98–111.

White, R. W. (1963). "Ego reality in psychoanalytic theory: A proposal regarding independent ego energies." *Psychological Issues* 3, 3 Monograph 11.

11 / Seduction

*I*T was this worry about the biological clock. Of course, the Professor remembered from her books that sex does not really have a biological clock, but perhaps the books were wrong. Once, a long time ago, she had lived by psychological books, but they had let her down so often that now she no longer believed in them quite so wholeheartedly.

And even without a biological clock, she would grow older and older and shrivel up, and by then the chances of finding a sexual partner who might appeal to her would be even more remote than they were at this moment.

The Professor had duly produced her required number of children, even somewhat exceeding the current quota, and being conscientious and ecologically minded, she frequently apologized and explained that it had been alright to have three children in her generation, when the pollution of the world had not yet become quite as obvious as it had since shown itself to be. In some ways she had enjoyed motherhood. She had had a husband and sometimes even enjoyed her marriage. But now the children were grown and she had left her husband, or maybe he had left her before she had left him; one could not be sure about such matters. She had certainly led a most privileged life. Once she had reached adulthood, her suffering and pain had been primarily of her own choosing.

She had even experienced some passionate love. She had passionately loved her children, later a woman, still later two honorably married men, and last of all her old and dying aunt. She had loved these children and women and men dramatically and fiercely with the core of her being. She had wooed them generously and persistently, and several of them were still in her life. She seemed to specialize in unrequited passions and often wondered whether she could actually love anyone who would fully respond to her love. The very idea made her uncomfortable, thinking that such extravagant love, if reciprocated, would quickly become a prison.

Especially in the sexual arena none of those she had loved had been suitable or even fantasied sexual partners. She did not think of herself as a sexual being. She thought of herself as a celibate woman, and sexual expression had never been her goal. Yet with the sudden freedom of her newly divorced status, the possibility of a sexual adventure had suddenly arisen in her mind. After all, many of her books had exhorted the possibility of postmenopausal awakening, and all of them agreed that the postdivorce period was especially auspicious for sexual experimentation. It was unknown territory that could perhaps be explored.

The Professor had absolutely no experience with sexual seductions and turned for advice to her daughter, who appeared to her quite knowledgeable in this area. On her daughter's next visit she looked up from her article on vaginal orgasm and the G spot and asked, "How does one go about seducing a man?" She knew how eager her daughter was to see her aging mother have some happy sexual experiences. "Do you have someone in mind?" the daughter asked hopefully. "Not exactly," the Professor equivocated. "It's hard to answer then," the daughter replied. "You see, the whole point is that it happens naturally. It's not a research project." The Professor insisted on getting some advice. "Okay," the daughter relented. "You could invite him for dinner and have some candles and music, you know." The Professor was not sure how this would work. "Why don't you go to the movies together, after dinner. It's an easy place for a first touch," the daughter added, "and then when you go home things just happen naturally."

The Professor decided to proceed in her usual methodical manner. She mentally reviewed her short list of unmarried and not too unattractive male acquaintances. She selected a particular man, who appeared to be considerate and even a bit playful and had the air of having serviced women, although not necessarily in sexual ways. The Professor knew that women need many services apart from sexual ones. The man gladly accepted her dinner invitation. He was an untenured part-time member of her faculty and seemed most eager to get her advice and support for his new academic career. Perhaps he too needed some servicing.

The Professor was not really the candlelight type, but she cooked this good enough man a nice dinner and he clearly appreciated her food. They had an interesting conversation about a scholarly article he was trying to get published. She advised him on which journals were most likely to accept his work.

Going to the movies seemed like a natural continuation of their evening. They sat together watching a film in which a man becomes mentally ill because his wife threatens to leave him. The Professor noticed how the man sitting next to her was full of pity for the poor husband in the movie. He had hinted at dinner that he had once been left by a woman whom he had loved very much. The Professor thought of her married men friends who pitied her husband. If her considerate, kind, and loving husband could be left by his wife, it could happen to any of them.

She herself took little interest in the movie. She was preoccupied with following her daughter's advice. When would the right moment arrive to put her hand into his? It seemed like a complicated and difficult decision. When she finally did it, his hand responded with some hesitation and surprise but with gentleness. He squeezed her hand receptively and held it in his. So this was how one seduced a man! The Professor felt pleased with her boldness.

After a while she started to feel uncomfortable in her position and took back her hand. She wondered what she should do next. She should have asked her daughter for more direction. Well, perhaps she had not done it in the right way.

The Professor tried it once again, more tentatively this time and with less conviction. This was rapidly becoming tedious and unmanageable. What on earth was she doing here, sitting in a movie, holding some stranger's hand? She abruptly took her hand back once again and decided to attend to the movie. The heroine was going to be blackmailed by her crazy husband. She was not going to gain her freedom; he loved her too much for that.

It got to be too late to have a cup of tea after the movie, and they said good-bye to each other in the driveway of the Professor's house.

The Professor thought that all people have possibilities that they do not develop. Some people could perhaps become great musicians, but they never even learn to play an instrument. There are millions of people with potentially great minds that go to waste. There have always been women who might have enjoyed motherhood, but destiny led them elsewhere. Not everyone could experience all that life might have to offer. She could bear to remain a celibate woman.

12 / The Paradoxes of Parenthood: On the Impossibility of Being a Perfect Parent

Voices of parents:

When my son was born I had hoped he would become president. Now I feel relieved if he does not become an ax-murderer.

My parents spoiled the first half of my life, and my children the second half.

I ENTERED young parenthood certain that I would rear my children in the best possible way. I saw myself as loving, generous, and infinitely patient. I planned to read the right books and faithfully follow their advice. Under my guidance my children would become emotionally healthy, happy, and productive human beings. I was convinced I would avoid all the mistakes that my parents had made. I had unbounded confidence in my ability to become a perfect parent.

Little did I realize at that distant time what hubris was involved in these presumptuous goals. Not trying to be the best possible parent within one's limited ability is thoughtless, unkind, and irresponsible. Yet reaching for perfection in the rearing of one's children is a self-defeating goal that can lead only to disaster.

I mean to explain to readers who are young parents why the road ahead, however well-paved with the best intentions, will be a thorny one. My thoughts are also meant to comfort myself and other middle-aged parents. I hope to dispel our guilt for not having succeeded quite as well as we had hoped. I want to comfort all of us who tried both too hard and yet not hard enough to be good parents, and convince us that it was not our fault if we failed in the impossible task of rearing our children perfectly.

There is the irksome matter of elusive goals. Indeed, there is no clear image of the ideal human being who might be the result of such perfect rearing. Moreover, even if we could devise such an image, we currently have no effective techniques to reach it, and it is a grave question whether we should use such effective techniques if we ever invented them.

Kundera (1984) has suggested that "the first rehearsal for life is life itself." (p. 8). No one can expect a first rehearsal to be an accomplished performance. I shall argue that the parental role involves a series of incompatible demands that defy satisfactory resolution.

Some Historical Reflections

The question arises whether the ambitious goal of becoming perfect parents could have arisen only in this individualistic Western culture, at this moment in time when rapid cultural change and extreme cultural diversity create both uncertainty and new opportunities regarding our child-rearing efforts. There is also a climate of anxiety in the air: Our children may not survive in this complex and difficult society unless we equip them so well in every way that they can defeat all obstacles short of nuclear annihilation.

We may look with nostalgia at our forebears, who, we believe, lived in stable, predictable times. They needed to devote little thought to the rearing of children, either because they were scarcely conscious of their parental responsibilities or because the cultural prescriptions for parental conduct were clearly outlined.

Recent historical research contradicts these envious fantasies. There is new evidence that an awareness of childhood as a special developmental period and the ensuing kindness to and concern for children are not recent cultural acquisitions. In *Forgotten Childhood*

(1983), Linda Pollock argued convincingly that people have known since antiquity that children had special needs and vulnerabilities and needed special protection. The evidence that "parents have always tried to do what is best for their children within the context of their culture" (p. 64) might be a blow to our twentieth-century ethnocentric presumptuousness. We are learning that some parents of different cultures across times have treated their children with great tenderness and cared deeply about them, while other parents, in history as well as currently, have been harsh, cruel, and neglectful.

There is also evidence that these parents assumed responsibility for their children's conduct and perhaps even for their future well-being. Sigmund Freud has been credited with establishing the impact of early child rearing on adult emotional health, yet the idea of parental responsibility for instilling the most important values of our culture is age-old. We find proverbs in the Bible, such as that urging parents to "train up a child in the way he should go and when he is old he will not depart from it" (Proverbs, 22:6).

Pollock argued that parents from at least the sixteenth-century onward were concerned with all the functions that we associate with parenthood today, such as educating, protecting, disciplining, providing, advising, training, and helping. She quoted one mother's diary from the eighteenth century to demonstrate the dedication and keen sense of responsibility felt by certain parents:

There is scarcely any subject concerning which I feel more anxiety, than the proper education of my children . . . The person who undertakes to form the infant mind, to cut off the distorted shoots, and direct and fashion those which may, in due time, become fruitful and lovely branches, ought to possess a deep and accurate knowledge of human nature. (Quoted by Pollock 1983, p. 117)

It seems that striving for "perfect parenting" has existed in some form for a very long time and is not unique to our age. Yet, it *is* possible that the striving has recently become even more complex, more self-conscious, and more frustrating than in former times.

Elusive Goals. As we imagine the wonderful human being our perfect parenting efforts are designed to bring forth, we immediately focus on the good values that such a person should embody, and we find ourselves on slippery ground. With respect to values, I think our ancestors did have a clearer vision. Until relatively recently we rarely questioned the desirability of patriotism that included a willingness to die for one's country, marital fidelity, premarital chastity, valor in battle, self-sacrifice and devotion to others, obedience and respect for one's elders, religious faith, ambition, and achievement through very hard work. All of these values have now been questioned and at times violently rejected, not just by isolated nonconformists, but by significant groups in our society. Parents who hope to do a perfect job will have to sift and choose among competing values and decide which ones they will at least try to transmit to their children.

I included both stereotypical masculine (valor) and feminine (self-sacrifice and devotion) values in my list. Not long ago it was taken for granted that boys and girls were reared to adopt different values in adult life. Now some people, although not the majority of Americans, advocate androgynous values with equal standards of sensitivity, assertiveness, courage, and warmth for both sexes. Yet these efforts can backfire.

I know parents who set out to raise an androgynous son but were defeated in their attempts to do so. When their little boy started to play with dolls in kindergarten, he was taunted by other boys and he started to cry. He had also been told not to fight. The mother did not want her son to be an outcast. She told him to stop playing with dolls and pointed out how nice it was to ride a nice red fire truck. The father did not want his son to be teased. He showed him how to punch anyone who teased him.

Another mother went on peace marches with her son and taught him to speak up against injustices. A group of Green Berets came to his high school to glorify the Vietnam War. He stood up and protested and created a dangerous situation for himself. "Don't speak up foolishly," his anxious mother told him. "You must learn to hold your tongue." Later in college, he participated in student sit-ins. "Don't get yourself into trouble," she told him, "think of your future and attend to your studies."

It is hard for parents to transmit unpopular values to their children. While parents may wish to teach their children certain values, there is also the possibly more urgent task of helping children find a secure and respected place in the society in which they will live. Perhaps parents should settle on a simpler goal of raising happy human beings, thus abandoning the attempt to teach children the "right" values and instead teaching them "useful" values that will promote their happiness or at least popularity and worldly success. The problem is that we live in such a rapidly changing society that even pragmatic values become unpredictable. The generation of women to which I belong was raised to the tune of "Cinderella and the Prince" and "they lived happily ever after," only to find themselves at midlife obsolescent, bewildered, and often alone.

Yet even if we could reach some agreement and certainty on *what* to teach our children, there would still be the problem of *how* to reach our goals.

Teaching and Learning. Loevinger (1959) pinpointed a major problem in the area of teaching values. She suggested that learning takes place in three major ways: through cognitive understanding, through watching models, and through rewards and punishments. The problem is that parents may choose to teach by one method and children may perversely and resistantly choose to learn by a different method, which may lead to a lesson the opposite of the intended one. Parents may choose to punish their children for a misdeed, acting on a reward and punishment principle, while children may decide in this instance to learn from watching models and conclude that power and justice rest with whoever is stronger. Or, alternatively, a parent may *explain* to a child what she or he has done wrong, using cognitive principles, while the child, adopting a reward and punishment framework, may conclude that misbehavior bears no consequences beyond words.

I think the problem can be posed in even more general terms. Behavior can be seen as forms of communication with various levels of messages, including those of content and relationship. Those who observe or listen to us can attend to whatever level they choose, and often it is not the one we intended or were even aware of transmitting. A scolding may be viewed at the relationship level as "caring" or "getting attention" and thus become a reward. Praise may be perceived as pressure for future performance and thus felt to be a threat. Even gestures of altruism may be ambiguous. Our help may be accepted as acts of kindness or alternately experienced as a form of condescension or an affirmation of helplessness.

Kegan (1982) told the amusing story of a father who indignantly confronts his adult son about being lazy and without ambition. The father thinks that he had been a model of hard work for his son, but the son had paid attention only to his father's stresses and complaints along the way.

The Right Discipline. How to teach children is thus clearly as much a problem as *what* to teach them, and many parents continue to imagine that "the right discipline" is the key to parenting success. They have somehow lost that key and turn to experts to find it. It is ironical that two current prominent writers, both claiming to be advocates of children, give us contradictory advice. In three consecutive books (1981, 1983, 1984), Alice Miller accused parents through the centuries of being determined to break their children's will, humiliate them, rob them of any sense of control over their lives, and destroy their spirit, curiosity, and vitality. Parents do all this, she thinks, for the sake of shaping obedient, conforming, and nonfeeling adults. Miller has contempt for every form of *Erziehung*, a German word conveying socialization, pedagogy, discipline, and education, viewing it as inevitably coercive and manipulative. She feels sure that mutual respect between the child and the caretaker as two separate human beings, and recognition of each other's authentic feelings with permission to express them, will ensure the development of a humane, whole, and vital human being.

Yet in *Children Without Childhood* (1981), Marie Winn was alarmed at the premature exposure of children to the ugly realities of adult life. She deplored the permissiveness of the current generation of parents, viewing lack of rules, structures, and firm expectations as destructive and dangerous neglect and an abdication of the protective obligations of parents. In direct contrast to Miller, Winn located the problem in too little parental control, rather than too much. She appeared nostalgic for the "benign dictatorship" of parents of olden days and called for more adult authority and less egalitarian relationships.

Both of these authors are passionate and convincing in their arguments. Where does this leave a well-meaning mother or father? Although Miller and Winn come to different conclusions, they both acknowledge the parent's psychic vulnerability: the dilemma of having to discipline children while also needing their love and approval. Miller thinks most parents are unwilling to acknowledge their children's pain, anxiety, sadness, or rage because such feelings would imply their own imperfections as parents, an intolerable possibility. The parents demand that such feelings remain unacknowledged, and the feelings become split off, only to reappear in adult life as self-defeating, self-destructive, or antisocial impulses.

Winn believes that some parents are unable to exert adequate discipline because they are, in these times of high divorce rates, so overwhelmed by their own struggle for survival that they turn to their children for emotional comfort and support, thus undermining their parental authority.

I believe both writers make valid points, but I see the dilemma between the need to discipline and the wish for love and approval as a universal dilemma of the parent-child relationship, rather than an instance of particular pathological conditions. We have come upon another paradox of the parenting role: parents' ability to discipline their children is based on a positive, loving bond between parent and child, yet discipline forever threatens disruption of that bond.

The New Good Enough Mother. Before I get carried away with the impossibility of the parental task, I need to stop and give credit to a new understanding of the parent-child relationship that has been achieved, providing new parental guidance. A generation ago, the emphasis was placed on unconditional love and attachment (Winnicott 1965), possibly even promoting overloving devotion. The current password to parental perfection is the synchronous dance (Schaffer 1977; Stern 1985). Attachment, it is said, grows through interpersonal sensitivity and attentiveness. Attention and stimulation that arises from the adult's personal agenda and is not geared to the needs and readiness of the young child is either useless or intrusive and in danger of provoking the infant's anxious withdrawal. Contingent responsiveness heeds the infant's needs for intimate contact as well as for some private space, signaled, for example, by gaze aversion. Parental love and devotion are best expressed by the willingness to get to know one's child and to respect his or her uniqueness, complexity, and otherness (Hamilton 1982).

There is no need for perfection. In contrast to the very best mother, the merely good enough mother is not always attentive. Sometimes she is casually preoccupied and turns her back to attend to her own needs. Sometimes she is in a hurry and imposes her own agenda, overlooks subtle cues, and becomes unreliable and unpredictable. The child needs to learn that the mother is still there even if she turns her back, and that both goodness and badness belong to one and the same mother. The good enough mother might ultimately be better than the very best mother, since it is one of the paradoxes of parenthood that loving too well ultimately means not loving well enough.

This dilemma of fostering simultaneous attachment and separation is perhaps the most difficult parental task. It involves promoting individuation and autonomy, essential life goals, while also offering the child an experience of attachment profound and meaningful enough to evoke a lifelong capacity to love, feel, and care.

Overloving Parents. We have learned that parents may damage their children through loving them too much rather than too little. The overloved child is expected to give meaning and reason for living. Overloving involves possessiveness, anxious overprotection, and intense involvement. The child's behavior and feelings are experienced mostly in terms of the parent's own needs, hopes, and fears. Even child abuse may be a form of overloving. Parents who are indifferent to a child who cries may simply ignore his or her distress. It is only with the confusion of boundaries that crying is heard as a personal accusation that must be silenced at all cost (Szasz 1959). We certainly know how desperately such parents will resist the removal of their children, like the violent husband who desperately clings to his battered wife.

Psychoanalytic theory has taught us that overloving is a cover for underloving and that an overprotective mother, for example, "spoils" her child as a reaction formation against hostile wishes. I have come to reject the whole concept of reaction formation associated with the assumption that one feeling (usually the more hateful one) is necessarily more basic than the other. One could also argue, as Searles (1965) has done, "that the most powerful driving force in human beings is the effort to express oneself in a loving constructive way" (p. 220). Indeed, for some people the expression of loving feelings is more to be avoided than hateful feelings, since they have learned to associate loving with overloving and therefore with dangerous consequences for self and other. Searle described how some mothers treated their schizophrenic children with indifference or hatefulness because they were afraid that their love might damage their children. We might say that they underlove their children out of fear of overloving them, once again pointing to the intimate connection between these two extremes.

Helm Stierlin (1972) discussed parents who delegate to their children the accomplishment of certain missions. Such children may need to achieve goals that the parents would have liked to pursue, consciously or unconsciously, but were prevented from doing so by inner or outer constraints. These might include professional success, sexual adventures, crimes, or perhaps acts of revenge or atonement. Overloving, binding, or delegating parents have not separated from their children. They intrude narcissistically into their children's life space, interfering with the formation of a separate independent sense of self.

As children we deeply resonate with such theories, but can we accept so much responsibility in our parental roles?

Who Is in Charge? With a new recognition that even infants participate in shaping parent/child interaction, we are becoming more respectful of the reciprocity and mutuality of the parent-child relationship. Once a particular cycle of interaction has been established, causes and effects become blurred.

Parents of all ages feel deeply dependent on their children's well-being, since the parenting role is quite central to most people's identity and "being a good parent" in one's own as well as in others' eyes is crucial to self-esteem. Success of the parenting enterprise may be judged by the child's ongoing welfare into adulthood as well as by the relationship that is maintained with the child.

A young mother thrives when her infant develops well, and her pleasure enhances her nurturing capacity. On the other end of the life-cycle, mothers and fathers in late midlife frequently evaluate their lives by how well they have done with their children. Children who fail in some important way in their parents' eyes may become a major threat to their parents' ability to invest their later lives with positive meaning. (Loewenstein et al. 1983) The fates of parents and children are interlocked across generations.

Many parents secretly feel that regardless of theories and appearances, their child was really in charge; but they may also acknowledge their guilt and failures. Indeed, the belief that parents are responsible for their children's ongoing life and ultimate fate is the grandiose fallacy this whole essay seeks to denounce. As parents we tend to ignore the innate emotional and intellectual dispositions of our children, since they are only potentials that are shaped by the care-taking environment. We tend to ignore the larger sociocultural context that constrains, distorts, and shapes our ability to be wise and loving parents. We insist that regardless of circumstances it is our parental responsibility to raise our children perfectly.

I view the parental role as one of "responsibility without authority," and every administrator knows that this creates a no-win situation. Responsibility ought to entail authority and control; and the more responsibility one feels, the more control one wishes to have. I believe the problem of parental control, which easily merges into overcontrol, arises from this dilemma.

"I have to protect you against your own mistakes," a friend of mine used to say to her children. "I have to control you for your own good." She would hound them into doing their homework, bribe them into good academic performance, coerce them into practicing their musical instruments, shame them into learning foreign languages. She would show them affection only if they met her expectations. Her children have become accomplished and successful professionals. Yet their sense of self-worth depends on their achievement, which they pursue relentlessly, while their self-esteem continues to elude them. They will never forgive her for loving them conditionally and for having been such a controlling mother.

Parents who have grown up under conditions of great hardship are often especially determined that their children should lead better lives. No sacrifice will be too great to achieve such a goal. They set out to control their children for their own protection, using guilt as their major tool. It is part of the drama of social relationships that excessive determination may defeat its goal.

Now that I realize that respect for the otherness of a child is the most important requirement for becoming a perfect parent, I harbor a secret conviction that I could do an excellent job if I were given another chance. On my next life journey I shall be so respectful of my children's autonomy that I will appear to be an irresponsible mother.

Another friend of mine believed in the importance of self-regulation above all else. She was extremely respectful of her children's decisions. She allowed them to discontinue their hobbies when the efforts momentarily seemed to outweigh the rewards. She allowed them to drop out of school since they learned only meaningless things and to follow their own stars. She allowed them to experiment with drugs when that was in fashion. I don't know what became of her children. We quarreled because I reproached her for being an uncaring and neglectful parent.

Letting Go. How can parents fill the requirements of a role in which they must learn to release control while being responsible for the success of the enterprise? We should not delegate our own unfinished life tasks to our children, yet children need some firm guidance, lest they lose their way.

"How have you changed as a parent?" My students and I asked the midlife mothers and fathers whom we interviewed. Many of the parents said they had learned to accept their children as they are, rather than continuing to involve them in the parents' own dreams and expectations.

Parents need to let go of expectations at the child's birth and to continue to do so throughout their lives. Parents (at least until the advent of amniocentesis) must accept the gender of their child, even if it disappoints their expectations. My black-haired mother and father wanted a blonde daughter. For three years my mother tinted my black hair as quickly as it grew in, and my early childhood photos show a blonde little girl. Later they had to resign themselves to a dark-haired child. Accommodations, resignations, and compromises occur in every area of a child's life. "My son, the future doctor" who becomes a nurse is only one obvious example. One of my friends looked forward to becoming a grandparent. Her son became gay, and her married daughter decided to remain childless. The epigraph about the ax-murderer at the beginning of this essay refers to this unexpected and astonishing process of having to give up one's fantasies and adapt to a real child.

Solnit and Stark (1961) have written about the mourning that must take place at the birth of a handicapped child. But the despair about the imperfect child only highlights the more subtle processes that are an inevitable part of all parenting. Some parents are conscious of their need to mourn, while most parents do so intuitively yet without deliberate intent, each in her or his own creative way.

Mourning involves facing one's loss—each disappointment being the loss of some hope—and "owning" one's sad and angry feelings rather than denying or suppressing them. Such acknowledging of feelings may involve sharing them with an intimate confidant or perhaps a therapist, who will accept them with understanding and without judgment. Sometimes sharing disappointments may be done in a group with similarly mourning parents who will provide support and validation to each other. Other parents might express their mourning artistically, or they might write a scholarly paper about perfect parenting.

Other parents become chronic mourners. They never learn to let go and to love their imperfect children in imperfect ways. They die without having forgiven their children for repudiating their religious upbringing, for having married a partner of the wrong race, or perhaps for having adopted a deviant sexual orientation. When parents experience such behavior as unforgivable personal betrayals, it means that they have not achieved differentiation from their children. When parents and children cut each other off emotionally, it is never because of excessive detachment, but rather because of overwhelming fusion. One needs to have separated from someone to complete one's mourning and forgive that person.

Preserving a bond with an unexpectedly "different" child may involve important changes in one's values and perceptions of the world, entailing a possible transformation of identity.

Separation and loss, with its necessary mourning, are actually built into the core of the parental role. The goal of the parent-child relationship from the very beginning involves a gradual separation and loosening of bonds. Parental love must be demonstrated by not loving too much and by introducing a measure of detachment into a relationship that is totally involving. The most devoted parent will send the child into the world, applaud the child's new attachments, and recede into the background. Success in the area of the child's well-being might mean defeat in maintaining a close and primary bond. The child who experiences defeat in the world continues to cling to her or his parents as primary attachments. Unfortunately, such relationships then become corroded by the mutual guilt and blame caused by the child's failure.

Letting go is not a one-sided parental task. I have referred earlier to the parents' double wish to see their child succeed and to maintain affectionate bonds as well. This confronts us with yet another paradox of parenthood: disenchantment with and rebellion against parents is a necessary part of the relationship; a relationship is flawed if it remains conflict-free and apparently totally harmonious.

The process of disillusionment with formerly idealized parents is a necessary developmental step of adolescence, but some form of self-assertiveness should be an ongoing aspect of the good enough parent-child relationship. We would be worried about a two-year-old who does not oppose parental demands and develop her own growing willfulness; we would be concerned about a schoolchild who never values her teacher's or peers' opinion above those of her parents.

The most permissive and tolerant parents are in the worst position. Their children have to go to greater lengths to be critical, disapproving, and provocative. Moreover, such parents may have such good will that they may even wish to help their children become rebellious, an effort doomed by its own internal contradiction.

In later life parents sometimes feel neglected and superfluous. Children get married, start their careers, move to another part of the country; they do not seem to need their parents any more. However, appearances may be deceptive. The parent-child relationship, with its ambivalent feelings of love and hate, the wish for and fear of dependency, the wish for approval and acceptance, continues throughout life and beyond. Even after parents die, the relationship remains alive and active in the children's lives. All parents are assured this form of immortality.

Failed Intent. It will always be impossible to be a perfect parent, because our actions do not always match our intent. Our internalized parents interfere with our intention to be the most enlightened and responsible parents. We tend to project these internalized figures upon our children, eventually repeating in some form old and familiar relationship patterns, saving us the pain of saying good-bye to our parents. Besides, while we may consciously wish to improve upon our parents, becoming a better parent than one's own would be such an act of disrespect and disloyalty that few of us could venture it.

Are we thus doomed to repeat our parents' mistakes through the generations? My students beg me to show them how to avoid this somber fate. There is evidence in the family therapy literature that honest conversations between parents and children can promote the needed separation. They should be conversations in which difficult questions can be asked and authentic feelings exchanged. An attempt must be made to settle intergenerational accounts so that children are not forever burdened with the emotional debts their parents have incurred. I believe such conversations would be useful.

My parents are both dead, and I did not have the courage to engage them in such conversations. My children care about me; they know how vulnerable I am to their opinions of me; they don't want to hurt me and they also do not engage me in such conversations. They are too difficult.

Conclusion

I want to make a last attempt to redress the balance between the impossible and the possible. Not everyting is possible. We must learn to respect impossibilities. The reckless determination of our technical culture to achieve the impossible has led us to the edge of an abyss. Excessive tenacity of purpose has disturbed the delicate ecology of our planet. The very idea that we are in charge of our own perfection, let alone that of our children, is grandiose and presumptuous. The goal of becoming a perfect parent carries the seeds of guilt, blame, disappointed expectations, and defeat.

I think, on reflection, that it is *possible* to become a perfect parent by tolerating, forgiving, and transcending imperfections—our own and those of our children. We shall become perfect parents by accepting the impossibility of such a goal.

References

Hamilton, V. (1982). *Narcissus and Oedipus.* London: Routledge and Kegan Paul.

Kegan, R. (1982). *The Evolving Self.* Cambridge: Harvard University Press.

Kundera, M. (1984). *The Unbearable Lightness of Being.* New York: Harper and Row.

Loevinger, J. (1959). "Patterns of child rearing as theories of learning." *Journal of Abnormal and Social Psychology* 59:148–50.

Loewenstein, S. F., et al. (1983). *Fathers and Mothers in Midlife.* Masters Thesis, mimeo. Simmons College School of Social Work.

Miller, A. (1981). *Prisoners of Childhood.* New York: Basic Books.

———. (1983). *For Your Own Good.* New York: Farrar, Strauss and Giroux.

————. (1984). *Thou Shalt Not Be Aware.* New York: Farrar, Strauss and Giroux.

Pollock, L. (1983). *Forgotten Children.* Cambridge: Cambridge University Press.

Schaffer, R. (1977). *Mothering.* Cambridge: Harvard University Press.

Searles, H. F. (1965). *The Collected Papers on Schizophrenia and Related Subjects.* New York: International Universities Press.

Solnit, A. J., and Stark, H. M. (1961). "Mourning and the birth of a defective child." *Psychoanalytic Study of the Child* 16:523–37.

Stern, D. N. (1985). *The Interpersonal World of the Infant.* New York: Basic Books.

Stierlin, H. (1972). *Separating Parents and Adolescents.* New York: Quadrangle Books.

Szasz, T. (1959). "The communication of distress between child and parent." *The British Journal of Medical Psychology* 32:161–70.

Watzlawick, P., Beavin, J., and Jackson, D. (1967). *Pragmatics of Human Communication.* New York: Norton.

Winn, M. (1981). *Children Without Childhood.* New York: Pantheon Books.

Winnicott, D. W. (1965). *The Family and Individual Development.* New York: Basic Books.

13 / On Time

THE Mother's heart leapt with recognition as the two towers of Jacobi Hospital loomed up in front of them. They had finally arrived after what seemed like hours of being lost and driving around in circles. "Oh dear, I think I took the wrong turn," said her daughter next to her in an anxious tone, as the towers receded once again into the distance. But the Mother merely laughed with relief, because not that much was at stake, not this time around, and besides they had allowed a great deal of extra time. There had been no reason to assume that this daughter of hers would find her way in this fearful maze of narrow streets and trapping super highways of the Bronx any better than she herself had found it, fourteen years earlier. After all, the Daughter had been a child who could not distinguish right from left until she was seven years old, who had learned to tell time only after years of strenuous effort, and who had failed her geography class in junior high school in spite of her tutoring the child nightly for a whole year.

Perhaps, however, she laughed above all because as much as she dreaded the roundness of life, she also treasured it. She found some solace in the thought that there was some order in a world that seemed frequently so arbitrary and meaningless. Here was her daughter taking off one day and a half from her hectic teaching schedule to drive her mother to a famous oncologist, while she herself, at the age of sixty-three, was in the process of taking on her own mother's life stance and life script. She had just got divorced, and now, like her mother, she would grow old alone.

There had been many years when she had avoided any serious conversation with her mother, lest she become confronted with the depth of her mother's emotional isolation. It was possible that her clinging so many years to the fiction of a man at her side was due to her effort not to repeat her mother's life. Yet once she was divorced, her own aloneness and her mother's as well had seemed less fearsome. It was a comfort to her that her older years would be similar to those of her mother. She was not sure in what direction her fate might lead her. She could foresee for herself a life in which respect would replace love and intimacy, a life in which needfulness and vulnerability would have to be carefully contained, lest they overwhelm herself and other people. She had finally accomplished her mother's urgent mission to attain professional recognition—how sad that her mother had not lived long enough to witness this—and she had also become her own mother. She had been a loyal daughter in every way. Was there anything else that still needed to be done? Perhaps this famous specialist they were about to consult regarding her mysterious bleeding would give her bad news and solve her problem of how to sustain a sense of purpose in her approaching old age.

"How silly for you to take a day off your work just to drive with me to New York," she said. "Do you think everything has to happen twice?" "I think I see the towers again," her daughter replied, "I'm sure we'll get there in plenty of time for your appointment."

Strange, the Mother thought, how her life had been punctuated by occasions in which she and this daughter had driven together to some destination where life seemed to hang on their getting there on time. There had been the many awful mornings when the child had missed her school bus, and she had driven her to school, filling the air with angry reproachful words. Then later, there had been her father-in-law's funeral, which also took place in New York City. "No," she had said to her husband, "I don't want to stay overnight at your mother's house. But I promise to get there in time for the funeral."

The funeral had been scheduled for 10:00 A.M., and she and her daughter had left Boston at four o'clock in the morning, allowing six hours for the four-hour drive to New York City. The drive to New York City that morning had reminded her of a poem by Schiller she had to learn by heart as a child in high school in Vienna. In the poem a man has to get back in time from a distant place to prevent his dearest friend's execution. As he rides along at full speed he is besieged by disasters. He has to cross a river in which a flood has broken the bridge, he is mugged by high-waymen, and his horse stumbles and breaks its leg. He does get there in time to rescue his friend. The Mother and Daughter encountered major highway construction; there was a six-car accident on the way, which stopped traffic for close to an hour; and they had a flat tire. They got to the door of the funeral home at the same moment as the rest of the family, but she knew that her husband had never forgiven her for being "almost late."

What she remembered best from that trip, however, was the fact that her daughter, a teenager at the time, did not choose to voice her own worries about getting there late. On the contrary, she had been full of amusing teenage gossip, easing her mother's almost unbearable tension. "I shall never forget how you sustained me on the day of Pappa's funeral," she now said to her daughter, "did I ever pay you back for that?" "Sometimes I think that first trip was a kind of dress rehearsal for that later trip we took together," her daughter replied.

She had been careful and deliberate, even then, fourteen years ago on the second trip that had also been to the Jacobi Hospital but not to the oncology clinic. Instead of facing a threat to life, they had dealt with the threat of an unwanted birth. They had driven into New York City the night before, so that nothing could go wrong at the last moment. It was easy enough to stay overnight in New York City, since her mother and sister lived there. They had decided, however, that her old mother must not be told upsetting news, and so she had stayed with her sister's family. "Well, how does it feel to be almost a grandmother" her brother-in-law had asked her in his usual joking way. "Don't you hate Uncle and his stupid jokes?" the child had later said to her. "He's just trying to be friendly," she had replied, "don't always be so oversensitive." But the poor man would never know that she had instantly, with that very funny question, crossed him off her list of friends. People were always telling her that she submitted them

to tests impossible to pass, but she had not invented this particular test, and she could not help it if people failed her at moments
of crisis in her life.

This particular crisis had started twelve weeks before their trip,
when the Daughter had come home from her nearby university
with tender and enlarged breasts and anxious premonitions of
pregnancy. It had been lucky that they had the kind of relationship in which the Daughter could turn to her immediately. It was,
in any case, definitely not an occasion for angry recriminations.
The Mother had been happy that her daughter, never popular
with boys, had fallen in love with an intelligent and caring young
man. She felt quite proud of herself for being a modern mother
who approved of sexual experimentation, and she had been
pleased that her daughter was growing up in every way. Besides,
she knew that the girl, and even the boy, had acted responsibly,
and that these accidents happen even to responsible people.

The Mother tried, even after all these years, not to remember
what she had finally said. "You manage to spare me nothing,"
she had said, probably in a self-pitying tone, and her daughter
had hung her head in shame and guilt. Now, after having lived
for many more years, she marveled how indignant she had felt
at having to cope with a rather common adolescent happening.
Meanwhile, some of her friends' children had had schizophrenic
breaks and needed to be hospitalized, dealt in drugs, or had committed suicide, and she had acquired quite a different notion of
the pain that children could inflict on their parents.

But there she had been, a forty-nine-year-old, apparently mature and competent woman, a social worker meant to help other
people with life crises, saying to her nineteen-year-old distraught
daughter, "You manage to spare me nothing."

The first pregnancy test turned out to be negative. Relief. Relief? Well, not quite, actually. The Mother knew that very early
pregnancy tests are unreliable; after all, her own pregnancy test
with this particular daughter had initially been negative. At the
time it had been a great disappointment, yet she had known then
that the test was wrong and her bodily sensations were right, just
as she knew this time as well, in her own body, that her daughter
was certainly pregnant. These events took several weeks.

The decision to abort had been an instant, obvious, and un-discussed decision for both of them. It had been inconceivable that the Daughter would have an unplanned baby in the middle of her college years. They were not that kind of family. It was the very year in which abortions had become legalized in New York State. So they did not need to fly to England, Sweden, or some other far-away land, and they did not even need to break the law. The Mother was an expert at getting the right informa-tion on what to do in various life emergencies. After many tele-phone calls, she was faced with choosing the best of many pos-sibilities. It was a lonely and burdensome choice. She determined that the efficient outpatient service set up at Jacobi Hospital by a doctor friend of a doctor friend of the family would be the very best place for their abortion.

The Daughter and her boyfriend had at first decided to take the matter in their own hands. The responsible young man had hitchhiked all the way from his distant university to meet the Daughter for her abortion at Jacobi hospital. However, the young couple was turned away in favor of more urgent cases, and the Daughter was given another appointment ten days hence, bring-ing her into her twelfth week, the last week of the first trimester, when a relatively simple outpatient suction abortion could be performed.

The boyfriend had to go back to his university, and she and the Daughter drove alone to New York City, which was just as well. It was clearly their common business and no one else's. Not the boyfriend's, and certainly not her husband's. True, he had been quite a loving and conscientious father, who worked very hard at all times. But never would she have considered even in her wildest dreams asking her husband to take a day off from his hard work to drive her and her daughter to New York City. They were not that kind of family, he was not that kind of father, and she was not the kind of wife who looked to her husband for sup-port. She too was working quite hard, but hers was the kind of work in which she could take some hours off to take her children to music lessons, pediatricians, psychiatrists and to listen to their teachers' complaints. And she had even managed to take off a whole day and a half for her daughter's abortion.

So Mother and Daughter had driven together to New York City. It had been quite a silent journey. She had made such an effort not to be reproachful that she had run out of things to talk about. They were in this together, yet the right words to reassure the frightened girl beside her had failed her, just as she had not been able to find any words to comfort her old mother when the latter had been dying. She had competently arranged for her mother's care and even still visited her at the last moment, and she had competently arranged an abortion for her daughter and driven her to New York City, but the right words of comfort had failed her on both occasions.

Well, the whole matter was actually quite routine. She had always fought for women's abortion rights. She had no moral compunction about this whole procedure. They were going to New York City for a minor medical intervention of little consequence.

"Are you scared about this visit?" her daughter was now asking. "No, of course not, don't be silly, this is just a routine medical check up," she answered.

On the night before the abortion they had had dinner with her sister and the sister's joking husband, and both had felt in alien country. Yet the sister's house in Queens was most conveniently located. The hospital appointment was at 9:00 o'clock in the morning and the Mother had been given careful directions by her family. They told her that the hospital was across the bridge and that the trip would take at most half an hour. She had decided, in her usual deliberate and foresighted way, to leave two hours early to get there. They left the sister's house at seven o'clock in the morning, with all the directions written on a piece of paper and placed firmly in the Mother's mind.

At the end of the bridge she had found an unexpected fork in the road with confusing road signs, and she had taken the wrong turn. She did not realize this immediately, although she soon started to feel uncertain while trying to combat the dread of feeling lost. Her directions no longer fitted the road on which they were traveling, but once on the highway she could not turn around for many miles. There were no service stations then, on those New York parkways. She blindly took the first possible exit and drove around the streets of Manhattan, or Queens, or the Bronx, she knew not which, until she found a garage where they gave her new directions.

She still remembered how she listened to the explanations with the utmost concentration, combatting the panic that was rising within her. She tried to get back on the parkway, in the opposite direction, but the New York rush hour had started by then, and traffic was crawling. When she finally reached the parkway entrance, it was barred by construction and detour signs. She had to find another entrance to the parkway that would lead her to the Bronx. It was eight o'clock.

She had found another entrance to the parkway, squeezed in through the traffic, and noticed after some time that she must be driving north rather than south. Or perhaps she was going south rather than north, but it was clearly not the right direction to the Bronx. Like her daughter, she lacked a good sense of direction. She had always been more interested in ideas than in her physical surroundings. There they were, trapped in the New York parkway system, driving in the midst of rush hour traffic to some unknown destination.

She had been sure that the hospital would not grant them another precious appointment for this same week. Her daughter would have to undergo a second trimester abortion and perhaps become traumatized for life because her mother had been too foolish to find her way from Queens to the Bronx. She started to go in desperate circles from parkway to parkway, taking the wrong exits, on the wrong parkways, in the wrong direction. It was 8:35 A.M.

She had grown up in Europe during the war years. She and her mother had lived for several years in mortal danger of being found and carted off to a concentration camp. They had sought refuge in ditches to escape German bombs during the French exodus out of Paris. None of these experiences had seemed unbearably frightening then. They had seemed mere adventures compared to the life catastrophe of being late for this abortion.

Perhaps her own mother had carried the fear for both of them at the time. She had never known how her own mother had felt. They had never talked about it; they were not that kind of family. Her mother had managed to bring her daughter from Europe to

America in the middle of a world war and a holocaust, and now this daughter, in her turn, could not manage to drive her own daughter from Queens to the Bronx.

She had looked at the girl next to her, who had been preoccupied with her own fears and seemed quite unconcerned about being lost. She knew that her child was often angry and disappointed with her, yet also saw her as a reliable mother who could be counted on to get people on time to the places where they needed to be.

There was a concrete wall ahead, no doubt another construction. She had thought then of closing her eyes, pushing the gas pedal all the way down to the floor, and driving into the wall. How lucky that she had always been a cool, efficient woman in charge of all situations, who rarely gave way to her impulses. Next to the concrete wall, invisible from a distance, there were road signs pointing to the Bronx. She took the next exit, found the way to Jacobi Hospital, and delivered the Daughter at 8:55 A.M. at the door of the abortion clinic. There was a wait of several hours before the Daughter's turn, but they were ready to drive home in the late afternoon.

"Here we are," her daughter now said in a triumphant voice. "I got you here exactly on time." The Mother laughed again and gave her daughter a kiss. "You are taking very good care of me," she said. "Thank you for taking the time to come with me." While they parked the car, she reflected that she would now have had a thirteen-year-old grandchild who would give her pleasure, or more likely pain, in the way of all children. She had always felt dread at the thought of becoming a grandmother. It had been such a relief when the children had grown up without a major misfortune befalling any of them. Why tempt fate a second time, in the next generation? Her daughter might have married the young man and been divorced by now, might have dropped out of and returned to college. Events that seem matters of life and death change shape at a distance.

"Welcome to Jacobi Hospital," said the doctor's secretary. "Did you have a hard time finding us?"

14 / Cowardice

"WE are indeed fortunate to have such a distinguished educator in our town," she heard the principal say. One had to sit through those endless introductions and appear neither too pleased nor too bored; behaving just right on such occasions was an art by itself. The mother looked around the room, which she remembered very well: a beautiful lecture hall, wood paneled, wall-to-wall carpeting, comfortable modern chairs, matching muted colors. Outside, the electric lights along the school building outlined snowy trees against the large picture windows. She could be proud that she had given her child the opportunity of attending such a fine school.

Curious how the room had been similarly decorated on her *first* visit to this school. Then too it had been close to Christmas and there had been holly branches and cut-out papers stars all over the room, with a brightly decorated tree and a crèche next to it in one corner. She remembered the crèche only all too well, because of the papier-mâché lamb on which Rachel, her daughter, had worked so feverishly, evening after evening at home. Rachel had wanted that lamb to stand in the stable next to little Jesus, but all of her lambs turned out to look like dogs, and Mrs. Fitzpatrick, the teacher, had not been about to put a lamb that looked like a dog in her beautiful crèche. The mother remembered Rachel's weeping, evening after evening, until she herself had finally produced a more lamblike creature. She had no special talents for making papier-mâché lambs, but she could do better than her eight-year-old child. Perhaps the difference was in the way it was painted to look like fleece.

Now they had a menorah standing next to the Christmas tree,

a silver menorah quite visibly displayed. Times had changed since her first visit to this school. The principal was now winding up his introduction. "Our guest is particularly well known for her expertise in counseling parents and teachers on how to promote creativity in children. She will be glad to answer any questions at the end."

Glancing about the assembled teachers and parents, the mother spotted Mrs. Fitzpatrick. Ah yes, she had heard about Mrs. Fitzpatrick's being called back from her retirement. The school simply had not been the same without those wonderful Shakespeare plays Mrs. Fitzpatrick had put on year after year. Nothing had ever gone wrong with Mrs. Fitzpatrick's plays. None of the carefully selected "top student" children had ever stumbled, or, God forbid, forgotten a line. Mrs. Fitzpatrick had seen to that. No doubt these plays, the pride of the school, were still being produced. Fortunately she did not have to go and see them any longer.

During their first year in this town, she had been summoned to this school at the end of the term. "I am so very glad to meet you, Mrs. Fleishberg. Please sit down," Mrs. Fitzpatrick had greeted her.

"Fleischman," she corrected automatically, thinking that she might as well have called this teacher Mrs. Flaherty, or Mrs. Finnerty or what not. One Irish name sounded like another, as far as she was concerned. Not that she was attached to the name Fleischman, since it was after all merely the name she had married into, not the one she had been born with. Even the inevitable "Mrs." grated on her nerves.

Mrs. Fitzpatrick motioned her to a chair opposite her desk. She remembered how even then she had detested sitting on the wrong side of the desk. She was already teaching a course on child development to college freshmen, and she was very careful to talk to her students without a desk between them. She was planning to get a Ph.D., after which she would not be called *Mrs.* Anything any more. But in her terror before this teacher who could destroy her child, she duly remembered that she was not there to pull rank and status, but to grovel in front of Mrs. Fitzpatrick and plead for her mercy.

At least Mrs. Fitzpatrick seemed to be interested in mercy. "The

Merchant of Venice" was her favorite play. Rachel reported that the class had been studying the "Quality of Mercy" speech, reciting it in unison. Rachel had been asked not to join the chorus because Mrs. Fitzpatrick thought it unsuitable for a Jewish child to be reciting the "Quality of Mercy" speech. At first she hadn't believed such an absurd story, but Sally, Rachel's blonde and blue-eyed friend, had confirmed it. "We missed Rachel's voice," she said. "She's so good at reciting things."

Funny how life had a way of repeating itself. As a little girl in Vienna she had joined singing the "Horst-Wessel" Nazi song, until the teacher had explained to her that she should not sing such a song. But that had been meant in kindness.

"First of all, Mrs. Fleischman, I want you to know that I am a mother too, and I know how much trouble a child can cause," Mrs. Fitzpatrick had said in a bright and sincere voice. That had been too much for her. "Actually, Rachel is a quiet child who is not all that much trouble," she had responded, knowing that it was the wrong comment. Had she not come to persuade this woman not to give Rachel a failing grade, which would exclude her in the next term from the advanced class and separate her from her friends?

"Believe me, Mrs. Fleischman, it hurts me more than I can say to give a child a failing grade."

Rachel's fatal poem with a large red *F* on it was lying on the desk between them. "I gave Rachel a chance to rewrite the poem with my corrections. She refused," Mrs. Fitzpatrick, continued. The mother knew perfectly well that she need only admit that Rachel was a stubborn, exasperating child, and together the two grown-up women would cow that child into submission.

She had wondered off and on during that interview whether she could choke another human being to death. She had seen it done in movies, with nylon stockings rather than with bare hands. She had tried placating this teacher. "Rachel respects you very much, and would like to please you. But this is the way she wanted to write her poem, and a poem is after all a personal expression."

The mother had known then, as she knew now, that she was a coward bent on surviving, getting along, not standing up for what was important to her. But unwittingly she had raised a child who at the age of eight years would not change a few lines in a poem in order to get a good grade.

"It would be a pity if she could not stay in the advanced section. She would hate to be separated from Sally," the mother said in a pleading tone, carelessly exposing her flanks. "Rachel may have to choose new friends who are more of her caliber," Mrs. Fitzpatrick replied. "I wonder whether you realize how poor her spelling is. Perhaps she is not used to speaking English at home?"

Even if the mother had had a gun in her purse it would have been useless because she would not have had the courage to pull the trigger. She did not even have the moral strength to punch Mrs. Fitzpatrick in the face or pour ink over her teased hairdo. She was a woman without courage.

They had moved into this elegant old Yankee suburb without any concern about whether there were other Jewish families in town. It was only important to get the child into a good school, and the country setting had seemed a miracle. A child of hers growing up among trees! She herself had grown up in a city, lulled to sleep at night by the clanging of trolley cars. She treasured the stillness of the morning with only bird calls to wake her. She treasured the open spaces and green meadows and watching from her window how the red sun rose over the lake. Now, after all these years, this place had become home.

It had not felt like home at first. She had been a young woman, struggling to climb the academic ladder, learning a foreign language in just a few years—a stranger to this country, to this town. As a foreigner she had tried to raise an American child who saluted the flag every day and recited the Lord's Prayer every morning at school. So what if Rachel rejoiced taking her turn reading a selected Bible reading?

She herself had grown up without religion. Let them teach religion in the schools, it had meant nothing to her and she knew Rachel would get over it. They had come to her house asking her to sign a petition against prayers in schools. The two other Jewish families in town had also wanted her to join in a request asking that a menorah be placed next to the Christmas tree. She had refused to get involved in these issues. She was a guest in this country, and not about to challenge its customs and laws. She was a guest in this town and trembled at the prospect of her child being singled out and perhaps persecuted by people like this teacher.

"Mrs. Fitzpatrick," she had said on that distant day, "I am a teacher too, and I also expect respect from my students. I will speak to Rachel and ask her to change her little poem."

What an opportunity today to take her revenge after all these years. It was a Walter Mitty dream come true. She would throw away her prepared speech. Instead she would simply tell the assembled parents and teachers the relevant story about Rachel and Mrs. Fitzpatrick.

Well, that was a preposterous idea. But perhaps, while talking about the danger of crushing children's creativity, she could stare at Mrs. Fitzpatrick as hard as possible?

The audience had begun to applaud. The mother got up. She thought what a friendly town this was, the last haven on earth in a violent and unsafe world. She would grow old here, and volunteers would bring her library books when she could no longer drive. How peaceful it would be to sit at her large picture window and watch the changing seasons.

The mother walked to the podium. "Dear colleagues and neighbors," she started. "I am honored to be asked to speak in the school of my own town. Coming back here brings back many happy memories of the time I was a parent in this school." She took a deep breath—and then she proceeded to read her prepared speech.

15 / Making a Difference

IN this time of physical and social deterioration of our society and indeed of our whole planet, with the threat of apocalypse forever in the background, we are in danger of succumbing to despair. This is especially true for mental health professionals, who often were drawn to their field in the hope of making a difference in the quality of life of other people and thus indirectly their own. I think many of them are vulnerable to viewing these efforts as insignificant, futile, or hopeless. I have thus decided to reflect on our ongoing need, responsibility, and capacity to make a difference to each other. I shall confine myself to simple, everyday interactions, leaving to others a consideration of other issues. I hope that focusing on the complexities of this life process, even in its more mundane manifestations, will help us sustain the meaning we find in our personal and professional lives.

I want to develop three thoughts: the theme of learning and teaching about the difference that one makes; telling others about the difference that they make; and limiting our desire to make a difference to others, lest such a wish turn into overcontrol and become self-defeating.

Taking Responsibility

Whenever I travel I become anxious after a while. I worry that I will not be needed when I return home. I then feel somewhat reassured when demands descend upon me as soon as I return to my place of work. I think most of us need to feel that we make a difference in order to preserve some basic sense of worth. The thought of feeling "disappeared" (Loewenstein 1984, p. 215), or the experience of feeling invisible, is very frightening. Even infants appear to have an inborn motivation to make an impact on their environment. Indeed, we learn from cybernetic theory that our sense organs are such that we can only perceive, hear, feel or smell a difference that is large enough to make a difference (Bateson 1972). And the biggest differences that have an impact on our lives and shape our fates are the kind of people we encounter, that we can recruit (Kegan 1982, p. 17), who take an interest in us, the messages we exchange with those people, and the meaning that we give those messages.

I had decided to write for once a gender-free essay. Both women and men wish to make a difference. Yet when discussing this theme with colleagues I had the impression that my struggle and uncertainty about my own attempts to make a difference seemed to be foreign to the men to whom I talked. They had not thought about this in the same way.

One scholar of great distinction told me that he used to hope his books would revolutionize the world, and he had to come to terms with their making just a small difference to some people. Men seemed to have to get used to making less of an impact than once hoped. Moreover, they focused on their creation of large monuments, books, or movies on social injustices that were to reform the world. As a woman, I had to get used to the realization that I might be making more of a difference than I had ever anticipated or been aware of. Moreover, my interest in making a difference had never focused on any papers I had written, but only on the impact I might be having on people during personal or professional encounters. Could it be that professional men and women not only take different roads, but might even travel in opposite directions when they try to come to terms with the impact they have on the world?

It is of course possible that other people are keenly aware of their impact on others, and that it was my self-doubts that got in the way. But it took me many years before I was fully in touch with the difference that I made to my students.

Learning in this area may thus be slow and difficult, but eventually vivid experiences through observation and through verbal feedback assure all of us that our intimate or public words, or perhaps our writing, or some public stand we have taken, have had profound and lasting influence on others. Most of us have had the experience of helping people in immediate dramatic and highly visible ways, as well as of hearing second-hand about long-range results. We have all had encounters with former clients who quote a sentence spoken ten years ago that changed their despair into hope. Or as teachers we meet former students who credit us with offering encouragement or showing some personal interest at a crucial moment that had opened new vistas of self-development for them. These are heady as well as unsettling experiences, especially if the quoted sentence had not been all that carefully considered or the student is long forgotten and her needs were not even clearly noticed at the time.

Many may have experienced the anxious overinvestment in the tone of voice, turn of phrase, small gestures, which occur in especially significant relationships in which we feel some doubt and uncertainty. In such relationships, minor forgetful or careless acts can assume major importance for the more dependent person. I sometimes think Freud's theory about the unconscious meaning of "Freudian slips" applies above all to the meaning those acts acquire in transferential relationships. Interpersonal happenings are never trivial in such relationships, and small acts such as the way we say or forget to say good morning can carry a great deal of weight. I shall never forget the student who was silent for a whole semester because, as she later explained, I had looked at my watch during her first classroom comment.

Taking responsibility, credit, and blame for the course of other people's lives is the fate of every parent, every mental health professional, and many others to varying degrees. Such power can be a heavy burden, raising the specter of disappointing others, betraying their expectations, profoundly damaging them through careless or thoughtless acts of commission or omission.

Once we are fully aware of our potential to make a great deal of difference we may become increasingly cautious. I used to tease my students a little, but I have become more hesitant as I realized the serious risk of being misunderstood. In my early years as a teacher I found the aspects of the role that called for evaluation, criticism, and challenge quite difficult, especially if they were met with tears and despair. The fear of having the wrong kind of impact can inhibit spontaneity, valid criticism, and honest confrontations. It took me some years before I could reframe these challenges as being as potentially helpful and caring as encouragements. I have faced and overcome my cowardice to some extent.

The other day I ran into a former student whom I did not recognize, but she certainly remembered me and approached me with eagerness. Ten years ago I had apparently told her that she was not a good enough student and would not become a good social worker, and she systematically and successfully proceeded to prove me wrong. At the end of the talk she emphasized how much she had learned from me. I had clearly made a big difference in her life. It is thus quite possible that some of our worst mistakes are not as fatal as we expect them to be. After we get fully in touch with the great differences that we make, it is an enormous relief to realize that we are not omnipotent after all, that we are allowed to make mistakes, and that our students and clients are resourceful and resilient.

Learning to draw new distinctions is the essence of growth and development. With the development of language, we learn to draw an almost infinite number of new distinctions that we could not have done without words. As we develop our sense organs, we learn to draw distinctions between beautiful and ugly things; we learn to appreciate music and to distinguish it from noise; we learn to draw distinctions between different ways that things feel and smell. Similarly, I believe our lives will also be richer and more exciting if we increase our awareness of the distinctions that our presence creates in other people's lives. As we understand this, negative effects may be changed and good differences can be embraced.

Making a Difference in Complementary Relationships. There is a curious illusion in our society that leaders make more difference than followers, even though one would be impossible without the other. Communication theorists (Watzlawick 1967) have termed relationships characterized by apparently unequal power but interlocking needs "complementary" relationships. We can examine three prototypical complementary relationships—parent/child, student/teacher, and therapist/patient—in terms of emotional care taking, rendering instrumental services, and exposure to narcissistic injuries, and look at the actual patterns of reciprocity and distribution of power.

In terms of emotional care taking, it is often unclear who takes care of whom. Early family therapy focused on the pathology of the "parentified child" who is expected to take care of his or her parents. More recently it has been recognized that family roles are flexible and that all the role functions in the family should be available to everybody in the family. A certain amount of emotional care taking by children of their parents strikes me as an inevitable part of a parent-child relationship, apart from the fact that many children give central meaning to their parents' lives. Elsewhere (Chapter 1, this volume) I wrote about the ways in which I took care of each of my three mothers, as one way of recruiting their love for me. I have found a most responsive accord to this idea, especially among women. I have the impression that it is daughters rather than sons who get selected for this vital care taking task.

Robert Langs (1982) wrote of the emotional care taking by patients of their therapists, so that the therapist can remain available to the patient. This is similar to the child's attempt to heal a parent to preserve or create a better relationship. Many patients never confront their therapists openly, not only because they may have trouble with anger or assertiveness but because they do not want to hurt the therapist's feelings.

It is also often quite uncertain who renders most service to whom. I have heard of an experiment in which high school students with reading difficulties were recruited to teach first-graders how to read. It turned out that the teachers, not the students, made the most amazing progress in their reading skills. From this example, it appears that if you want to learn something thoroughly it is best to become a teacher. It is also true that many become therapists in a quest for self-healing. Indeed, in order to be healed it might be safer to become a therapist rather than a patient.

Confidence in our ability to make a desired difference helps us to be more effective. I therefore try to teach my social work students that they have the power to make a great deal of difference. I start this lesson in our classroom. They sometimes think because there are so many of them and only one of me that each of them makes very little difference. My students undoubtedly need me, but their need for me does not compare to the enormity of my need for them. Without me, they would merely lose a teacher, while without students, I could not be an educator, and I would thus lose my very identity. As a matter of fact, my worst nightmares—and I think they are not atypical teacher nightmares—revolve around coming to a classroom and finding it empty, or starting to talk and noticing that students leave one by one while I talk.

Communication theory (Watzlawick 1967) also suggests that conflict in a complementary relationship results in disconfirmation of the partner with lower social power. While we must be acutely aware of the vulnerability of this one-down position, people who are in one-up positions also need to pay attention to the possibility of disconfirmation of their own roles. Children, clients, students, and employees can assault the self-definition of a parent, therapist, teacher, or boss. In our school students are evaluated by teachers and teachers by students. Both stake their self-confidence and sometimes even their professional survival on the other's evaluation. I have seen repeated instances of students' "killing" a teacher. And, in other cases, one finds autistic children defeat a mother's readiness to love and clients disempower their therapists. The narcissistic injuries to the one-up partner in these admittedly Pyrrhic victories can be profound and lasting.

We must thus conclude that there is mutual vulnerability, reciprocity, and interdependence, in all ongoing significant relationships. Making a difference is not a one-sided process.

In my classroom, I comment on the absence of any student. This angers my students yet also flatters them. Once, when they had an examination in another course in the afternoon, several students did not come to my morning class, and I asked them how they would have felt if no one had appeared. They looked stricken. I do not want them to become social workers without acquiring a deep conviction that each of them makes a great deal of difference and accepting responsibility for that fact.

We need to assume that each of us can make the world a better place for others. It is not safe to plead that our actions are insignificant. Society consists of tightly interconnected networks of people in which any action affects everyone else in a ripple effect. In the infamous Milgram (1974) experiments it was found that the presence of one other person who refused to give dangerous electric shocks to the supposed victim/learner radically reduced the number of people who were willing to do this. The first person who refused to go along with the experiment introduced the idea that people have more choices than they are aware of. We know that even a single person speaking up against an act of injustice, such as Rosa Parks refusing to take a back seat in a bus, can perhaps make a difference in world history.

It is not always easy to maintain the assumption that one does and can make a difference. If I did not have the inner conviction that my teaching makes a difference, I myself could not insist on regular attendance. To take responsiblity for making a difference one must feel good enough about oneself. It could be viewed presumptuous to think of oneself as that important. Often we make less difference, or as I have already suggested, a totally different kind of difference from what we intend or imagine. There seems to be a thin line between being grandiose on the one hand and taking responsibility for one's place in the world on the other hand. It is one of the many tightropes on which we walk. I shall come to other similar tightropes.

As mental health practitioners and educators, we are thus not only called upon to teach students or to help clients solve their problems of living, but more importantly, we must help them gain greater awareness of the differences that they are already making and of the new differences that they could make. Helping people with such a process of empowerment could be the greatest difference that we make to them.

I would have welcomed more help in gaining awareness of my impact on clients or students when I started out in these professional careers. Even with my own children, I was more aware of how much they meant to me than of my importance to them. I have therefore thought of three ways through which we might be able to help other people and ourselves gain more conviction about the differences that we all make.

Teaching Others that They Make a Difference. The first is to recall people who have made a difference to us. First of all, there are our parents. We might help parents become aware of the profound effect they have on their children by reminding them of the profound effect that their parents' lives and messages to them had on *their* lives; like messages of validation that sustain through the years, or approval withheld, creating lifelong self-doubts. It is also true, however, that our parents' messages take on different meanings as we grow older, especially after their death.

Then there are our mentors, toward whom we may feel profound and ever-lasting gratitude, perhaps less ambivalently than toward our parents. Many may feel that we would not have succeeded in life if it had not been for the support our mentors have lent us. My social work mentor, Virginia Turner, offered her loving, caring, steady support throughout my doctoral studies, and later became a close friend. Unlike Levinson's men (1978, pp. 97–101), some women do not need to reject their mentors to become autonomous. Instead, they often form lifelong friendships in which the roles of lending and receiving support may later become reversed.

Most of us carry images of favorite or feared and hated teachers in our heads. I had in my first three years of grammar school an enthusiastic young man teacher whom I, along with the seventeen other little girls in that class (and I think the four little boys as well) passionately loved. Ever since, school has been associated with happy feelings for me. I have loved any teacher who was the least bit lovable. Finally I became a teacher so I would never have to leave the classroom.

In junior high school I had a teacher of religion whom I also loved very deeply. When Hitler entered Vienna, I asked him why God allowed Hitler. He explained that if my grandfather made a decision, we would all accept it without question. It was the same for God's decisions. It turned out that God, my grandfather, and Hitler would all make a great deal of difference to our century.

I have not mentioned the difference made by friends because it would take a whole essay by itself. Each of our friends draws an important new difference in our life. A student told me of an incident when she suddenly followed her impulse of calling a childhood friend with whom she had not been in touch for many years. It turned out that her friend was contemplating suicide at the time of her call. Let this incident stand for the life-sustaining role of friendships.

The second way we can get in touch with the differences that we make is to focus on the myriad small differences that people make to each other and that shape the quality of our daily lives. I go out of my way to buy stamps at a particular post office because I enjoy the helpful advice and friendly exchange I have with the postmistress there. She makes a difference to my life. Our whole town is ready to go into mourning as she threatens to retire.

We often grow accustomed to the impact we have on each other, in our families, our places of work or recreation. There is a danger that we take these people for granted. During travels or in other situations in which we lack our usual support system, we may become suddenly aware of the small exchanges that make a difference in our daily lives. I missed a boat this summer, and an Italian couple who watched my distress offered in broken German to give me a ride to the city, where I could take a train. During the ride the husband and I conversed in German and the wife and I in French. He was retired and was apparently urging her to retire as well, although she loved her job as a teacher. I tried to intervene on her behalf. As we waited together for my train she embraced me with tears. I had felt quite lonely before, and suddenly all of Italy had became illuminated for me. I told them I would never forget them, and I am herewith keeping my promise. All of us, like Tennessee Williams' Blanche Dubois, must often depend on the kindness of strangers.

The third and most dramatic way in which we can affirm our own unique differences is to think about people who were close to us and who have died. We know from experience that they left a permanent hole in the fabric of our lives. My mentor Virginia Turner died. I often find myself longing to tell her something; no one will ever replace her. Such thoughts will make it clear that each person has a unique place in the world and that no one can truly replace anyone else.

Revising Societal Distinctions. When teaching about the possibility and responsibility of making a difference, we could also raise the awareness of our colleagues, clients, students, or others that many of our assumptions about our society are not part of a "natural God-given order" but are only socially agreed upon distinctions. This would then raise the possibility that individuals and groups could draw new and different distinctions for the sake of building a better society.

We might, for example, challenge our society's distinctions of such basic categories as race, gender, and sexual orientation. If there were thirteen categories of skin color, rather than just three or four (which in any case is closer to reality), discrimination against people of color might become more complicated. If there were nine genders based on various combinations of stereotypical masculinity, femininity, and sexual orientations, it might become more difficult to define who is deviant and who is normal. I am very intrigued by Langer's (et al. 1985) idea that much of the concept of deviance would virtually disappear if we drew more, rather than fewer, distinctions among human beings. We could even imagine a society in which any of the categories that currently defines our very identity would be merely of minor interest, and new categories would become important.

I offer these ideas as examples of the extent to which making differences, changing things, is a sociocultural process in which we can all participate, rather than taking the differences we perceive as rigid and immovable. Such changes would entail a great many other social changes, such as a new language, since a changed world view and a changed language are intrinsically interrelated. I think the current attempt to create a less male-oriented language has made much difference to women.

A Two-Way Street. Social workers and teachers try to help and "enable" others. We try to make a difference by offering knowledge, information, concrete services or things, or else by offering attention, comfort, advice, and encouragement. We might help to change clients' social context so that they have more choices. Yet on a deeper level we can only make these good things available to other people; we cannot truly give them. It is the other person who determines in which way our efforts will make a difference to him or her. It is often difficult to people with different maps of the world to have an impact on each other. I have known people who have said they loved me, yet I could not feel their love because our notions of what it means to love or care were too different. It is quite possible that our professional ways of conveying caring and interest and helpfulness to our clients and students are often incongruent with some of their definitions of helpfulness and caring. It is good that we have recently tried to find ways to adapt our methods to reach our clients better.

Our skill and inventiveness in reaching out and helping are another important factor. Most people can be reached, given patience and respect for their differences. We may be hurt when our students or clients are not always open to our efforts. We transform this hurt into labeling such people as "resistant" or "hopeless," and we feel discouraged. Yet the ability to decide for oneself when to accept or reject other people's efforts at making differences can be viewed with respect, as a source of strength. The power to allow us to teach or help them is within our students' and clients' minds, not within our own.

In my attempt to analyze this process of making a difference, I have distorted it and talked about professional efforts as if they were one-way streets. It is interaction and dialogue that create the atmosphere for making a difference, and one-way streets do not lead to dialogue. I suggested earlier that we find affirmation and identity through our complementary relationships, but that is not the whole picture. We know that our clients offer comfort and give us emotional strength, and the main joy of teaching is the opportunity to learn from our students. I think it is only through openness to the differences that others make to us and acknowledgment of these differences that we might hope to make some difference to them.

Even in our personal lives we need to be careful as professional helpers not to become so involved in making a difference to others that we lose sight of others' efforts to make a difference to us. We must seek situations in which we can take turns between helping and being helped, choosing and being chosen, loving and being loved. It might be best when these polarities happen within the same relationship, but perhaps that is too much to expect. If we show any kind of openness we find that the world is full of people who wish to recruit us as a friend, mentor, substitute parent, or an extra child. Yet helping professionals are in danger of being drained by other people's needfulness, and like our students and clients, we must make choices about when and with whom we exchange differences.

I am confining my thoughts here to openness toward people, bypassing the world of objects and ideas that can make a difference to us with its infinite possibilities for learning, growth, and renewal of spirit.

Unintended Differences. I suggested earlier that many of the differences that we make are unintended. For example, other people can choose to attend either to the content or to the interpersonal message of our communications. I used to think that my primary activity was to teach developmental theory to my students. After years of student feedback and personal observations, I have concluded that the content is important, yet a matter of course, while my students attend with at least equal interest to the degree of my sensitivity to their unique needs, to my level of fairness, my openness or defensiveness to their complaints, and other such urgent messages. A younger friend of mine is taking a course for college faculty on teaching methods. "What are you learning?" I asked her eagerly. "There are many important professors in my course. I am learning to conquer my timidity and speak up," she answered.

It seems as if the most effective yet unintended way we made a difference to each other is simply the way we live our lives and present ourselves to the world. All of us are forever looking for models as well as being models for other people. Intergenerational Modeling is particularly important, because we need some guidance for future life stages. At this time of my life I watch my elders die—my mother, my aunts—and I am assembling good and bad images of how one dies. I did not know that before. One of my mentors lives with a chronic increasingly disabling illness. I watch her courage and I learn from her.

We often look for models of people who have found new differences that may not have occurred to us. I have the impression that many black children started to play tennis after Arthur Ashe had shown them that this sport was a viable option for a black person. Acts of courage, kindness, and generosity invariably spawn similar acts; unfortunately, negative acts of violence and cruelty have the same effect.

I want to mention a completely trivial but funny example of how I once was inspired. I heard quite an unenterprising woman of my age discuss riding a motorcycle; suddenly I knew that I had always wanted to do this, and if it was possible for her, I could do it as well. I started to ride a motorscooter to work, which solved my parking problem and gave me a fame of sorts in my school. Later I learned that the woman whom I overheard had only once taken a ride on the back of her husband's motorcycle, but by then it did not matter any more. We can use people as models who don't even carry the role all that well. Sometimes we need only a spark, an inspiration, to get started.

While we all seek models to admire and emulate, we need just as desperately people who validate us through their imperfect lives. I think women have served as both kinds of model for each other. We can look to a generation of pioneers who have blazed new trails. Women have also exposed shameful secrets, doubts, and imperfections, exploding myths with which we have lived too long and which have clouded our visions. It is very important that we continue this sharing. Each time a woman comes out of her particular closet, whether it deals with her sexuality, her motherhood, her marriage, her experience of madness, incest, or rape, many other women breathe a sigh of relief, feeling that they are not alone, feeling less shame, less guilt, less humiliation. Our willingness to share our secret selves can make a great deal of difference to others.

Telling Others About the Differences They Make

It is quite unfortunate that we are often unaware of the difference that we make to each other because we are not accustomed to exchanging this information, especially in our professional lives. Often we hear how much difference we have made to a person, a group, or an institution, only when we are ready to leave them, often with resentment and discouragement that we have not been appreciated.

Many institutions customarily give good-bye parties at which speeches are made about the departing person's wonderful contributions. This is the wrong time to make speeches of appreciation, especially if it has not been done before. I think one should express public and private appreciation for people who stay with organizations, rather than wait until people leave. I extend this idea even to funerals. I once had a friend who had been a famous child psychiatrist in Boston; as she got older and troubled in her mind, she had to go to a nursing home, where she spent several extremely bitter and lonely years. After she died, the whole Boston mental health establishment turned out for her funeral and gave one eulogy after another. I was consumed with the irony of the situation, because my old friend had yearned for such recognition; her sense of being abandoned and forgotten had contributed to corroding her spirits. As individuals and as a society we need to find new ways of telling intimate others, parents and children, friends and colleagues, those for whom we work and those who work for us, that they are making a difference—before they depart.

It is also a healing process to tell people what they have meant to us, even if the relationship was difficult. Sometimes, after we tell people about a negative difference they have made, we can suddenly remember the good parts as well and perhaps find ways to forgive. The angry student I mentioned before must have felt great satisfaction to tell me after ten years how much I had injured her.

I had a father whom I experienced as uncaring (See Chapter 17, this volume). When someone close to him once told me that he had spoken lovingly about me, it was a great surprise to me—but he was dead by then and nothing could be resolved. I wish my father could have told me before he died what difference I had made to him, and I wish I could have told him what bad and good differences he had made to me—it might have helped us both.

Making Too Much Difference

Although the process of living can be equated with making a difference, the important cybernetic principle that more is *not* better fits well into our theme. It is said that even too much health or happiness can become ecologically unsound. Our occasional wish to make too much of a difference threatens to defeat our best intentions.

The temptation of making too much difference is often connected with our wish to help and our readiness to love. It is quite baffling to realize that love and helpfulness can become toxic when they grow beyond a certain limit. I have coined the word "overloving" to convey the wish to possess, protect, control, and coerce people for their own good, because one loves them so much. Some readers might object to my misuse of the concept of love, which is after all the most hopeful emotion in this world. You might say to me that I confuse narcissistic overinvestment with love. You might point out that self-sacrifice and overprotectiveness of our children, clients, or students arise out of our narcissistic need to use others as ornaments and reassurance of self-worth. I claim that overinvestment is one particular form of love that has grown toxic because it has grown out of bounds. We can equate it to the sorcerer's apprentice phenomenon or to a cancerous growth that may have started from the body's efforts to heal a wound through new cell production.

The word overloving is phenomenologically correct for both the person experiencing the feeling as well as the person receiving it. Indeed, if the emotion that is expressed and received were not defined as love by common agreement, it would not create such havoc. Possessiveness that is not defined as love could be repudiated without guilt. And people who feel overprotective and controlling would not be so hurt by rejection if they had not defined their feelings as love.

The word "overloving" is not only economical, graphic, and evocative, it is also extremely useful in clinical situations. A woman whom I shall call Mrs. Kennedy consulted me regarding her adolescent son. She wanted me to recommend a group therapist. She had already arranged numerous tutorial and other therapeutic services for him, trying "to fix him" in every possible way, but he was not responding appropriately. I said she clearly loved him too much and adolescents were allergic to mother-love. Her next demonstration of love would be to release her control and let him mess up his own life. Mrs. Kennedy was very grateful to me for understanding her so deeply. She promised to follow through on this idea. She also explained that her former therapist had accused her of covert hostility toward her son, which had missed the point completely.

It is true that the essence of love is recognition and respect for *the otherness* of the loved partner, while narcissistic overinvestment is the very opposite. Yet opposites meet on the emotional continuum. Think of the Inquisition, where people were tortured and killed to glorify God; the enemies of abortion who will kill to preserve the sanctity of life; or of the arms race for the sake of peace. It seems that every ideal escalated to a fanatic level defeats itself. Why not love?

The world has become a frightening place, and I cannot stop the disasters that expand all around me. I feel powerless. It is only in the classroom that I feel I can make some small difference to a few students. But I sometimes feel I make too much of a difference in the classroom. I bring a great deal of energy and life and enthusiasm to my students. I wake them up each week and encourage them to learn. It works. But sometimes when I am tired or depressed I cannot mobilize that energy and then nothing happens at all—everything and everyone collapses. So perhaps it is better to distribute the responsibility of bringing life into a situation.

Langer (1983) has alerted us to the danger of overloving in

nursing home care. Many old people in nursing homes are not encouraged toward maximum self-care. I am not referring here to situations where the staff takes the easiest, least troublesome way out, but to situations of genuine care, expressed in the misguided notion that the most complete care taking is also the best. In this process old people become debilitated and increasingly helpless and demoralized. Autonomy and self-regulation are important life goals from infancy to old age, even if they involve extra effort.

There are many other examples illustrating how a potentially good thing can become dysfunctional. Therapy that extends too long can become addictive and create excessive dependency upon another human being. Such therapy may be encouraged by overloving therapists who may not have been able to make enough of a good difference to their parents when they were children. Perhaps some of us have become therapists to make up for having failed in this way.

Benevolent interest can become intrusiveness, which seems to be an especially toxic phenomenon in all its forms. I have discussed elsewhere in this book (Chapters 7, 11, and 15) how the effort to make too much difference as a parent, therapist, or teacher can backfire, since fostering independence and autonomy is the foremost goal in growth-promoting relationships.

The hazard of making too much of a difference is especially problematic in child-welfare work, although this is also a field in which social workers can make the most dramatic life-saving difference. But our need to rescue can lead to excessive interference. Child welfare is a field in which it is agonizingly difficult to make neither too little nor too much of a difference. It is also a field that illustrates the importance of drawing the right kinds of distinction, those that include the whole context of a child within a family, within a community, rather than a narrow focus on an individual child. I have seen instances where a great deal of attention was focused on one particular child by a child-welfare agency, while no consideration was given to the child next door (and sometimes even to the sibling), who may have had similar needs. It is very important that social workers insist on carrying out differences in accord with our own professional vision and code of ethics. If we succumb to community pressures that are based on ignorance, scapegoating, and bigotry rather than on the best differences for children, we fail in our professional mission. I am thinking here in anger about a recent Boston case in which community pressure resulted in the removal of two children who had been placed with a gay couple. I find myself wishing that the whole social work community had gone on a protest strike. That might have made a worthwhile difference to our society.

We thus expect therapists, teachers, and parents to control their narcissistic needs, and yet the demands of these roles are so great that we surely could not meet them adequately without some personal narcissistic investment, by which I mean involvement of our self-esteem in the success of these relationships. When we use others to meet our needs for emotional nourishment, self-affirmation, feeling alive rather than dead, feeling useful rather than useless, being in control rather than being controlled, then the relationship is in danger of becoming one of emotional exploitation. Yet it is hard to imagine a situation in which some of these factors do not exist. It is thus more a problem of balance, and it is the tipping of the balance in the direction of too much narcissistic investment that ends up in overloving—making too much difference.

Making a difference consists of a process: "making," and a goal: "a difference," and I suggest to you that the goal should never overshadow the process. At times we may be so focused on some end result that the process is neglected and viewed as unimportant. Single-minded tenacity of purpose can easily become a self-defeating and even destructive enterprise. When discussing creative parenthood, Anthony (1983) warned of the danger of parents' cultivating creativity in the child as an end in itself, suggesting that such efforts may actually interfere with a child's spontaneous creativity.

I tell my students on the first day of class that they should not go through social work school merely to get a degree. I try to suggest to them that the journey is as important as the destination, especially since any destination inevitably only leads to another journey. Our clients may come to us with some particular wish for a change, but I think the way we help toward this goal could be viewed as significant as the goal itself.

Although the process of living inevitably entails making differences, we can ask ourselves whether the wish to make a difference is necessarily the best life goal. Perhaps it is as important to do things for the pleasure of doing a good job or curiosity, rather than for the sake of changing the world. Raising children so that we can be proud of them or helping others in the hope that they will be grateful is apt to result in disappointment. Does this mean that it is less narcissistic to try to make a difference to oneself rather than to others?

The whole situation creates an insoluble dilemma. On the one hand we know that excessive dreams of glory and admiration interfere with genuine artistic creations. On the other hand we need to believe in our talent in order to engage in the discipline and effort to nurture it, and we need to believe in our message in order to risk self-exposure. How can we both transcend our narcissism and yet rely on it when our belief in ourselves is precarious? Artists face this dilemma at all times. We turn with relief to Bateson for some thoughts on this difficult problem. "The artist may have a conscious purpose to sell his picture, even perhaps a conscious purpose to make it. But in the making he must necessarily relax that arrogance in favor of a creative experience in which his conscious mind plays only a small part" (1972, p. 138).

Even a relatively modest enterprise may raise similar issues. It had not been in my life script to publish a book. Then, when the possibility arose, the project became so important that I felt anxious, empty, and unable to sustain it. I had to give up my wish to make a difference with a book. "Here goes nothing," I finally thought, and started to write.

References

Anthony, J. (1983). "Creative Parenthood." In R. S. Cohen, B. J. Cohler, and S. H. Weissman (Eds.). *Parenthood*. New York: Guilford Press.

Bateson, G. (1972). *Steps to an Ecology of Mind*. New York: Ballantine.

Kegan, R. (1982). *The Evolving Self.* Cambridge: Harvard University Press.

Langer, E. J. (1983). *The Psychology of Control.* Beverly Hills: Sage Publications.

———, Bashner, R. S., and Chanowitz, B. (1985). "Decreasing prejudice by increasing discrimination." *Journal of Personality and Social Psychology* 49:113–20.

Langs, R. (1982). *The Psychotherapeutic Conspiracy.* New York: Jason Aronson.

Levinson, D. J. (1978). *The Seasons of a Man's Life.* New York: Knopf.

Loewenstein, S. F. (1984). *This Place.* London: Routledge and Kegan Paul.

Milgram, S. (1974). *Obedience to Authority.* New York: Harper and Row.

Obholzer K. (1982). *The Wolf-Man. Sixty Years Later.* New York: Continuum.

Watzlawick, P., Beavin, J., and Jackson, D. (1967). *Pragmatics of Human Communication.* New York: Norton.

16 / Making a Difference as a Therapist

*T*HE title of this essay is borrowed from the ideas of Gregory Bateson, who said that we can perceive only a difference that makes a difference (1972, p. 315). Being perceived and having an impact on the world is a basic wish of every human being. Whether we truly make a difference as psychotherapists, and how we do it, are thus a core issue for all of us.

As therapists our first task is to learn to believe that we can indeed make a difference to other people, and I have addressed myself to that issue (chapter 14, this volume). But once we have acquired the conviction or at least the illusion that we do indeed make a difference to some people, we then have to face the fear of making the wrong or excessive difference. Both the fear of being ineffective and useless or alternately, omnipotent and perhaps dangerous, lead to self-doubts and anxiety, and they may both interfere with our ability to have a "good enough" effect. We seem to do best when we have some inner assurance that we can indeed make a difference, without having an overwhelming need to do so.

The concept of "difference" also refers to the evolving constructivist idea that the world is created by human beings drawing distinctions—or differences—among perceptions and sensations in a chaotic world, thus making us human beings the creators of our own world. In the process of growing up in a particular culture and family, we learn to draw certain kinds of distinctions, such as the distinction between self and other, and all the other distinctions that the language in which we were raised imposes on us. These distinctions ultimately make up our assumptive world.

As individuals we are to a large extent constrained by the distinctions that others have drawn for us. Yet an appreciation of the arbitrariness of that process might allow us to enter the assumptive world of another human being without concluding that they are mad, bad, or sick. We can appreciate that their experiences have led them to draw different distinctions, creating a different reality that may be neither more nor less true than our own. We would thus never challenge the truth of a particular reality, but only its usefulness in leading a good enough life according to the client's hopes and wishes. Simply approaching a therapeutic encounter in this spirit of inquiry might have therapeutic results.

In this understanding of the world, education and therapy are both processes that help people draw new distinctions or give up old and useless ones. Perhaps my title should therefore read "Teaching to Draw New Differences as Therapists."

The process of learning new distinctions is so fundamental that it can be encompassed within such different thought systems as structural change in ego psychology, the building of a coherent self in self psychology, the acquisition of semiotic competence in communication theory, or learning new behavioral responses in behavior therapy. But even if we thus define the central task of therapy as teaching to see new patterns, new frames, new possibilities and options, the question remains how therapists actually succeed in this task. In this time of paradigmatic change, new questions are raised and new tentative answers are being proposed to this very basic issue.

In order to bring freshness to these perennial questions, I collected from my doctoral students, who are all experienced therapists, and from other students and friends whom I could enlist, some positive or negative incidents from their experience as patients and therapists that seem to have made an important difference to them. I also reread a large number of papers that adult students enrolled in a university extension course on the psychology of women had written over the years about their therapeutic experiences. These papers explored helpful themes rather than significant incidents. I shall use this case material selectively to illustrate, perhaps in somewhat procrustean fashion, some of the new ideas about psychotherapy that seem to be in the forefront of current practice.

Process Versus Content

Communication theory (Watzlawick 1967) suggests that every verbal exchange contains both a substantive and a relationship message. Freud split these two levels of messages, calling one of them transference and countertransference and the other free associations and interpretations. He seems to have assumed that the two levels did not contaminate each other. As cybernetic theory gives us a greater appreciation of the recursive, complementary nature of process and structure, substance and form, we challenge this assumption. I think the concept of transference is seen as too separate a dimension in psychoanalysis and psychotherapy, obscuring the process in which the expectation and opportunity for self-disclosure in a help-seeking relationship create certain kinds of strong feelings that then shape and color everything that goes on in treatment, including the patient's dreams, free associations, and selective recall of the past. In turn, the therapist's reactions are also not neatly divided into objective interpretations versus countertransference, but can better be viewed as part of a coevolving relationship.

We have come to appreciate ever more deeply that food given to infants outside a relationship context is essentially sterile. It barely nourishes an infant's body, and certainly not its mind and spirit. Similarly, it took me many years as a teacher to appreciate the central importance of the relationship between myself and my students. (See Chapter 7 this volume). When this relationship is troubled, the interpersonal aspect of the teacher's messages becomes foreground, the information conveyed becomes background, and the student cannot learn. Relationships have always been recognized as very important in psychotherapy, yet it is still an effort to appreciate fully to what extent content in therapy may be background to process.

The matter of therapeutic compliance, for example, has created

interesting dilemmas. We feel hurt and frustrated when our patients resist our creative insights and our subtle guidance, and
yet assertiveness and autonomy are frequently key therapeutic
goals. Our client has made progress when she refuses to attend
her assertiveness classes. An anecdote from one student will illustrate her appreciation of resistance as therapeutic progress.

Her mildly retarded client comes in every week announcing that
she is not in a talking mood. My student agrees that there are
days when one does not feel like talking much, and, perhaps,
things one just does not wish to share, and says she really respects the client for making a decision about what to share and
what not to share. After that the client is eager to share whatever
she has on her mind even if what she says is not particularly
revealing. But once she has defined herself as an autonomous
person who does not wish to get pushed around, and has been
reinforced and respected, the rest of the hour becomes merely
background.

The themes drawn from the psychology class of adult students
tend to cluster around relationship factors. Many of them express
appreciation of a creative relationship that was caring or perhaps
even loving, validating, supportive, nonexploitative on any level,
nonjudgmental, in which the person felt listened to, deeply
understood, and appreciated for her strengths. Psychotherapy at
its best appears to be the kind of relationship that one would
ideally want to have with family, lovers, or friends, but that seldom seems to work in this way, given the personal, usually competing needs of other people. Therapists get paid for putting their
needs aside, and they succeed in doing this to varying degrees.

In addition, therapy offers a situation in which irrational projections and interpersonal conflicts, which often seem insur-
mountable in our intimate relationships, can be addressed and
worked out. Some students of psychotherapy (Levenson 1983) have
suggested that this process is the very heart of psychotherapy.

Psychotherapy as Reparenting

Since most of us may have vainly hoped to have this kind of ideal
relationship with our parents, psychotherapy becomes in an im-

portant measure a reparenting experience. Reparenting may be very partial, filling in some particular deficits, or it may be a totally encompassing experience, as in the following situation reported by a therapist. She saw an adolescent for eight years, from the age of thirteen until twenty-one. The client was a severely emotionally deprived girl with no relationships, who was withdrawn into a fantasy world. The therapist taught her how to feel and label emotions, how people care for each other, how they communicate. The client felt as if everyone else had been taught a language from birth that she had never learned. She eventually learned the language, but she will always have an accent. This therapist seems to have taught her young client many of the essential distinctions made by our culture.

Many respondents said that the therapist was a better instrumental and expressive parent, who taught the practical aspects of living while also paying due attention to the whole range of emotional issues. Women therapists, for example, were welcomed as new role models, different from the clients' own mothers. Generally the therapeutic relationship was seen as an opportunity to expand horizons, to gain a firmer, more authentic sense of self, to take new risks, to lead an examined rather than an unexamined life. Above all the respondents had gained new understanding. Matters that had appeared senseless and puzzling had now acquired meaning. Therapists had given many women courage and hope, as expressed by this forty-seven-year-old former student: "He taught me to laugh at my depression and to believe in the possibility of love. During a hard time in my second marriage my relationship with him was the most important thing in my life."

Another client mentioned that one of the most important moments in her therapy occurred when the therapist gave her a cup of tea on a rainy day, an especially significant gesture, since she knew that "feeding" clients was against the rules. It proved to her that her therapist really cared about her. Important also to respondents were therapists' statements that protected the client's health and welfare. One respondent said she always came late to her psychoanalysis due to serious car troubles. Her analyst recommended one day that she buy a safer car, eschewing any dynamic interpretations of her lateness. My friend purchased a new car, generally started to take better care of herself, and was never late again.

There is a definite feeling in these examples that "transmuting internalizations" (Kohut 1977) have taken place. The therapist's caring becomes transmuted into self-caring. Many respondents appreciated therapeutic permission to be more selfish, self-caring, or self-loving, reflecting the conflicts that women have in these areas.

Several other critical incidents involved transgressing the rules or going beyond the call of duty, letting the client feel that the "caring" was more than purely professional. One suspects that it is important to have rules just so we can transcend them.

Being touched, not routinely or seductively but at significant moments, was also interpreted as caring and could be seen as part of reparenting techniques. Several women experienced it as a powerful and deeply meaningful contact, a gift of love, perhaps most especially again in situations when the therapist was taking some risks. In one instance reported by a therapist, a comforting holding of the shoulders released the client's secret of her sexual molestation by a staff member on her hospital ward and broke through her silent, sullen withdrawal.

Yet, it is also true that touching is such an immediate way of reaching another human being that we must view it with caution. The example reported by a former student made me uneasy.

Suzanne is a thirty-four-year-old, divorced, free-lance editor. She finds it difficult to relate intimately to others. Her warm, trusting four-year-long relationship with her psychiatrist, a married man of about her age, is currently her major significant relationship. She feels that she has made great progress in treatment and expresses respect and admiration for her doctor. They have an "exquisite understanding about the nuances of communication." After two years of never touching, they had a particularly hard and successful session; he shook her hand, and after that they started to shake hands regularly. A year later he started to enfold her hand in both of his to show appreciation and empathy, and half a year later he started to give her bear hugs on special occasions. "I am proud of you, thank you," was the message that she read into them. Then the bear hugs started to feel different, more like tender holding; one day he made an erotic noise while he held her and then kissed both her hands. Meanwhile, they have discussed these happenings and they both agree that they want to avoid "sexual involvement." Suzanne feels happy, appreciated, and loved in this relationship.

The eventual outcome of this therapy experience remains uncertain. We wonder how termination will be handled if it ever becomes a goal in the future.

There was also one example from a prison setting, where inadvertent touching of hands created unrealistic expectations.

We can see that touching can easily backfire, but therapy is a risky enterprise in any case. We may need to reconsider the taboo about touching in traditional psychotherapy and apply it selectively.

Validating and Invalidating. Although many women express a strong wish to be loved and cared about, they wish even more urgently to be affirmed and validated, which is one good way of showing love and caring. Validation takes different forms for different clients.

I believe that the benefit of sharing past suffering is not so much a cathartic emptying of personal pain, but the act of bearing witness to one's suffering, being believed, listened to, and understood without judgment, all of which are affirming experiences. The sharing of shameful, often sexual secrets may also be a test of ultimate acceptance, perhaps followed by the therapist's implicit or explicit reassurance and an attempt to relieve the client of guilt and shame.

Sometimes being asked "good questions" is experienced as profoundly validating, especially if the questioner is interested in the answer. Good questions imply an effort to understand, a gift of genuine interest. Questions may lead our thoughts in unexpected and astonishing directions. "Did you hope that he would die?" a therapist might ask, implicitly giving permission for taboo feelings and even suggesting that murderous feelings against "loved ones" may be quite commonplace. "How did you feel when your mother died?" Questions about things that are sometimes taken for granted also imply that we need not have the kind of conventional feelings and reactions that others expect of us.

Interestingly, this category of validation included most of the profoundly negative critical therapeutic experiences, in which the women felt invalidated or disbelieved. One of my doctoral students reported how misunderstood she felt when her therapist insisted that her view of her father as critical and distant was merely a reaction to his loss, while their real relationship had been involved and loving. Her therapist was a kind, protective, and fatherly man who could not be challenged, and who ended up being as disconfirming as her own father, in his own benevolent way.

Even more serious, however, is a therapist's defensive reaction to a patient's critical perception of the therapist. The following episode came to my attention.

Miss A. accused a male therapist of preferring another woman in the therapy group to her. The therapist interpreted Miss A.'s accusation as related to her old jealousy that her father seemed to prefer her sister. But Miss A. was furious and demanded that her perception be validated. During a consultation the therapist admitted that there may have been grounds for her to see him as preferring the other group member, but he insisted that what was important for Miss A.'s own therapy was that she face her feelings toward her father. The situation ended with Miss A. leaving the group.

I believe this vignette raises interesting therapeutic issues. I mentioned earlier that we are currently more inclined to view transference and countertransference as the feelings and habitual distortions aroused in an intense and intimate human encounter.

Some recent writers suggest (Levenson 1983) that psychotherapy at its best is not an archeological expedition, but an effort to examine honestly and in a nondefensive manner the total therapeutic transaction. This dialogue enables both client and therapist to distinguish a client's misperception and distortion from a justified reaction to what might have been very subtle cues by the therapist. It is useful to become aware how hypersensitive we all are to nonverbal signals in emotionally charged relationships, and how adept we often are at reading those signals correctly. The debate continues on the wisdom of acknowledging therapeutic flaws rather than focusing on the client's excessive vulnerability, need to attack, find fault, and focus on minute negative trivia rather than on the therapist's helpfulness. It is my own strong impression that the acknowledgment of errors, whether in the role of therapist, lover, friend, parent, or teacher, is more beneficial than defensive or deflective maneuvers, no matter how well-justified. There is even evidence that the acknowledgment of therapeutic error and careful reflection of why it occurred and how it was experienced can be a vehicle for major therapeutic movement. Clients with invalidating, mystifying parents who taught them not to trust their own perceptions may find it truly liberating to feel confirmed. This raises the therapeutic paradox that we want to be perfect therapists, yet the most important therapeutic progress might occur when we make mistakes, as long as we admit and discuss them.

Responding to strength rather than weakness was an important way in which therapists validated my respondents. It is an axiom of social psychology that belief creates reality (Snyder 1984). Children build their identity through others' reflected appraisals, their expectations of the child; once an identity is formed it reinforces these expectations, which in turn confirms identity, creating once again a benign or vicious cycle. As therapists we can be significant others who break this cycle, challenge a particular presentation of self, and create quite different expectations.

One of my students presented her work with a woman with a "fragmented self," who had been a neglected and abused child of alcoholic parents. While Al-Anon and AA had framed her patterns as a consequence of a disease process, the therapist bypassed the victim role and relabeled her experience as one that had provided her with special strengths and survival skills. She blossomed under this approach and used more effective coping patterns. Similarly, a therapist started to see a chronic borderline woman who had been acting out in self-destructive ways for many years. After a few sessions of long stories about her abusive mate and a long litany of complaints of never getting anything she needed for herself, the therapist said firmly that she was actually an expert at getting what she needed. The client was startled, confused and then laughed. She asked: "Do you mean I think I need the things I get? Then maybe I have to define what I need differently." Soon after she left this abusive relationship, a dramatic move for her.

I have the impression that our interest in pathology and diagnostic labels sometimes reinforces an old reality, rather than creates a new one. One very troublesome paper from a psychology student seemed to suggest that an initial perhaps hasty psychiatric hospitalization during adolescence reinforced or even created a "patient identity," which lead to vicious cycles of increasing incapacity, increasingly frequent hospitalizations, and deterioration. It remains a question whether the deterioration led to the hospitalization or quite the opposite. We need to be extremely aware of the possible damaging effects of our well-intentioned interventions.

Validation may also consist in normalizing experiences, locating distress, for example, in universally upsetting circumstances and thus dispelling guilt and shame, rather than calling it an abnormal reaction. One client, burdened with a harsh superego, described her therapist's insistence that she was entitled to feel upset and depressed in her situation; this alleviated her habitual self-blame and started to create a soothing rather than scolding inner voice. One of my students reported a therapist's comment to her, when she was a young woman: "It sounds like you have all the obligations and none of the pleasures in your marriage." She had hung on to that sentence through many years of a socially correct but sterile marriage, giving validation and justification to her secret dissatisfaction.

Popular psychological literature often has such normalizing goals. Many women felt great relief after the feminist literature on the myth of blissful motherhood appeared, universalizing the stress, ambivalence, and isolation experienced by many mothers. Validation like this leads us into the whole area of making meaning of one's life, which is often considered the central purpose of psychotherapy. Human beings strive to make meaning, and create patterns and organization from the moment of birth. Loss of meaning creates profound uncertainty and anxiety, and people turn to therapy to restore meaning. Some years ago I conducted groups for recently separated people in which I tried to give psychological meaning to the fact that most group members unexpectedly felt distress after leaving an unloved and sometimes even hated spouse. These unanticipated feelings made people wonder whether they had made the right decision. I offered them the prevalent psychological theories about the general difficulty of life changes, the need for mourning the end of even bad relationships, and the idea that attachment may continue after love has died (Weiss 1975). People felt reassured and comforted.

One of the essential functions of psychological theories is to offer a structure for making meaning for both therapist and client. Our theories of mourning have served us extremely well in that respect. One of my students described how she had lost several loved persons and found herself engulfed by despair:

Within my therapy I was encouraged to express the feelings that had seemed so frightening, and they were labeled as normal "mourning." Once the feelings had a name I began to feel some sense of relief. Though the sorrow of the losses remained, having a label for what I experienced gave the process some meaning. The darkness surrounding me was now contained by boundaries and limits. Knowing this I was able to find the courage to squarely face and explore it.

This woman's temporary despair may or may not have actually been related to her losses, but she felt better once her feelings were normalized as well as given "a good reason."

People tend to become embedded in a particular way of making meaning. Reframing is a powerful device though which we draw new distinctions and offer alternate meaning. I have already given two examples of reframing, when I talked about addressing strengths rather than pathology. The following two reframing illustrations greatly pleased me because they made a difference to people who were important to me. They also suggest that therapeutic interchanges are not mysterious technical events but simply thoughtful ways of approaching difficult situations that may occur inside or outside of therapy.

A student announced that she had to drop out of social work school, because the material she was learning had brought up so much old baggage and distress that she needed time to process it all. After a lengthy exploration I asked her if she could consider the next summer as an alternate time for attending to the baggage. She changed her mind after the interview and explained during our graduation party that the idea of using the summer had been decisive in our exchange.

After my old aunt had a stroke she felt extremely distressed to have become so dependent on other people for the simplest life tasks. I told her that she had worked hard all her life and had earned enough money to hire a nurse, which meant that she was not dependent but simply buying services. She announced the next morning that she had considered this during the night and agreed with me. After that she seemed to find it easier to accept her dependency.

Metaphors, Interpretations, and Paradoxical Prescriptions

Often we create meaning through the introduction of metaphors. Psychoanalysis gave us oedipal metaphors, which served us well for a long time but have now become too commonplace. Different times need different metaphors. Just as anorexia nervosa has seemingly replaced hysterical paralysis, oedipal metaphors are giving way to new "myths" in which the misbehavior of one person is linked in some way to the behavior of others in his or her life. A troublesome adolescent, for example, is said to sacrifice herself for the sake of keeping her parents united in blaming her. Metaphors about intergenerational loyalties currently have a special emotional appeal. It may be that using metaphors as a way to create new meaning is replacing interpretations that are slowly falling into disrepute. Some have suggested that interpretations are linked to the linear idea of finding the one and only truth, located in the patient's past life. It is now suggested that the past is mutable and is constantly being invented and reconstructed during the process of recalling it (Spence 1982).

Writers have also looked at interpretations for their interpersonal rather than their content message, viewing them as potentially intrusive upon the patient's autonomy (Hamilton 1982) or else as therapeutic one-upmanship. In the field of psycholinguistics of psychotherapy (Mahrer [1985], p. 142), interpretations have also been seen as indirect prescriptions for change rather than mere explanations about interconnections in the client's life experiences. In cybernetics, prescriptions become descriptions that turn into prescriptions, and it is impossible to punctuate this cycle. While none of my respondents offered illuminating interpretations as critical incidents, my data contain a number of sentences that seem to have had catalytic impact. "Students as clients" identified the following sentences as instrumental in moving them from feeling stuck in their marriages to initiating separation:

"You can live in a coffin forever, if you like."
"He will find someone else to service him."
"Now you know that *he* wants to stay with you, and you can start thinking of what *you* want."

These sentences were experienced as dramatic, challenging statements that verbalized the patient's latent but unformulated feelings and could thus be seen as an interpretation. One of them is also a powerful metaphor that made the client think of herself as a corpse. All three sentences are forms of advice couched in some other linguistic form.

Resistance

A move to seek change through therapy threatens the way one has made sense out of the world and thus creates a wish for sameness. Therapists call this conflict between wanting a new situation but fearing change "resistance." Due to this conflict, many therapeutic encounters become subtle contests in which the therapist wants to promote change and the client wants to stay the same. In order to avoid such a defeating struggle in which a therapist ends up being more invested in change than the client, new approaches that bypass this struggle are being used. We have discovered that the paradox of a "no change" prescription in a context that is defined as change-oriented can create a powerful unbalance. The therapist joins the client's reluctance to change and rather than urging change, she or he suggests that change might be too difficult and perhaps inadvisable. Suddenly the "no change" position becomes so top-heavy that the client has to adopt a change position in order to restore the balance. Other explanations of the effectiveness of this paradoxical move involve the negation of the client/therapist power struggle, the creation of benign double-binds, and rendering the symptom ineffective as an interpersonal manipulation and others. Here is an instance where I have "prescribed the symptom": A student complains that she no longer enjoys classes because she feels she ought to participate but she is too shy to do so. Instead of paying attention she agonizes all through class. I forbid her to participate in discussions for six weeks, we both laugh, and the problem is instantly cured. This was effective therapy, either because I prescribed the symptom, or because tension between us was reduced, or because I addressed her agonizing about not talking, her solution to her problem, which had become more problematic than her symptom. Perhaps it was simply our common laughter that interrupted the cycle.

Quite a dramatic example of the effectiveness of an unintentional paradoxical intervention is an amusing story told by the eighty-six-year-old Russian Freud had called the Wolf Man, to a journalist during a review of his life (Obholzer 1982). After being Freud's "most famous patient" the Wolf Man became a lifelong patient of other psychoanalysts with unimpressive therapeutic results, except for one dramatic cure of his obsession with some nose deformity. Dr. Ruth Mack Brunswick, his analyst at the time, labeled his obsession as paranoid symptom, which so enraged him that he overcame it. We could give many other examples of situations in which the action of a therapist will have a totally different effect from that intended.

I very much like the definition of pathology as a process of escalating sameness (Keeney 1983, p. 123), in which patterns stay the same and feelings escalate. The secret is to disrupt the circular sameness in some creative, inventive, and startling way.

I know that this powerful technique raises ethical issues. Disobedience with therapeutic intentions could be seen as an expression of autonomy for which one could congratulate a client, such as in the earlier example with the retarded client. That example also showed how easy it was to trick this client and create inadvertent compliance with our intentions. The dilemma between promoting autonomy and promoting therapeutic cooperation is yet another paradox of psychotherapy.

Traditional psychotherapy has always been attuned to the need to avoid the therapeutic power struggle between change and no-change positions, and prescribing the symptoms has always been, although perhaps inadvertently, a central ingredient of effective psychotherapy. When we ask our clients to talk about their depressive feelings rather than cheering them up, or to express their angry or irrational feelings rather than swallowing such feelings, and when we listen to these feelings with empathy and interest, we are essentially in the business of prescribing symptoms (Loewenstein 1979). We even specify that they should occur during the therapeutic hour rather than some other time. It is also true that many people who seek psychotherapy are preoccupied with obsessional broodings or absorbed in narcissistic preoccupations, and we might well characterize psychoanalysis or many forms of psychotherapy as permission and invitation to do just that, with an attentive listener. There are therapists (Russell 1986) who feel that psychotherapy is an opportunity to relive the drama of the relationship with original parental figures, by reexperiencing it in therapy. In this formulation we might view therapy as prescribing the symptom of repetition compulsion.

Therapeutic Neutrality

The issue of too little or too much love in psychotherapy is currently debated under the heading of therapeutic neutrality. Some feminist therapists have recently suggested that unresponsive, frustrating neutrality is a typical male invention, but many male therapists currently denounce traditional therapeutic neutrality as a potentially sadistic defense (Hoffer 1986). We are told that Freud himself was seldom neutral and that neutrality does not mean lack of warmth, empathy, or active engagement, but only neutrality in relation to the patient's conflict. I have described earlier how many of my women respondents sought in therapy the kind of love, approval, and caring that they had missed in their childhood and had perhaps never received. Is it possible that this current debate was sparked by consumers' dissatisfaction with unresponsive therapists?

Overloving Therapists. I do not know whether patients receive more help from loving, caring, and warm therapists than from more neutral ones, but I am convinced of the destructive effects of overinvested therapists. My experience suggests that many of us are still trying to recover from overloving parents, and overloving therapists will hardly help us toward this goal. Indeed, the therapeutic experience seems to lend itself to the development of intensely passionate feelings, especially in the male therapist/female patient encounter. As with parents, the concept of overloving therapists may suggest benevolent yet excessive therapeutic zeal and narcissistic overinvestment, and it may result in quite a similar form of emotional exploitation. Patients become addicted to overloving therapists and separation is endlessly delayed or becomes a life-wrenching trauma for which more therapy may even be needed. Even worse, anger and criticism are misplaced in such a relationship, and the patient is trapped in one more ostensibly mutual albeit caring bind. As one woman wrote, "I became the person I wanted him to see."

Overloving in therapy is a potentially serious therapeutic issue that deserves our further consideration. Much has been written from different perspectives about the potential betrayal experience in the therapeutic encounter (Chesler 1972; Ferguson 1973; Freeman 1972; Freeman and Roy 1976; Mitchell 1973). I do not want to dwell here on the increasingly popular subject of sexual seduction in therapy, because I feel that some of the anger women have expressed against psychiatric sexual seduction is really anger about emotional seduction displaced into the sexual arena. "You touch me emotionally constantly, and wanting the other kind of touching comes from that," is a quote from a love letter written by a woman to her male therapist.

A poignant human document on this subject is Sarah Ferguson's (1973) book addressed to her dead psychiatrist, yet another long love letter vividly portraying the hazards of intensive therapy even with a devoted therapist who would have had contempt for sexual seduction. Ferguson appears to have been in a Laingian type of psychoanalysis, where deep regression and total dependency are tolerated and even encouraged (Barnes and Berke 1971). In the course of her analysis Sarah Ferguson's entire affective life came to revolve around her analyst. Nothing and nobody else held any meaning for her any longer, much as people lose interest in other aspects of their lives when they are in love. The analyst suddenly died of a heart attack, terminating the analysis prematurely; her life became totally empty and she nearly died as well.

In my own research on passionate love experiences (Loewenstein 1980), I found many examples of women who had loved their therapists too much and consequently experienced various emotional disasters. Sometimes these women had gone into therapy in the first place because of a loss, betrayal, or rejection related to some overloving experience in their lives. Among the ninety-one women in my sample who reported a nonsexual "passion experience" for their therapists, fifteen mentioned considerable pain, often in such muted ways as the following: "I found it very difficult to give him up"; "I finally had to leave since I couldn't do anything about it"; "I became totally involved in therapy and finally had the strength to sever the dependency"; "We had a reciprocal identification and feelings for each other. We kept our friendship after therapy but he broke it up and left the country. My passion continued for three years when he said he could not continue relating to me." The last respondent reported feeling rage, damaged self-esteem, and extreme emotional upset. A thirty-two-year-old single social work student reported: "I saw him for three years and left him one day," and then described a long period of deep despair and suicidal thoughts following this experience. I have learned from suicide hotline volunteers (Hilt 1977) that a number of calls come from women patients who feel suicidal about their unhappy passions for their therapists.

Two respondents had an intense passion experience when each consulted a psychiatrist again after an interval of some years. Their passion, which had been present but subdued in their initial treatment, seemed to have lain dormant but not forgotten in the intervening years, and perhaps motivated the later consultation. A professional woman, married and in her early fifties, returned to a therapist whom she had seen six years earlier over a three-year span for help with her depression. Although he had not really helped her with her symptom, the therapy had been an emotionally positive experience for her. This time she told her therapist of a brief extramarital affair in which she had been quickly rejected, leaving her with a sense of inadequacy and isolation. The therapist had expressed great pleasure in seeing his old patient again. He compared her life situation with his own midlife loneliness and disappointment in his marriage. The patient misinterpreted these confidences. They precipitated a flood of passionate emotions in her and led to fantasies of a possible mutual love relationship, which she had formerly kept under control. She started pursuing the startled therapist in socially inappropriate ways, which was very unusual for this socially conforming and inhibited woman. The experience ended with her feeling ashamed, humiliated, and rejected.

Finney (1975) discussed the ambiguous nature of these "after therapy" relationships from the therapist's point of view, admitting that there are no precise guidelines for such situations. From an ideal human standpoint, a creative therapeutic encounter might result in a beautiful in-depth friendship; this is not an unusual situation in same-gender therapeutic experiences, but it might be more difficult in cross-gender therapies.

I shall present yet one more vignette to dramatize the truly disastrous results of an overloving therapeutic relationship. This episode was told to me by a forty-six-year-old divorced friend, a professional woman. While it had happened ten years earlier, the whole story had been a major life trauma and remained extremely vivid in her mind. She had gone into therapy after a stillbirth at age thirty-six, seeking help with an extremely unhappy marriage. She too experienced exceptional and unique communication with her psychiatrist. For the first time someone taught her to verbalize her feelings, which was a liberating experience for her. She felt deeply heard and understood in a way that had never been possible with her husband. She had graduated from the same high-status university as her therapist at about the same time, and she saw him somewhat as a peer. Sometimes they had violent arguments about money, and she experienced these symmetrical engagements as highly involving. They teased each other and had private jokes, and she felt that he was also attracted to her.

It was, however, only when his wife died after three years of therapy, something they never discussed in therapy, that her passion for him became unmanageable. He reassured her, explaining that this was a normal expected transference reaction, but she felt she was losing her sanity. On her insistence they both saw a consultant, who advised an immediate change of therapist. However, she was desperately in love and saw no way to turn this off. She could not relate to her new female psychiatrist nor to the subsequent male psychiatrist, neither of whom could apparently understand her desperation. She made four suicide attempts in eighteen months, two in her first therapist's car. She repeatedly invaded his waiting room, threatening to hurt herself if he did not talk to her, until he called the police one day. My friend grabbed the policeman's gun to shoot herself and ended up in court, accused of armed assault.

I reported this unusual case because it gives us several useful warnings. One lesson is that a sudden separation is not always indicated when transference "runs amok." Actually, it is distressing that some of the practices from the days when Breuer abandoned Anna O. (Freeman 1972) still continue. My friend feels that a third person in the treatment situation and an opportunity gradually to work through her violent emotions would have been a solution. Even today she still longs to talk out this whole experience with her therapist, and she hopes he will read my report. A second lesson is that the importance of the wife's death in giving full rein to this woman's fantasies was not sufficiently appreciated. Perhaps therapists often overlook the importance that events in their private lives can have for their patients. The fact that the therapist is a high-status intelligent man who is probably in reality a highly suitable love object for the woman patient is yet another real problem. In comparison with a husband, a therapist may appear to be a much better alternative. The relationship does not become corroded by the discouraging aspects of sharing one's daily life.

My friend was diagnosed as having a borderline personality with a transference psychosis. Like Sarah Ferguson, she was certainly particularly vulnerable to fusion and loss experiences. Ten years later my friend has divorced her husband, is entirely self-supporting as a high-level computer scientist, has successfully steered two sons through adolescence, and enjoys a network of friends. She has come to feel that her mental health depends on managing without a husband or psychiatrists.

The last two vignettes also document Langs' (1974) contention that a patient's excessive transference reactions are usually due to therapeutic errors and countertransference problems and are not necessarily a manifestation of the patient's emotional problems. While some of the women I have quoted could be viewed as hysterical or borderline, characterologically the kind of women who tend to have negative therapeutic reactions (Stone 1985), a closer description of the interaction suggests that a therapist might bear serious responsibility for such "therapeutic passions" even if he is not blatantly seductive.

Freud sanitized the strong emotions that arise in therapy, calling them transference. However, he admitted (perhaps in a weak moment, since he later retracted this, probably for political reasons) in a paper (1915) that transference love, with its irrational infantile projections, addictive features, dependency, and obsessional longing for fusion, was not much different from other kinds of love. He did not minimize the risk of psychoanalytic relationships, admitting that "the psychoanalyst knows that he is working with highly explosive forces and that he needs to proceed with as much caution and conscientiousness as a chemist" (1915, p. 170). *The Secret Symmetry* (1982), edited by Aldo Carotenuto, an Italian Jungian analyst, further documents the problematic nature of transference love, or love that arises in the course of psychotherapy. It consists of actual diary entries and letters of a young Russian woman, Sabina Spielrein, which were discovered in the basement of a Swiss clinic. She had been brought by her parents to Burghölzli, the Swiss sanatorium in which Carl Jung had started his psychiatric career, to be treated for an emotional illness, and had become Jung's patient. The title refers to the secret passion between Carl Jung and his patient, perhaps in the assumption that such passion creates a symmetrical relationship. Spielrein's diaries and letters describe her desperate love for her therapist, which seems to have been cautiously reciprocated. Jung had rescued his patient from her emotional illness—she later became a productive psychoanalyst—but she paid the price of having tormenting feelings for Jung for many years. Carotenuto commented on the dilemma: " . . . if the analyst is happy and his love is outside the analysis, then he is 'dead' for his patient. If instead he wants to experience love in the analytic relationship, then death is imparted by the dissolution of the analysis" (p. 172). Carotenuto thinks that Spielrein inspired Jung with some of his most creative ideas, reminding us of Bertha Pappenheim (Anna O.), who invented "the talking cure."

The power and drama of addictive transference love does not seem to reside exclusively around sexual desires. I have already referred to the Wolf Man earlier in this essay (Obholzer 1982). We find that his entire life had been overshadowed by his love-hate dependency relationship to his famous analyst. He had a lifelong passion for Freud, quite as absorbing in its own totally different way as Spielrein's passion for Jung.

Actually, the life history of the Wolf Man, one of the most written about yet insignificant men of the twentieth century, is a stunning example of Langs' (1982) point that the therapeutic relationship can repeat and even reinforce rather than resolve certain earlier relationship conflicts. We might say, stretching the point a bit, that from an overloved child, the Wolf Man became an overloved and overloving patient. In fact, he was both underloved and overloved by his mother, whom he described as very cold yet very possessive, and maybe he was underloved and overloved by Freud as well. In any case, he transferred his unresolved dependency needs from his parents to Freud and on to a series of other psychoanalysts, never growing toward a sense of wholeness or of being in charge of his own emotional life.

I am not an advocate for unresponsive therapeutic neutrality. Proper regulation of emotional distance is the most difficult task in human relationships, including the therapeutic one. We have seen the pendulum swing between traditional unresponsive psychoanalytic neutrality to Kohut's tender loving empathy to Davanloo's (1979) aggressive intrusiveness. There is thus a large range of therapeutic distances, on which each of us can find a comfortable spot that combines the best interest of our clients with our own emotional preferences. Parents learn these days that the best way of showing their love is emotional attunement, attentiveness, and respect for the child's individuality (Stern 1985). Since we have decided that much therapy is some form of reparenting, this seems quite a good formula.

Therapy is not a one-sided effort. The dichotomy between therapist as helper and client as the helped is one of the many faulty dichotomous distinctions that we have created. It might be more useful to see a circular connection between helper and helped, in which the helping and being helped are alternate processes for both participants. This is certainly true of the teaching process; this essay, for example, is as much my students' as mine, but it is also true of psychotherapy. Furthermore we cannot make a difference in isolation. We cannot help, comfort, educate, or change anyone unless he or she is open to our efforts. Therapists at best can only motivate people to use their own resources to expand their lives.

Finally, making a difference is a process—"making"—and a goal—"a difference." Here again, we can appreciate to what extent the goal and the process are interrelated and inseparable. In therapy as in life, the goal is the journey, and the journey is the goal.

References

Barnes, M., and Berke, J. (1971). *Two Accounts of a Journey Through Madness*. New York: Harcourt, Brace Jovanovich.

Bateson, G. (1972). *Steps to an Ecology of Mind*. New York: Ballantine.

Carotenuto, A. (1982). *A Secret Symmetry*. New York: Pantheon.

Chesler, P. (1972). *Women and Madness*. New York: Doubleday.

Davanloo, H. (1979). *Evaluation Criteria for Selection of Patients for Short-Term Psychotherapy*. New York: Spectrum, pp. 9–34.

Ferguson, S. (1973). *A Guard Within*. New York: Pantheon.

Finney, J. (1975). "Therapist and patient after hours." *American Journal of Psychotherapy* 29:593–602.

Freeman, L. (1972). *The Story of Anna O.* New York: Walker.

——, and Roy, J. (1976). *Betrayal.* New York: Stein and Day.

Freud, S. (1914). "On narcissism." In J. Strachey (Ed.). *Standard Edition of the Complete Psychological Works of Sigmund Freud.* vol. 14. London: Hogarth Press, 1957.

——. (1915). "Observations on transference love." In J. Strachey (Ed.), *Standard Edition of the Complete Psychological Works of Sigmund Freud.* vol. 12. London: Hogarth Press, 1957.

Hamilton, V. (1982). *Narcissus and Oedipus.* London: Routledge and Kegan Paul.

Hilt, T. (1977). Personal communication.

Hoffer, A. (1986). "Neutrality: The therapist's compass." Colloquium, Psychiatry Grand Rounds, Mt. Auburn Hospital, Cambridge, Mass., April 28.

Keeney, B. P. (1983). *Aesthetics of Change.* New York: Guilford Press.

Kohut, H. (1977). *The Restoration of the Self.* New York: International Universities Press.

Langs, R. (1974). *The Technique of Psychoanalytic Therapy.* vol. 2. New York: Jason Aronson.

——. (1982). *The Psychotherapeutic Conspiracy.* New York: Jason Aronson.

Levenson, E. (1983). *The Ambiguity of Change.* New York: Basic Books.

Loewenstein, S. F. (1979). "Inner and outer space in social casework." *Social Casework* 60(1):19–29.

——. (1980). "Passion as a mental health hazard." In C. L. Heckerman (Ed.). *The Evolving Female.* New York: Human Sciences Press.

Mahrer, A. R. (1985). *Psychotherapeutic Change.* New York: W. W. Norton.

Mitchell, S. (1973). *My Own Woman.* New York: Horizon Press.

Obholzer, K. (1982). *The Wolf-Man: Sixty Years Later.* New York: Continuum.

Russell, P. (1986). The role of paradox in the repetition compulsion. Mimeo.

Snyder, M. (1984). "When belief creates reality." *Advances in Experimental Social Psychology* 18:247–305.

Spence, D. P. (1982). *Narrative Truth and Historical Truth.* New York: Norton.

Stern, D. N. (1985). *The Interpersonal World of the Infant.* New York: Basic Books.

Stone, M. H. (1985). "Negative outcome in borderline states." In D. T. Mays and C. M. Franks (Eds.). *Negative Outcome in Psychotherapy.* New York: Springer.

Watzlawick, P., Beavin, J., and Jackson, D. (1967). *Pragmatics of Human Communication.* New York: Norton.

Weiss, R. S. (1975). *Marital Separation.* New York: Basic Books.

17 / What Does Woman Want? Developing New Theories for Feminist Counselors

The Need for Feminist Counseling

*F*EMINIST therapy, or feminist counseling, developed as one aspect of the women's movement. It quickly seemed of special relevance to social workers as well as other mental health professionals who see predominantly women clients. Our clients are single mothers in poverty (who are harassed and depressed); mothers of troubled children (who feel guilty and responsible); women who have been betrayed by love experiences (who are depressed); depressed middle-aged housewives; abusive mothers (who are desperate, guilty, and defensive) and their abused children; impregnated teenagers who need abortions or who want to keep their babies to meet their dependency needs; and women who have been raped or sexually molested by their fathers, battered by their husbands, or emotionally abused by the men in their life. There are other clients, but it is primarily these women who come to us, out of necessity, out of courage, out of desperation.

Many different approaches developed within feminist counseling. Some writers have criticized any kind of therapy that assumes that problematic behavior and the possibility of change are located primarily in the inner space of people, rather than between people, in institutions, and above all in the social fabric of our society. In her fine book *A New Approach to Women and Therapy* (1983), Miriam Greenspan criticized not only psychodynamic therapies, but also behavioral therapy and even so-called growth therapies such as Gestalt or Transactional Analysis because, in her eyes, they are not sufficiently attuned to the constraining sociopolitical context in which behavior takes place. The emphasis of such writers is on outer space rather than inner space. Their emphasis in therapy might be on preparation for political action and social change. They insist that feminist counseling is a unique body of theory and practice done "of women, for women, by women."

Yet other feminist counselors believe that feminist counseling consists above all of certain values and attitudes and can be combined with any other kind of therapy, even psychoanalysis. To them, feminist therapy is simply good, nonsexist, humanistically oriented therapy. We are thus not talking about a monolithic belief system. It might be useful to distinguish feminist counseling from nonsexist gender-sensitive counseling (Marecek and Kravetz 1977), the former having individual change and the modification of personal behavior as its focus, the latter concentrating on political change and on critique of society and social institutions. Both approaches, however, are often loosely called feminist counseling (Williams 1976), and I believe in actual practice they overlap.

In order to explain the growing interest in feminist counseling, we must understand the major criticisms that feminists have raised against traditional counseling. It is my perception that many of these criticisms were so trenchant that they first weakened the edifice of psychoanalysis and subsequently affected and changed the entire field of therapy. As women's consciousness was raised, tolerance for sexist counseling decreased. Some might even say that all therapists and therapies changed so radically that we are no longer in need of specific feminist counseling, while others would disagree and point to subtle aftereffects of traditional psychoanalytic and patriarchal thinking.

Phyllis Chesler (1971) was one of the early critics of traditional psychotherapy; she pinpointed many of its major dangers for women. She thought that therapy was an institution in which predominantly women patients went to see predominantly male therapists "with the same urgency and despair" (p. 747) with which they entered the other socially approved institution for middle-class women, namely marriage:

For most women the psychotherapeutic encounter is just one more instance of an unequal relationship, just one more opportunity to be rewarded by expressing distress and be helped by being expertly dominated. . . . Both psychotherapy and marriage enable women to safely express and defuse their anger by experiencing it as a form of emotional illness, by translating it into hysterical symptoms, frigidity, chronic depression, phobias and the like. . . . She wants from a therapist what she wants and often cannot get from a husband: attention, understanding, merciful relief, a personal solution—in the arms of the right husband, on the couch of the right therapist. (1971, pp. 746–59)

This first criticism so eloquently voiced by Chesler thus deals with the unequal power relationship in cross-gender therapy, which duplicates the one found in society between men and women. Obviously this criticism, along with several others, applies most to cross-gender counseling, and there are indeed increasing number of women who seek out women counselors.

Second, Chesler and others have claimed that therapy has been a form of social control meant to keep women in their place. Women were taught in therapy that the problem was within themselves, what I call their inner space, rather than in society and in the possibly pathological context in which a particular woman had to survive. The feminist protest is encompassed in the slogan: "Women are messed over rather than messed up."

Third, feminist writers have pointed out that therapy has traditionally been pathology-oriented, and the medical model encourages diagnostic guessing games rather than capitalizing on a person's health and strength.

Fourth, it has been claimed that many male therapists were focused only on women's relationships, especially their relationships to men, leaving out the importance of women's friendships to other women, not to mention their working lives, their career goals, their autonomous self-development, and so on.

Fifth and perhaps most important, psychoanalytic theory has an antifeminist theoretical bias. In his phallocentric, "little-boy-view" (Horney 1926) of women, Freud saw them as castrated and therefore inferior creatures whose development as people was shaped by penis envy, love and admiration for the father who did have a penis and contempt for the castrated mother. Women were seen as either grudgingly submitting or aggressively protesting their anatomical and therefore psychic inferiority. The "fact of their castration," as Freud tended to say, was said to have many negative psychological consequences. Freud also defined women's sexuality for them, and it took women a long time to recover from his theoretical mischief, which was then elaborated and perpetuated by men and women psychoanalysts. Anatomy was destiny, and inferior anatomy presumably deserved inferior social status and opportunities.

Although Freud made repeated attempts to understand women with dubious results, his infamous exasperated question: "What does woman want" seemed to concede his own puzzlement. His theory of human beings, while perhaps relevant to men's behavior, did not explain women's motivation. It has become an urgent task for women writers to question the popular mythology that grew out of psychoanalytic theory and to develop a new psychology of women which would illuminate women's true experience and form a new theoretical basis for counseling women. I shall try to contribute to this task. In considering some of the myths that my generation of women were raised on, I shall select those that have diminished in important ways the quality of my own life. I have been privileged in many ways, and women who have been raised and lived in poverty might emphasize different, probably even more destructive myths.

Myths in Women's Lives

The Myth of Cinderella and the Prince. We all cling to the belief that we live in a just society. Women therefore conclude that their powerlessness and low status in society are due to their own deficiencies. "They develop traits typical of minority groups: dislike of their own sex, negative self-image, insecurity, self-blame, a submissive or 'shuffling' attitude, identification with males, and low aspirations" (Kirsch 1974, p. 330). Most women I have known harbor deep self-doubts about being intelligent, attractive, loving, and lovable. The infamous need to please others, seen as a typical female characteristic, is the obvious result of such an insecure self-concept. Men too seem to be plagued by self-doubts, perhaps endemic in our society, but men may be more dependent on appearing competent than on being loved. Women's entire lives are dominated by their anxious need to love and be loved by men as the one major road to happiness and possible self-love.

How do we see this throughout the life cycle? Adolescence is overshadowed by the agony and shame caused by the "popularity" contest. Heartbreaking episodes of unrequited love, betrayals, and rejections can leave their marks for life. Here is what one woman tells about a love experience when she was nineteen years old:

I was working at my first job. He was my boss. I was in an emotionally vulnerable position, not knowing where I was going. After eight years I still feel unresolved. The ending was extremely abrupt and involved another woman. I developed a kind of shell and bitterness, which is probably still with me. The experience still hurts. I am still discovering things which grew out of it, like a fear of involving myself totally with anyone. Also a constant battle with depression and feelings of worthlessness and inadequacy.

After adolescence comes young adulthood, with the dread that no suitable prince will come to the rescue to act out the fairy-tale script. I still remember how I was haunted, during my late adolescence, with worries that I might not find a suitable man. Why would an attractive and intelligent woman, such as I must have been, be beset with such anxieties? Women are socialized to believe that their private nightmares are unique and deeply neurotic, and I thought for many years that I was burdened with abnormal fears about not finding a husband. Only recently have I realized that these very same fears haunt many women. How grateful we are to men who are willing to love us with all our imperfections.

In addition, many women enter marriage, or at least they did in my generation, with a deep conviction that their husbands will protect them from the pains, anxieties, and problems of life. The reality of marriage can only be a rude awakening. My own parents had a disastrous, loveless, and quarrelsome marriage, and my maternal aunt, who was a second mother to me, felt nothing but contempt and pity for her husband. Yet I entered marriage with a total conviction that we would live happily ever after. Cultural myths seem to outweigh our own observations of life around us.

Once married, each woman continues to worry whether her husband loves her enough and she hopes that he will not beat her, drink, or be unfaithful. "I guess I can't complain. He's a steady worker; he doesn't drink; he doesn't hit me," responded working-class wives when asked by Rubin (1979) "what they valued most about their husbands" (p. 93). As women age, they hope their husbands will not leave them for younger women. Some women get divorced and are faced again, in the middle of their lives, with the tasks of man hunting, man finding, and man keeping that will pursue them to their graves.

Clearly, things have changed in recent generations. Women will now take the initiative in divorcing these days, if they are economically independent. Their rejected husbands suffer deeply, but according to statistics, unlike their middle-aged wives they remarry quickly and easily. And modern young women postpone marriage until their late twenties (Lipman-Blumen 1976); yet they seem to undergo the same terror and agony that my generation suffered when we were younger. I saw a young woman of twenty-eight for consultation. Both her parents had died and she felt alone in the world. Would she have to spend a lonely life without loving or being loved by a permanent mate? She was a highly accomplished young woman and she knew exactly why she had not found a mate. No, she did not blame the shortage of interesting young men for highly educated women, or circumstances, or the difficulty of finding an interesting man at any age. She blamed her various shortcomings. She thought she had a crooked nose and she was a bit too fat. Being a woman, she was depressed and she said she was too depressed to get her house in order, go on a diet, or to go out and seek a man, all projects her male counselor had urged her to pursue. I had only two major prescriptions: to stop the attempt at dieting because she was quite attractive enough, and to live triumphantly in her messy house, which she did not have to clean up for any man. No doubt I cheered her up temporarily, but I could not find her a man.

If women felt strong, independent, confident, and even ready to face with some equanimity life without a permanent mate, then they could relax and simply be open to the encounters with women and men that life might bring them. Some women want children more urgently than a man, and the new revolutionary trend among some professional women to have a child without a father may ease the desperation about finding a man. Perhaps matters would also be easier if most of us did not believe in the next myth I will discuss:

The Myth of the Lonely Spinster. Research on comparative life satisfaction in the last two decades has consistently shown single women as a group to be in better mental health than married women, while the opposite is true of single men, who as a group have the lowest life satisfaction and the highest incidence of alcoholism, mental illness, and criminality (Campbell 1975; Gove and Tudor 1972). This finding was in total contrast to our common assumption regarding happy bachelors and lonely spinsters. Bernard (1972) commented:

It is not necessarily the magnitude of the statistical differences between the mental health of married and single women or between married men and married women that is so convincing: it is, rather, the consistency of the differences. . . . The poor mental health of wives is like a low-grade infection that shows itself in a number of scattered symptoms, no one of which is critical enough to cause an acute episode. And so, therefore, it is easy . . . to dismiss. Or to blame on women themselves. There must be something wrong with them if they are psychologically so distressed. (p. 37)

Intrigued by these findings, my students and I (Loewenstein et al. 1981) studied the life satisfaction of sixty never-married, divorced, or widowed women aged thirty-five to sixty-five, whose children, if any, no longer lived at home. We found that the great majority of women in our sample were either highly satisfied with life (50 percent) or reasonably content (30 percent). Only 15 percent, nine women in our sample, as compared to about 10 percent of the general American population (Campbell 1975) felt deep dissatisfaction with the quality of their lives. We were particularly stunned to find that life satisfaction was highly related to work satisfaction and good health and only minimally related to a good sex life, to having a steady man friend, or to the presence of young adult children in their lives. We could only conclude from our study that neither marriage, sex, nor motherhood is a necessary component of high life satisfaction for women in midlife.

The Myth of the Family as "Haven in a Heartless World." (Lasch 1977) This myth was particularly damaging for me. Once, long ago, I used to believe experts unquestioningly and take their writings very seriously. I remember reading in a sociology book that the family was the institution from which people drew enough comfort and strength to function in the world of work. Since I had always considered working less stressful than raising children and since I always looked forward to work as a relief from family life, I felt that something must be very different and very wrong with our particular nuclear family. Later, it was almost a relief to realize that most nuclear families are jungles of brutality (Lystad 1975), islands of despair, or breeding grounds of madness (Henry 1965; Laing and Esterson 1964). My own family compared rather favorably once the myth was dispelled.

Each year my social work students choose to write about their own families as part of an assignment on family theories. These usually well functioning, competent, and caring graduate students often come from families in which there had been alcoholism passed down through generations; some of them had been sexually molested as children; many are from divorced or blended families; and a number report mental illness in a sibling or parent. I feel newly astonished every year. Here again we face an urgent need to revise our assumptions about the actualities of family life. Berman (1973) captured this well:

The system promulgates overload. It places too many emotional eggs in the family basket and then proceeds to crush them. . . . The very features that would seem to nominate the conjugal, nuclear family for this adaptive function (referring to industrial society)—its privacy, small size and binding love ethic . . . run counter to the need to discharge rage and displaced hostilities. The small size means that a few persons must bear the overload of tension and emotionality and antagonism that they did not earn. . . . Our small, claustrophobic nuclear family is explosively and exquisitely oedipal. It makes weekend neuroses the rule, and the creed of surrounding privacy ensures that . . . each family resides with consuming guilt in the unshaken conviction that theirs is a special and lonely private hell. (p. 269)

Moreover, there is unquestioned documentation that women are more often the victims of family violence (Goodstein and Page 1981), suffer more from depressions (Weissman and Klerman 1977), and have more schizophrenic breakdowns (Chesler 1972) than men.

The destructiveness of family living is displayed most dramatically when we view women who live in unfavorable economic circumstances. In her study of forty low-income families, Belle (1980) described the alarmingly high incidence of depression and other psychic disturbances among low-income mothers. She found that single mothers and mothers with large families and preschool children generally led exceptionally stressful lives and had consequent psychiatric symptoms. Belle wrote:

It is instructive to consider the nature of some of the highly stressful live events experienced by our small sample of women. These include: rape, beating by the husband, robbery, nervous breakdown, appearance in court, husband stabbed to death, children claimed by their father after many years, and desertion by the husband. Violence is not rare and husbands and lovers are frequently the perpetrators of violence. (1980, p. 87)

It is also arresting to learn that "for every age bracket the more income a girl or a woman has, the lower the rate of marriage, a situation just the reverse of that of men" (Bernard 1972, p. 35); high-status women are also the least likely to remarry after a divorce (Lipman-Blumen 1976). The assumption is that those women have a choice.

It could well be, however, that it is frequently not marriage per se, but the housewife role and raising children that seem to create so much stress, and that these somewhat dated statistics no longer describe the situation of working wives and mothers. However, they were valid statistics ten years ago, and it behooves us to remember the recent past, given that the social pendulum swings in a pattern. Moreover, I believe women continue to be held responsible and to hold themselves responsible for the emotional disturbances that the system creates in the children. This brings me to my next myth.

The Myth of Blissful Motherhood. It is most fortunate that this myth is finally being exploded, because at least today's young mothers need not add guilt about their natural ambivalence toward their children to the list of motherhood stresses. Sociological (Bernard 1974), autobiographical (McBride 1973; Radl 1973; Lazarre 1976), and feminist (Rich 1976) writings all concur that the greater prevalence of depression among women may be at least partially related to the stresses of being a mother. Studies of depression repeatedly find a strong correlation between motherhood, especially young and multiple motherhood, and the incidence of depression (Weissman 1980).

I feel bitter that the knowledge of the "postpartum blues" as a commonly expected phenomenon has only recently been publicized (Weissman and Klerman 1977). I still remember the surprise and guilt I felt as a new mother when I found myself acutely anxious about the new baby and quite depressed during what I had expected to be "the happiest period of my life." My conviction that I was an unnatural mother—a conviction that pursues women throughout life (Rubin 1979)—was a worse burden than the depression itself.

Many women are now asking their husbands or mates to participate more fully in the initial nurturing tasks. This will dilute (for better or for worse?) the mother's passion for her infant and protect the father from becoming a jealous outsider. (See Chapter 3, this volume). Common parenting may also facilitate the infant's early identification with *both* genders, protect mothers and daughters against excessive fusion, and help sons to acquire an early male identification and avoid the excessive and effortful repudiation of their primary identification with their mother (Stoller

1974; Dinnerstein 1976). It is also hoped that such shared parenting may shape the development of androgynous human beings who are more whole, and that it may even in time disrupt the masculine/feminine polarity of human behavior.

It seems quite natural that working women actually become better loving mothers, protected as they are from pouring all their life energies, hopes, and ambitions into their children, a situation that is almost bound to create some forms of "overloving." We have learned that one effective way of stopping child abuse is to send a mother to work (Justice and Justice 1976). How ironic that mothers of my generation had been promised by Dr. Spock (and other men who teach women how to take care of their children) that we would have perfect children if we stayed home and took care of them twenty-four hours a day (Wortis 1971). Slater's (1970) seemingly wild speculation that American mothers were angry at these false promises and did not rally around Dr. Spock when he went into politics may have some reality.

As a young mother, I worked to preserve my emotional and intellectual equilibrium. Belle found that for low-income women as well, employment is not only a vital economic necessity, but also a buffer against depression. She continued: "Jobs represented a bright hope for many of these women. Research . . . suggests that employment can actually protect women's mental health when other circumstances are difficult. To several of the women with whom we worked, the future looked dismal without a job to provide some way out of poverty, isolation and low self-esteem" (1980, p. 90). Most married and unmarried women work for sheer financial survival. Many middle-class women and most working-class women then face the bitter reality that working conditions are permeated by low status, low salaries, and various forms of discrimination and stress (Lemkau 1980).

The unmitigated bliss of motherhood was not only emphasized for the young mother, but social science literature perpetuated the illusion that women could not bear to separate from their children. This resulted in the creation of the next myth.

The Myth of the Empty Nest. I remember telling a childless woman psychoanalyst how relieved I was, when watching children's birthday parties in the neighborhood, that those days were over. She promptly suggested that my sense of loss for the days when my children were young was so profound that I had to deny it completely. At the time I felt uncertain and confused. My feelings about the passing stream of life are so ambiguous that I find it difficult to distinguish relief from regret. We have since learned that excessive grief about the children's departure from home is confined to women who were exclusively invested in mother-hood and who arrive at midlife and menopause with no other available roles (Lowenthal, Thurnher, and Chiraboga 1975). Even for these women, depressive feelings focus more on lack of al-ternate meaningful activity than on the loss of children or repro-ductive capacity. The newer research findings suggest consis-tently that women tend to feel a sense of relief from the burden of motherhood (Radloff 1975; Rubin 1979; Loewenstein 1980a), es-pecially after getting children through the stresses of adolescence. In a study my students and I undertook on fathers and mothers in midlife (Loewenstein et al. 1983), we found that most mothers experience distress not when children leave home, which is after all a long anticipated event, but when young adult children re-turn home during periods of unemployment, marital separation, or mental instability.

The myth of the empty nest is just one of the areas of mis-understanding of the midlife woman; it is not as diminishing as earlier statements by Deutsch (1945), who described her as "en-gaged in an active struggle against her decline" (p. 459) or ridi-culed her for displaying youthful enthusiasm (pp. 461–64). More recently such women are being scolded for neglecting their grandmotherly duties in favor of more frivolous pursuits (Frai-berg 1977). It is a great comfort to hear women of substance speak out against these stereotypes. "The most creative force in the world is a postmenopausal woman with zest," stated Margaret Mead at a talk (1977).

Midlife women have been particularly maligned in the area of their sexuality. Popular writers such as David Reuben (1969) have falsely equated the capacity for reproduction with the capacity for sexual lust and enjoyment. Fortunately, here again the newer voices of women researchers have swept aside these distortions and given older women full permission to remain, or even to become, sexual beings (Huyck 1977). A striking finding from the Kinsey Institute suggests that widowed and divorced women "had a higher percentage of orgasm during their postmarital life than in their former marriage" (Gebhard 1970, p. 102). Actually, the whole area of female sexuality has been particularly prone to value-laden distortions by "experts."

The Myth of the Sleeping Beauty. Men have not only instructed women on how to rear their children, but, already long before Freud, they have defined women's sexuality for them. It is surprising how reluctant women have been to claim their own sexuality, apparently feeling uncertain about what they felt, what they thought they should feel, and whether they were unique and therefore abnormal (Loewenstein 1978a). Women in consciousness-raising groups have been willing to share their sexual experiences, and women finally revealed themselves to women researchers (Hite 1976; Seaman 1972), thus ending the pluralistic ignorance in which each woman individually bore the secret shame of her particular assumed sexual inadequacy. Freud and some of his women disciples suggested that mature femininity depended on the transfer of erotic sensitivity from the clitoris to the vagina, and moreover, the vagina was downgraded as an organ much inferior to the priceless penis. Female development, as mentioned earlier, was therefore organized around penis envy. It is comforting to know that some of Freud's early disciples, such as Karen Horney (1926), had already suggested that penis envy, when it occurs, might be a reaction to the superior status of men in our society, perhaps even starting with the preferred position of brothers in the family. Horney was also the first woman psychologist who talked about womb envy, which Freud never once mentioned.

Not until Masters and Johnson's (1966) research was the role of the clitoris in adult female sexual functioning restored. We now understand that women may indeed have either a vaginal orgasm or a clitoral orgasm or the combined orgasm that Masters and

Johnson studied in their laboratory, and that these diverse patterns of female sexuality are neither related to emotional maturity nor even to some ill-defined "femininity" (Loewenstein 1978a; Singer 1973).

While psychoanalytic literature defined lack of vaginal orgasmic experience as "frigidity" and a neurotic rejection of the feminine role, social scientists have pointed out that "the human female's capacity for orgasm is to be viewed as a potentiality that may or may not be developed by a given culture" (Mead, quoted in Seaman 1972, p. 65). This capacity is said to be a learning process that involves considerable deinhibition (in our culture), sexual experience, and skillful lovers. The Kinsey researchers (1953) found that it took some women many years, if ever, before they had their first orgasms. For generations women have passively waited, like Sleeping Beauty, for men to awaken them, teach them about sexuality, and "give" them orgasms. It is now clear that men, far from being competent teachers, are not familiar with women's needs and preferences and need to be taught themselves. Effective communication between partners may create mutual guidance, exploration, and experimentation with both partners taking active and passive roles. The stereotype that equated femininity with passivity is destructive to women.

It thus becomes very obvious that the romantic ideal of chastity and virginity until marriage is highly dysfunctional for both women and men. In our new feminist language women will be said to gain sexual experience with their first sexual encounter, rather than lose their virginity. Feminist writers have also tried to exorcise the guilt traditionally associated with masturbation. They urge women to masturbate as a way of becoming disinhibited, as a primary form of female sexuality (Dodson 1974), and as a potential bridge toward vaginal orgasmic capacity (Barbach 1975). Feminists have thus urged women to take their sexuality into their own hands (!), to learn to experience comfort with their own female bodies, and to communicate their needs to their lovers. These have been hard lessons to learn.

While technical skill training has been an important part of this thinking, the importance of feelings and of the emotional aspects of the sexual relationship has not been denied. Female sexuality

is not confined to heterosexuality, and that brings me to the myth
of homosexual pathology.

The Myth of Homosexual Pathology. When Eleanor Roosevelt's correspondence with Lorena Hickok (Carmody 1979) was published,
speculation about her sexual orientation was rampant. Western
culture thrives on false polarities. It is very important in our society that people not only be sharply divided into men and women,
but also be viewed as having either homosexual or heterosexual
orientations. Harry Stack Sullivan, an important pioneer in rejecting this insidious dichotomy, wrote:

> This results in seventy-two theoretical patterns of sexual behavior in sit-
> uations involving two real partners. . . . From this statement, I would
> like you to realize . . . how fatuous it is to toss out the adjectives "het-
> erosexual," "homosexual," or "narcissistic" to classify a person as to his
> sexual and friendly integration with others. Such classifications are not
> anywhere near refined enough for intelligent thought; they are much
> too gross to do anything except mislead both the observer and the vic-
> tim. (1953, p. 294)

The actual frequent bisexual behavior widely documented (Kinsey et al. 1948, 1953; Bell and Weinberg 1978; Riess 1974, Loewenstein 1985) is often dismissed in the psychiatric literature as
"limited" or "situational experimentation" (Saghir and Robins,
1973). Marriages of women who later identify themselves as lesbians are retrospectively defined as "doomed to failure," eschewing the alternate explanation that women who are disappointed
by men may turn to other women for emotional and physical satisfaction (Loewenstein 1980b). In our new, more fluid culture and
somewhat more permissive life-styles, changes in sexual orientation throughout the life cycle have become less infrequent. "The
evidence supports a theory of multipotentiality of sexual expression" (Bleier 1979, p. 55). Several of the women in my research
on passion had changed their sexual orientation at least once, and
two women had done so twice, in addition to a number of women
who defined themselves as bisexual (Loewenstein 1985). Gender
orientation of sexual and emotional responsiveness among the
women in my research fell along a continuum from exclusive het-

erosexuality, to heterosexuality coexisting with women-oriented sexual or nonsexual passions, to self-identified bisexuality, to self-identified lesbianism with histories of heterosexual passions, to exclusive lesbianism at the other end. Other researchers have confirmed this finding of at least secretly mixed orientations (Blumstein and Schwartz 1976), although women and men in our society are almost forced to make an allegiance to a particular network of social relations, which then reinforces and sharpens their allegiance to one particular sexual and emotional gender orientation.

Most destructive has been the mental health professionals' insistence that homosexuality is a severe emotional problem, in spite of all the research evidence that "homosexuality is simply not a clinical entity" (Riess 1974, p. 19) and that "there is no evidence whatsoever that homosexuality represents either a biological or an emotional aberration" (Bleier 1979, p. 55). Thomas Szasz formulated a positive view of homosexuality before it was fashionable to do so:

Our secular society dreads homosexuality in the same way and with the same intensity as the theological societies of our ancestors dreaded heresy . . . Thus has the physician replaced the priest, and the patient the witch, in the drama of society's perpetual struggle to destroy precisely those human characteristics that, by differentiating men from their fellows, identify persons as individuals rather than as members of the herd. (Szasz 1970, pp. 242, 259)

The American Psychiatric Association removed homosexuality from the category of mental illness in 1973, apparently under political pressures, but the stigmatization persists. Homosexuality has been alternately or simultaneously labeled a crime, a sin, or a sickness, three labels that have oppressive guilt- and shame-producing consequences. Lesbian women have tended to avoid using traditional mental health facilities and social agencies for fear of discrimination. However, as women (and men) courageously come out of their closets, we realize that "lesbian women are everywhere." (Diamond 1979, p. 81) "Everywhere" includes social work faculties, social work students, and mental health professionals in general. It has become crucial for all social workers to resist stigmatization of lesbians and to become aware of their particular life stresses, such as discrimination in jobs, housing, and child custody fights; heartbreak when a love relationship ends; and all the practical hardships faced by women who are not "protected" by a man. Counselors of lesbians need to regard their life-style as a valid and potentially gratifying choice, and to separate it from the problems that the lesbian brings for help.

There are two last myths I would like to discuss, leaving them for last because they pervade in subtle ways all the issues that we have discussed.

The Myth of Natural Inferiority of Women. It is ironic, but perhaps not accidental, that we women were just recovering from psychoanalytic insults when new curses were laid on our lives, this time in the guise of sociobiology or biosociology. Instead of anatomy, it was now evolutionary biology that became our destiny. Our genes and our hormones, we were told, meant us to be passive, maternal, submissive to our more aggressive and therefore more successful mates. The social organization of hordes of apes was suddenly held up to us as a cultural ideal.

Once again we read that women and men are profoundly different in ways other than cultural programming. Little girls are less aggressive than little boys, apparently right from the cradle. Girls have better verbal skills, but only until adolescence, while boys' better-developed visual spatial skills remain superior throughout life (Maccoby and Jacklin 1974). These traits are connected with greater field independence, which amounts to a higher capacity for abstract, analytical thinking, nothing less than the most highly prized attribute of our culture. While nineteenth-century "craniology" was not able to prove women's intellectual inferiority (Hubbard and Lowe 1979), modern research about differences between the right and left hemispheres of the brain raises once again the specter of inferior female intelligence. This research has produced highly confusing and contradictory speculations, suggesting that females think less (or more?) holistically and less (or more?) intuitively than males (Star 1979). Of course, women did not lose out completely in this research. "Women are better than men on . . . a number of other tests of visual matching and visual search which are predictive of good performance on clerical tasks" (Buffery and Gray, quoted in Star 1979, p. 123)! I feel grateful to women and men scientists who have accepted the task of critically examining sex-role research. They explain the biased perspective and the deficient methodology on which most of this research is based. They have commented that the scientists who did the research

> did not acknowledge that the ways in which observations are made and, indeed, what one sees, are strongly colored by the hypotheses one uses and by the framework in which one's observations are made. If one is sure that there are innate behavioral differences and tries to demonstrate this, then facts which do not support this belief are often simply not seen or even are unconsciously distorted or misinterpreted. (Hubbard and Lowe 1979, p. 12)

Finally, we have learned that Cartesian duality between mind and body, nature and nurture, does not correspond to reality. Social biologists seem to neglect modern genetic and cybernetic wisdom, which states that behavioral outcomes are the result of "processes by which traits are maintained in the transactions between organism and environment" (Sameroff 1976, p. 21), each modifying the other in a continuously circular feedback process. Moreover, geneticists say, two populations with different environments can simply not be compared. We have encountered the same basic methodological fallacies in the comparison of differences between black and white children. Hubbard and Lowe summarized this situation well:

> There is no theory at present that enables one to determine the origins of behavioral differences between the two groups in two different environments. This theoretical limitation invalidates all attempts to distinguish between genetic and environmental sources of sex differences, race differences, or any other *group* difference in behavior. (1979, p.145)

A great deal of passion surrounds the study of "differences" among groups, because the concept of "different but equal" tends itself to be a myth in our society. Inevitably, "when a difference is established between groups that have different positions in the social hierarchy, the attributes of the dominant group are the 'right ones' to have" (Hubbard and Lowe 1979, p. 30). An intriguing example, which illustrates much of the controversy in this area of "differences," is the polemic about women's moral judgments. Freud claimed that women had different, less pure and absolute moral judgments than men (Freud 1933), while Gilligan (1982), agreeing with Freud's impression that women's moral judgment is indeed different, defined it as more contextual and challenged Freud's assumption as to what is "better." Gilligan's research is based on decisions women made regarding abortion. We could see these women's decisions as a result of moral judgment or simply as a result of conflicting desires and pulls. From asking whether men or women have better moral judgments, which simply perpetuates the old game turned upside down, we are led to wonder whether woman or man can ever make any judgments that are not dictated by the immediate or larger social contexts in which they take place. Let us remember the research on jury selection (Wrightsman 1978), which suggests that a person's socioeconomic, ethnic, religious, and political allegiance is highly predictive of his or her final judgment. Are moral judgments located in the inner space of people, or are they dictated by the social forces that surround us? This question pervades the entire gender-related research and leads us to an examination of the myth of "inner space" psychology.

The Myth of "Inner Space" Psychology. To lead "examined" lives, we certainly must pay attention to our feelings and emotions. Yet we also need to be alert to some of the fallacies of the "inner space" (Rabkin 1970; Loewenstein 1979) approach. We cling to the belief that the mainspring of our actions lies within ourselves. Yet ingenious social psychological experiments (Milgram 1974; Asch 1955), not to speak of the dramatic lessons of history, teach us that the behavior of many (including mental health professionals) is ruled by obedience to authority and conformity to the social expectations of their reference groups. This holds true regardless of whether we consider the trivial corruptions of Watergate, our behavior toward minority groups, or the horrifying events of the Holocaust.

But if we persist in our belief that our motivations are found primarily within our inner space, by which I refer to the unconscious, or critical developmental periods, or genetic and biological predispositions, the logical conclusion is that the reasons for our misfortunes also lie within us.

Am I mistaken in thinking that women have been particularly prone to take responsibility for all the misfortunes and betrayals that tend to befall them? Would a man's first impulse be one of self-blame if he had a retarded child, were raped, if his mate were alcoholic, beat him, or left him for a more attractive partner? Perhaps it would. Women have no monopoly on guilt, shame, and self-blame, and we are perhaps only leading the way when questioning how the profound assumption of individual responsibility affects our lives. Besides, it is easier to blame oneself than to condemn the entire fabric of our society; it gives us some illusory sense of control over our lives, and it preserves the concept of a just or at least minimally meaningful society, an idea without which we might not be able to survive.

It is perhaps mainly in the realm of psychoanalytic theory that this inner space psychology has damaged women more than men. Freud's disciple Helene Deutsch, who was for a long time the major authority on the psychology of women, defined women as masochistic, passive, and narcissistic. Many feminist writers have addressed themselves to these psychoanalytic allegations in a voluminous literature, to which I have also contributed.

It is tempting and easy to find explanations for women's greater narcissism. We could argue that women have less opportunity to sublimate their primitive narcissism into mature forms, a universal maturational task (Kohut 1973), thus gratifying it through bodily display as implied by Freud, or through narcissistic investment in their children. Or we might say that mothers love their daughters more narcissistically because of the closer identification with a child of their own gender, thus transmitting female narcissism through the generations. Or else, using narcissism in a somewhat different sense, we could refer back to women's self-doubts, which create their own form of narcissistic vulnerability. If we were to use Reik's definition of narcissism as "the desire of the self to be loved," (1944, p. 31) we could argue that women have learned that their psychological survival is based on being loved, and that their narcissism is therefore an adaptive trait. Yet I reject all these easy speculations, because I think it is not women's vanity, but men's grandiose needs for heroism, power, admiration, and adulation, as dictators, statesmen, kings, and warriors, that have brought this world to the edge of extinction (Loewenstein 1977).

Quite similar to narcissism, the concept of feminine masochism has also undergone many conceptual transformations in its journey from inner space to outer space. Moral masochism is usually considered self-defeating readiness for self-sacrifice. Freud equated feminine masochism with the sexual act and saw it as a truly feminine characteristic. Deutsch viewed feminine masochism as the association of pleasure with the painful experiences of feminine sexuality. But both Freud and Deutsch see masochism only partly as the result of constitutional and anatomical differences; they also recognized the role of society, and particularly the father, in teaching the adolescent girl to turn her unacceptable aggressive forces against herself, which then results in masochism (Deutsch 1944, p. 251).

Horney (1935), on the other hand, suggested that masochism was a response to socioculturally defined inferiority. She saw it as an attempt of an intimidated individual to gain safety and satisfaction in life through inconspicuousness and self-effacement, a willingness to suffer pain as the price for affection, and a natural consequence of neurotic dependency on someone else for magical support. Most interesting, perhaps, is the view of feminine masochism as the power of the weak, a subtle form of manipulation and emotional blackmail exerted by people who do not have more direct access to power (Johnson 1976).

As we gain deeper understanding of the interconnectedness of such polarities as active/passive or masochistic/sadistic, we can see that one pole cannot exist without the other. Most human beings have the potential to experience the full gamut of opposite feelings at different times. Yet men and women have reached many arrangements in which one gender carries predominantly one pole and the other gender the other pole, to the possible greater disadvantage of one partner, but ultimately to the detriment of both. Lerner (1983) made an excellent case for female dependency as an example of an unfair division of labor. She thought that women learn early to pretend weakness and dependency as an ego service to the men in their lives, thus indirectly meeting their men's dependency needs. This could well be one of the many unsung sacrifices that women have made to men. As a young married woman I was very grateful for the many services that my husband was willing to perform for me. As I gained increasing independence and less interest in being serviced, he felt increasingly hurt and assaulted in his masculinity. We could not find some other way of dividing the emotional tasks of living between us.

These multiple myths and betrayals of expectations have made each woman feel that she is deficient, inadequate, and uniquely responsible for not measuring up to the various unrealistic cultural ideals.

The systemic cybernetic view implied in the discussion of polarities is more oriented toward blending of inner space and outer space than psychoanalytic theory. This view's three basic tenets—that nothing can be understood outside its context, that everything in the world is interconnected, and that behavior happens between people rather than inside people—seem consistent with a feminist perspective of the world. However, system theory draws our attention to the interlocking function of different family members, while the feminist perspective emphasizes power differentials. The former emphasizes equal responsibility of all members for the functioning or malfunctioning of a social system, while the latter leads to a view of women as victims, trapped by their economic needs and their responsibilities to their children. I see validity in each perspective and feel personally caught between them.

The "woman as victim" orientation is tempting, its accuracy in terms of group inequality indisputable, and its superior moral position comforting. I think it is a perspective that must be recognized yet ultimately rejected, because it does not give us strength and courage to change our lives.

I believe that most women are plagued so deeply by self-doubts that they need to accept them as a life condition. I advise my women clients and students to do what I practice myself: Pretend to love yourself better than you really do and it will serve you well enough. We need to accept the paradox that a pretense at more self-confidence, more power, and more control over our lives than we either feel or can realistically assume, may become a self-fulfilling prophecy. Ellen Goodman recognized very well that Joan Kennedy's "journey toward self-confidence is . . . part of that mass migration known as the women's movement" (1980, p. 30).

It is thus important that women recognize their own competence and mastery. We must learn to reject a view of ourselves as defective, passive, powerless, and helpless. While all human beings must lead responsible and considerate lives, we must learn to avoid self-blame for our misfortunes of fate, and excessive responsibility for the welfare of others. We need not become self-absorbed in a negative way; self-love rather than self-doubt and healthy rather than unhealthy narcissism should be primary therapeutic objectives. Feminists have tried to formulate therapeutic practices that are conducive to these goals.

Can Men Counsel Women?

This essay has reviewed a multitude of "sins" committed by traditional therapists, many of whom were and are men. Indeed, many feminist counselors, among them Chesler and Russell, are very skeptical about the possibility that men can overcome the many years of socialization experiences of a patriarchal society. It is also suggested that in a sexist society one should expect even normal, considerate, and sensitive men to be sexist, and that it is most likely that men counselors will either identify with the men in the women's lives, or alternatively, may get excessively angry at other men who misbehave against their wives, when they themselves try so hard to be good husbands. It is suggested that men's and women's sex-role orientations and life experiences are so different, and sexism so pervasive and subtle, that only women can understand other women's experiences. It might be difficult to validate the experiences of someone who lives in a totally different world, especially since there is seldom any attempt in the training of men mental health professionals to sensitize them to the different emotional reactions that women have to many issues. Writers who prefer same-gender counseling also point to the need for role models, especially for younger women. These are important arguments against cross-gender counseling. I shall suggest some additional considerations.

In my research on passionate love experiences I found that disappointment, betrayal, rejection, and disconfirmation in love experiences inside or outside of marriage were the major reason the women I studied entered psychotherapy. In such a situation there is every possibility that women were inclined to fall in love with their therapists, who were bound to listen, understand, and empathize better than the women's own disappointing men, at least in this professional situation. The likelihood that a woman would fall in love with her therapist was thus very great. There is then a potential in these cross-gender encounters to evoke once again those elements of unrequited yearning, passion, dependency, masochism, and intense ambivalence from which the women are trying to recover. Therapy is often meant to arouse these feelings, but they tend to be quite hard to "work through," especially if the woman is emotionally deprived. Langs (1974) commented on the difficulty of these situations:

For many patients the therapist is in reality one of the few truly concerned and consistently helpful persons in their lives. The patient's response to this is usually only partly transference—that is based on past longings and relationships; it is also quite appropriate. This can also create very sticky ties to the therapist for the patient and make final resolution and termination of treatment quite difficult, especially for deprived and lonely individuals. (p. 223)

I am confining myself to a consideration of situations where no obvious sexual seduction took place and where the therapist acted in an ethical and benevolent manner. Yet men therapists may not be aware of their own subtly seductive acts, or those acts may be misunderstood. The male therapist has the extremely difficult task of not responding to a woman's loving overtures while still accepting, sustaining, and supporting her. Since human beings have difficulty compartmentalizing feelings, and since one person's caring is another person's loving, it is perhaps no wonder that he does not always succeed. I have even known situations where a woman needed to have a second therapy to recover from the unhappy passion aroused by her first therapy, turning the solution to her problem into a more serious problem. The boundaries between caring for someone, liking him, loving him, and passionately loving him are fine lines that are difficult to maintain. I have also known situations in which lesbian women had quite similar problems with their female therapists.

Some might say that the relationship with a caring, sensitive, and understanding man might give a woman who has been disappointed by men a chance to forgive men and to learn to love them, and there could be a point to that. On the other hand, the real goal of therapy is not to learn to love men, but to love oneself.

I also think that women are raised to protect men, and they have a very hard time getting angry at male therapists. Women are afraid to overwhelm men with their rage, whether it be murderous fantasies against the men in their lives or rational or irrational rage directed at the therapist. Many women have told me that it was very important to them not to hurt their therapist's feelings, even if he had upset them. When I have encouraged women to confront their male therapists with some major complaint, they have been unwilling to do so. They respond:

"He is very well-meaning and I don't want to hurt his feelings."

"He is just not the kind of person who could tolerate much anger."

"He might stop seeing me if I told him how much I sometimes hate him."

Women look up to men, but paradoxically they also often perceive them as weak, vulnerable, and in need of protection, especially from women's rage. Thus the probability is great that a woman will become an obedient and protective pseudodaughter, pseudomother, pseudowife, or pseudolover to her male therapist. I don't think men realize how protective women feel about them and how conscious women are of a woman's obligation to support the potentially fragile ego of the men whom she encounters. A woman in therapy with a man might end up taking emotional care of yet one more man in her life.

Finally, I believe women are more easily ashamed in front of men than in front of other women. Women clients might withhold issues that may cause embarrassment, humiliation, or shame when shared with a man. However this is only a guess, and it would be interesting to see whether it could be supported by research.

I know that many women, expressing typical minority-status self-contempt, prefer male therapists (Schwartz 1974), male pediatricians, and male obstetricians; but times are changing, and we hear from mental health clinics that many women request female therapists.

Yet other feminists will emphasize the need for certain attitudes in a therapist rather than gender. The increasing tendency to think that counselors need to be similar to clients in gender, race, religion, or sexual orientation is a little sad, narrowing the possibilities of potentially enriching explorations of human differences. Therapy at its best is a mutual learning experience, entailing openness, respect, and curiosity.

While women therapists can be models of competence and assertiveness, they also need to avoid certain traps. There is the danger of all too quick understanding, which blocks careful exploration. Overidentification might also lead to premature reassurance (indirect self-reassurance) and fear of exploring some of the more frightening aspects of certain experiences, such as rape or incest. McCombie (1975) warned:

In an effort to reduce stress, the counselor may inadvertently . . . [offer] reassurance [and] without giving the victim the opportunity to explore and master conflict, the counselor can end up fostering regression. . . . The counselor needs to be sensitive to feelings of shame and guilt. If left unattended, such feelings may lead to self-punitive acting out in an unconscious effort to expiate guilt or to bolster claim to legitimate victimization. (p. 156)

Another possible temptation for women therapists is getting angry on behalf of the client. Women must be allowed to feel and express their own rage, even if it is not directed at the "true enemy," but, for example, at other women. A feminist counselor may be "distressed by the frequent histories of indifference, hostility, and cruelty in the mother-daughter relationship. She may find herself rushing to the defense of the mother, pointing out that the mother herself was a victim" (Herman and Hirschman 1977, p. 755). It might be similarly painful for a feminist counselor to listen and give credibility to mutual betrayals among straight and lesbian women. They do happen. Intimacy is difficult not only between men and women, but in all close, intense relationships. Political ideologies must not be allowed to pervert therapeutic needs.

Both Menaker (1974) and Nichols (1977) commented on the frequently deeply distorted relationship between mother and daughter in our society; they suggested that some women may need substitute mothering that is neither hostile nor suffocating and allows for the experience of both nurturance and gradual differentiation. Women therapists could be ideally suited to be such new kinds of mothers, who give their clients/daughters permission to be autonomous and strong.

I look forward to a time when counseling of men and women by women and men will be attuned to the particular needs of the other gender. There will be knowledge, respect, and delight in the other's differentness. Feminist counseling may be a transitional phenomenon, but it will have charted the way.

References

Asch, S. (1955). "Opinions and social pressure." *Scientific American* 31–5.

Barbach, L. G. (1975). *For Yourself: The Fulfillment of Female Sexuality.* New York: Doubleday.

Bell, A. P., and Weinberg, M. S. (1978). *Homosexualities.* New York: Simon and Schuster.

Belle, D. (1980). "Mothers and their children: A study of low-income families." In C. L. Heckerman (Ed.). *The Evolving Female.* New York: Human Sciences Press.

Bequaert, L. (1976). *Single Women, Alone and Together.* Boston: Beacon Press.

Berlin, S. (1976). "Better work with women clients." *Social Work* 21(6):492–97.

Berman, E. (1973). *Scapegoat. The Impact of Death Fear on an American Family.* Ann Arbor: University of Michigan Press.

Bernard, J. (1972). *The Future of Marriage.* New York: World.

——. (1974). *The Future of Motherhood.* New York: Dial.

Bleier, R. (1979). "Social and political bias in science: An examination of animal studies in their generalization to human behavior and evolution." In R. Hubbard and M. Lowe (Eds.). *Genes and Gender.* New York: Gordian Press, pp. 49–69.

Blumstein, P., and Schwartz, P. (1976). "Bisexuality in women." *Archives of Sexual Behavior* 5(2):171–81.

Carmody, D. (1979). "Letters by Eleanor Roosevelt detail friendship with Lorena Hickock." *The New York Times,* Oct. 21, p. 34.

Campbell, A. (1975). "The American way of mating." *Psychology Today* 9:37–43.

Chesler, P. (1971). "Women and psychiatric and psychotherapeutic patients." *Journal of Marriage and Family* 33:746–59.

——. (1972). *Women and Madness.* Garden City, N.Y.: Doubleday.

Combs, T. D. (1980). "A cognitive therapy for depression: Theory, techniques and issues." *Social Casework* 61 (6):361–66.

Deutsch, H. (1944). *Psychology of Women.* vol. 1. New York: Grune and Stratton.

——. (1945). *Psychology of Women.* vol. 2. New York: Grune and Stratton.

Diamond, L. (1979). *The Lesbian Primer.* Somerville, Mass.: Women's Educational Media.

Dinnerstein, D. (1976). *The Mermaid and the Minotaur.* New York: Harper and Row.

Dodson, B. (1974). *Liberating Masturbation.* New York: Betty Dodson.

Fraiberg, S. (1977). *Every Child's Birthright: In Defense of Mothering.* New York: Basic Books.

Freud, S. (1933). "The psychology of women." In *New Introductory Lectures on Psychoanalysis.* Lecture 33. In J. Strachey (Ed.). *Standard Edition of the Complete Psychological Works of Sigmund Freud.* vol. 22. London: Hogarth Press, 1957.

Gambril, E. D., and Richey, C. A. (1980). "Assertion training for women." In C. L. Heckerman (Ed.). *The Evolving Female.* New York: Human Sciences Press.

Gebhard, P. (1970). "Postmarital coitus among widows and divorcees." In P. Bohannon (Ed.). *Divorce and After.* New York: Doubleday.

Gilligan, C. (1982). *In a Different Voice.* Cambridge: Harvard University Press.

Goldner, V. (1985). "Warning: Family therapy may be hazardous to your health." *Family Therapy Networker* 3:19–23.

Goodman, E. (1980). "Portrait: Joan Kennedy." *Life* 5:29–30.

Goodstein, R. K., and Page, A. W. (1981). "Battered wife syndrome. Overview of dynamics and treatment." *American Journal of Psychiatry* 138(8):1036–43.

Gove, W. R., and Tudor, J. F. (1972). Adult sex roles and mental illness." *American Journal of Sociology* 78:812–35.

Greenspan, M. (1983). *A New Approach to Women and Therapy.* New York: McGraw-Hill.

Hare-Mustin, R. T. (1978). "A feminist approach to family therapy." *Family Process* 17(2):181–94.

Herman, J. and Hirschman, L. (1977). "Father-daughter incest." *Signs* 2:735–50.

Henry, J. (1965). *Pathways to Madness.* New York: Random House.

Hite, S. (1976). *The Hite Report.* New York: Macmillan.

Horney, K. (1926). "The flight from womanhood." In J. Strouse (Ed.). *Women and Analysis* New York: Grossman, 1974, pp. 171–86.

——. (1935). "The problem of feminine masochism." *Psychoanalytic Review* 12:241–57.

Hubbard, R., and Lowe, M. (1979). "Introduction." In R. Hubbard and M. Lowe (Eds.). *Genes and Gender.* New York: Gordian Press, pp. 9–34.

Huyck, M. H. (1977). "Sex and the older woman." In L. E. Troll, J. Israel, and K. Israel (Eds.). *Looking Ahead.* Englewood Cliffs, N.J.: Prentice-Hall.

Johnson, P. (1976). "Women and power: Toward a theory of effectiveness." *Journal of Social Issues* 32:99–110.

Justice, B., and Justice, R. (1976). *The Abusing Family.* New York: Human Sciences Press.

Kinsey, A. C., et al. (1948). *Sexual Behavior in the Human Male.* Philadelphia: Saunders.

——, et al. (1953). *Sexual Behavior in the Human Female.* Philadelphia: Saunders.

Kirsch, B. (1974). "Consciousness-raising groups as therapy for women." In V. Franks and V. Burtle (Eds.). *Women in Therapy.* New York: Brunner/Mazel.

Kohut, H. (1973). "Thoughts on narcissism and narcissistic rage." In R. Eissler, et al. (Eds.). *The Psychoanalytic Study of the Child.* vol. 27. New York: Quadrangle.

Krause, C. (1971). "The femininity complex and women therapists." *Journal of Marriage and the Family* 33(3):476–82.

Laing, R. D., and Esterson, A. (1964). *Sanity, Madness and the Family: Families of Schizophrenics.* London: Tavistock.

Langs, R. (1974). *The Technique of Psychoanalytic Therapy.* vol. 2. New York: Jason Aronson.

Lasch, C. (1977). *Haven in a Heartless World. The American Family Besieged.* New York: Basic Books.

Lazarre, J. (1976). *The Mother Knot.* New York: Dell.

Lemkau, J. P. (1980). "Women and employment: Some emotional hazards." In C. L. Heckerman (Ed.). *The Evolving Female.* New York: Human Sciences Press.

Lerner, H. (1983). "Female dependency in context." *American Journal Orthopsychiatry* 53(4):697–705.

Lipman-Blumen, J. (1976). "The implications for family structure of changing sex-roles." *Social Casework* 57(2):67–79.

Loewenstein, S. (1977). "An overview of the concept of narcissism." *Social Casework* 58(3):136–42.

Loewenstein, S. F. (1978a). "An overview of some aspects of female sexuality." *Social Casework* 59(2):106–15.

———. (1978b). "Preparing social work students for life-transition counseling within the human behavior sequence." *Journal of Education for Social Work* 14(2):66–73.

———. (1979). "Inner and outer space in social casework." *Social Casework* 60(1):19–29.

———. (1980a). "Toward choice and differentiation in the midlife crises of women." In C. L. Heckerman (Ed.). *The Evolving Female.* New York: Human Sciences Press.

———. (1980b). "Understanding lesbian women." *Social Casework.* 61(1): 28–39.

———. (1985). "On the diversity of love object orientations among women." In M. Valentich and J. Gripton (Eds.). *Feminist Perspectives on Social Work and Human Sexuality.* New York: Haworth Press, pp. 7–24.

———, et al. (1983). *Fathers and Mothers in Midlife.* Masters thesis, Simmons College School of Social Work.

———, et al. (1981). "A study of satisfactions and stresses of single women in midlife." *Sex Roles* 11:1127–41.

Lowenthal, M. F., Thurnher, M., and Chiraboga, D. (1975). *Four Stages of Life.* San Francisco: Jossey-Bass.

Lystad, M. H. (1975). "Violence at home: A review of the literature." *American Journal of Orthopsychiatry* 45(3):328–45.

Maccoby, D., and Jacklin, D. (1974). *The Psychology of Sex Differences.* Stanford: Stanford University Press.

Marecek, J., and Kravetz, D. (1977). "Women and mental health: A review of feminist change efforts." *Psychiatry* 40:323–29.

Masters, W. H., and Johnson, V. (1966). *Human Sexual Response.* Boston: Little, Brown.

McBride, A. B. (1973). *The Growth and Development of Mothers.* New York: Harper and Row.

McCombie, S. L. (1975). "Characteristics of rape victims seen in crisis intervention." *Smith College Studies in Social Work* 46:137–58.

Mead, M. (1977). Comment made during a talk at the Harvard School of Public Health, April 7.

Menaker, E. (1974). "The therapy of women in the light of psychoanalytic theory and the emergence of a new view." In V. Franks and V. Burtle (Eds.). *Women in Therapy.* New York: Brunner/Mazel.

Metzger, D. (1976). "It is always the woman who is raped." *American Journal of Psychiatry* 133:405–12.

Milgram, S. (1974). *Obedience to Authority.* New York: Harper and Row.

Mitchell, J. (1974). *Psychoanalysis and Feminism.* New York: Pantheon.

Nadelson, C. C. (1978). "The emotional impact of abortion." In M. T. Notman and C. C. Nadelson (Eds.). *The Woman Patient.* New York: Plenum Press.

Nichols, B. B. (1977). "Motherhood, mothering and casework." *Social Casework* 58:29–35.

Parkes, C. M. (1971). "Psycho-social transitions: A field for study." *Journal of Social Science and Medicine* 5:101–15.

Rabkin, R. (1970). *Inner and Outer Space.* New York: Norton.

Radl, S. (1973). *Mother's Day is Over.* New York: Charterhouse.

Radloff, L. (1975). "Sex differences in depression: The effects of occupation and marital status." *Sex Roles* 1(3):249–65.

Radov, C. G., Masnick, B., and Hauser, B. (1977). "Issues in feminist therapy: The work of a women's study group." *Social Work* 22(6): 507–11.

Reid, W. J., and Shapiro, B. (1969). "Client reaction to advice." *Social Service Review* 43(2):165–73.

Reik, T. (1944). *A Psychologist Looks at Love.* New York: Farrar and Rinehart.

Reuben, D. (1969). *Everything You Always Wanted to Know about Sex but Were Afraid to Ask.* New York: Bantam.

Rich, A. (1976). *Of Woman Born.* New York: Norton.

Riess, B. (1974). "New viewpoints on the female homosexual." In V. Franks and V. Burtle (Eds.). *Women in Therapy.* New York: Brunner/Mazel.

Rubin, L. (1979). *Women of a Certain Age.* New York: Harper and Row.

Russell, M. N. (1984). *Skills in Counseling Women.* Springfield, Ill.: Thomas.

Saghir, M. T., and Robins, E. (1973). *Male and Female Homosexuality.* Baltimore: Williams and Wilkins.

Sameroff, A. J. (1976). "Early influences on development: Fact or fancy?" In S. Chess and A. Thomas (Eds.). *Annual Progress in Child Psychiatry and Child Development.* New York: Brunner/Mazel.

Schwartz, M. C. (1974). Importance of the sex of worker and client." *Social Work* 19(2):177–85.

Seaman, B. (1972). *Free and Female. The Sex Life of the Contemporary Woman.* New York: Coward, McCann and Geoghegan.

Seiden, A. M. (1978). "The sense of mastery in the childbirth experience." In M. T. Notman and C. C. Nadelson (Eds.). *The Woman Patient.* New York: Plenum Press.

Singer, J. (1973). *Goals of Human Sexuality.* New York: Norton.

Slater, P. (1970). *The Pursuit of Loneliness.* Boston: Beacon.

Star, S. L. (1979). "Methods, limits and problems in research on consciousness." In R. Hubbard and S. Lowe (Eds.). *Genes and Gender.* New York: Gordian Press.

Stoller, R. J. (1974). "Facts and fancies: An examination of Freud's concept of bisexuality." In J. Strouse (Ed.). *Women and Analysis.* New York: Grossman.

Sullivan, H. S. (1953). *The Interpersonal Theory of Psychiatry.* New York: Norton.

Szasz, T. (1970). *The Manufacture of Madness.* New York: Harper and Row.

Taggart, M. (1985). "The feminist critique in epistemological perspective: Questions of context in family therapy." *Journal of Marital and Family Therapy* 11:113–26.

Thomas, S. A. (1977). "Theory and practice in feminist therapy." *Social Work* 22(6):447–54.

Weissman, M. M. (1980). "The treatment of depressed women." In C. L. Heckerman (Ed.). *The Evolving Female.* New York: Human Sciences Press.

——, and Klerman, G. L. (1977). "Sex differences and the epidemiology of depression." *Archives of General Psychiatry* 34(1):98–111.

Welsey, D. (1975). "The women's movement and psychotherapy." *Social Work* 20(2):120–22.

Williams, E. F. (1976). *Notes of a Feminist Therapist.* New York: Dell.

Wortis, R. P. (1971). "The acceptance of the concept of the maternal role by behavioral scientists: Its effect on women." *American Journal of Orthospychiatry* 41(5):733–46.

Wrightsman, L. (1978). "The American trial jury on trial: Empirical evidence and procedural modifications." *Journal of Social Issues* 34:137–64.

18 / On Daughters and Fathers

ONCE upon a time there was a king to whom a daughter was born. At first he was sad that she was not a son, but the baby was so lovable, smiling at him when she was only a few weeks old, that after a while he forgave her for being only a girl and fell in love with her. Even though he had much work to do in the kingdom, he played with her every day, half an hour before she had to go to sleep. He threw her into the air and caught her safely in his strong arms, never did he let her fall. As she grew up, he read her beautiful stories, and soon she learned to read, and sometimes she was allowed to read stories to him as well. When she did, he gave her a big kiss and said: "Nobody reads stories the way you do." Once a month on Sunday, he had his big black horse and her little white pony saddled, and together they rode through the wild heather and the dark forests. He showed her everything that lived and grew in nature and taught her the names of different animals, flowers, and trees. The king was very proud of his little princess-daughter who did all she could to please him. Sometimes she was even allowed to sit next to him on his throne. The courtiers all admired her beautiful golden locks in order to flatter her father.

But as time went on and the princess found more interesting things to do, she grew tired of brushing her curls for hours every day. Besides she was used to having her own way, and so one day she just cut off all her curls.

"What have you done with my beautiful curls?" screamed the

king in sorrow and rage. "You have become ugly!" The princess looked at her father in shock and disbelief. He still looked liked her real father, and he had the same voice, yet it seemed as if a malicious magician had secretly exchanged him overnight, and he had turned into a wicked stepfather.

Now she was no longer allowed to sit on the throne next to him because her new father was ashamed that she no longer had such beautiful curls like all the other maidens in the land. Yet they continued to take rides together, especially during the yearly "King's Hunt" in the fall. But when the princess observed one year how harassed the poor does and stags were, being chased by dogs for hours, and what a cruel sport this was, she refused to participate in the hunt. Instead, she went into the village to makes speeches against hunts. After all, her father had taught her to love animals, and as a king's daughter she felt a duty to express her opinion.

The king now had to go hunting all alone, and some of his subjects even thought he was cruel to shoot deer. How sad, lonely, and betrayed he felt. It was true that his daughter had already failed him when she cut her curls, but never had he expected that she would criticize him in public and bring shame on her own family. He sought comfort with the queen, but since he had neglected her through the years, she could now no longer find any time for him.

The poor king. He could not bear to have his own daughter rebel against him. He banished her from the kingdom and expelled her into the world without a penny. The Kingdom was, in any case, in debt and so this was not altogether inconvenient.

From that day on the princess wandered through the world to look for her real father, the big, strong, clever, mighty father who had always caught her in his arms. It was hard to find such a wonderful man; besides, she was not sure whether the king was perhaps right and she was after all only an ugly, ungrateful girl. That doubt made her search more difficult. But she was a stubborn princess and she continued her quest perhaps even until today.

I had to invent a fairy tale myself because I could not find an authentic one in the literature. We read about witches and wicked stepmothers, but where are the stepfathers? Is it that way because men invented the old fairy tales, just like the men who wrote the Bible and decided that God created a man first?

In fairy tales and in modern literature, mothers have been thoroughly confronted with their multiple sins, but fathers have been relatively spared, especially by their daughters. After all, as Dworkin (1974) pointed out, the poor father of Hansel and Gretel was persuaded by his wicked wife to send the children into the forest, and he was overjoyed when they returned safe and sound. Cinderella's and Snow White's fathers as well cannot be blamed if their malicious wives persecuted their beautiful daughters. It is true we do find darker pictures of fathers in legends. There are fathers who order all their daughters' suitors killed because they cannot solve some riddles, but they do that only for their daughters' sake. No man is good enough. And if Agamemnon sacrificed Iphigenia to the gods, it was done for the sake of winning the war for his country. We know that no sacrifices are too great for winning wars.

I feel it is time that we daughters interrupt our usual complaints against our mothers for a few minutes and focus on our fathers. It is not my goal to insult men. I am personally surrounded by well-meaning men, and some of them may love me, although rarely in the way I want to be loved. I cannot hold these men responsible for my father's never having kissed me; for his not having been concerned about me; for his not having contributed to my education. Besides, I showed my father that I could make a place for myself in this world without his help. I am very invested in forgiving the men in my world. But before one forgives one has to have an opportunity to accuse, and this I wish to do for myself and for other daughters. I used as sources women's biographies and autobiographies, stories from friends and clients, and students' papers in which they write about their fathers. I shall thus express our love and our hatred, our disappointments, betrayals, and pity.

The psychological literature has been dominated by Freud's contention that little girls are in love with their fathers, and indeed, Freud, as the father of three adoring daughters, experienced this first hand. Later, he would choose a daughter over his sons to be his spiritual heir. His disciple Helene Deutsch (1945) suggested that a father's continuing love for his adolescent daughter is predicated on her renouncing her competitive strivings, and on a readiness to subordinate herself to men. "The bribe offered to the little girl by her father, as representative of the environment, is love and tenderness. For its sake she renounces any further intensification of her activity, most particularly her aggression" (p. 251). Deutsch wrote this thirty-five years ago. I hope circumstances have now changed.

More recently, the life cycle of the father-daughter relationship has been described by psychoanalyst Rudolph Ekstein (1980) in the following way. As a little girl the daughter feels herself unconditionally loved, prized, and admired. Her father awakens her sensuality for men by kissing her, caressing her, and holding her on his lap. Of course, a wise and caring mother is in the background to help maintain sexually appropriate boundaries at all times. As the daughter grows up, her father stands at her side, protects her against the injustices of the world, offers advice, and encourages her developing talents. He stimulates her intellectually and respects her opinions. He does all he can to support her independence and her autonomous plans. Later the roles change, and the daughter becomes a good mother for him, one who lovingly stands by at all times.

There are indeed daughters who speak of their fathers with love, respect, gratitude, and trust. No doubt these women have enviable marriages and brilliant careers. But for the great majority of daughters this story is only a daydream. Where does it fall apart, Ekstein's male fairy tale?

The father is an overpowering and formidable figure to his little daughter. He is not only a grown-up, one of the giants of her world; he is not only a parent on whom she is totally dependent; he is also a member of a superior gender to whom women look up. A boy is of course also deeply vulnerable to treatment by his parents, but as soon as he grows older he learns that his mother is only a woman and that he will one day grow up to be a giant like his father. This equalizes the power relationship with his mother to some extent. The father-daughter relationship is a model for the girl's future heterosexual relationships in terms of power, while the mother-son relationship does not serve similarly as a model. At least in this respect, a boy's dependency on the opinions of the parent of the opposite sex is somewhat less intense than a girl's. The daughter will never forget her early childhood and adolescent experiences with this shining knight. His feelings and attitudes toward her, verbally or nonverbally conveyed, will penetrate her bones and stay there and determine her fate, because self-esteem is fate.

One of the most painful relationships is with a father who is never available to his daughter. Whether he is overworked, avoids his family because of marital conflict, is otherwise preoccupied, or lacks the ability to love, his daughter will imagine in all cases that she is not worthy of his attention. In this category also belong the daughters who have grown up without fathers, or who have lost their fathers in childhood or youth through illness, war, or marital separation. Each generation seems to suffer from its own kind of father abandonment. Each situation is unique because of the differing reasons for the emotional and actual absence of the father. But being abandoned means being abandoned in the unconscious, whether the father was in charge of his own life or not. Among these daughters we find a common mourning for the lost or absent father, a common yearning to be loved, to be acknowledged, to be appreciated, by a father. "Dear daddy, please, please, write me soon," entreated Charlotte Perkins Gilman of her separated father in each of her childhood letters (Hill 1980). Such a yearning can become a leitmotif that the daughter can play out in many ways in her life, through her relationships or through her work. She may be forever seeking for this perfect father of her fantasy, or she may drive herself in her work, hoping to show herself worthy of her father's love, even after he has died.

Eleanor Roosevelt was ten years old when her father died from an alcohol-related accident. After the death of her mother, her father had written her many touching letters, in which he assured her of his ardent love and planned with her how the two of them would live together some day (Roosevelt 1937). Eleanor carried his letters with her throughout her life. He was the first man who betrayed her. Perhaps her husband's subsequent betrayal and her reaction to it are somehow connected to this earlier experience. Lash (1971, p. 58) thought that Eleanor's admirable life represented her effort to justify her father's belief in her.

Sylvia Plath seems never to have surmounted the grief that her father's death, when she was eight years old, had caused her. We do not know whether it contributed to her suicide as a young woman.

Some fathers do not find their little daughters pretty or clever, or they cannot love them, and that always seems to slip out. "Daddy, do you like my new dress?" "No, the strong color does not go with your pale complexion." "Daddy, I got the best grade in my class." "The other students must be really stupid." "Daddy, I am going dancing." "I am sorry for your partner's feet." It is hard to hold on to self-esteem if one seems devalued by a father who knows everything and is always right. One can either crawl into a hole or else set out on a lifetime of proving to one's father and other fathers that one is neither as stupid, ugly, or useless as he had always thought. At times these proofs can become very hard work, and in one's innermost self one wonders whether father was right, after all.

Why would a father hurt his little daughter's feelings in this way? Perhaps he displaces his self-doubts on her, or he projects his bad mother on her, or he is jealous of the relationship that she has with her mother, a relationship that may exclude him.

Most fathers, however, are tender and loving toward their little daughters. But when a daughter becomes adolescent, her father may begin to feel betrayed. He feels threatened by his daughter's awakening sexuality, meant for someone else, her new-found independence, and her new opinions. Simone de Beauvoir (1959), Margaret Mead (1972), Golda Meir (1975), Svetlana Alliluyeva (1967), and many other less well known women have described how their fathers, just as in my fairy tale, were suddenly transformed from supportive friends to harsh, disapproving enemies. Simone de Beauvoir (1959) expressed this transformation with particular eloquence:

As long as he approved of me I could be sure of myself. For years he had done nothing but heap praises on my head. But when I reached the awkward age, he was disappointed in me; he appreciated elegance and beauty in women (p. 113) . . . my father thought I was ugly and harbored resentment against me because of it (p. 118). . . . I kept wondering what I had done wrong (p. 200). . . . I had counted on his support, his sympathy, his approval; I was deeply disappointed when he withheld them from me (p. 201). . . . by adopting opinions and tastes that were at variance with his own, it seemed to him as if I were deliberately rejecting him (p. 201). . . . all he wanted was to find fault with me. (p. 203)

"Take a look at yourself. Who'd want you? You fool!" (Alliluyeva 1967, p. 181) Stalin screamed at his beloved "little housekeeper" when she fell in love with the wrong man. When Svetlana later decided to marry a Jewish man, Stalin cut off their relationship altogether.

What is the matter with these fathers who have to control their daughters at any price with an iron hand? In *Ghostwaltz* (1980), Ingeborg Day recounted how her self-righteous Nazi father absolutely forbade her to divorce her American husband. When she disobeyed him he cut her off forever without another word. He was a man of principles.

Conflicts are often expressed through money because it lends itself exceptionally well to the expression and manipulation of feelings. After all, it is usually the father who owns the money. Margaret Mead, Golda Meir, and Simone de Beauvoir, after receiving years of intellectual encouragement from their fathers, suddenly found that there was absolutely no money available for further education.

"It does not pay to be clever," Golda Meir's father warned her. "Men don't like smart girls" (Meir 1975, p. 41). Golda left home at age fifteen to live with her married sister and go to school. "In the two years I was to spend in Denver, my father, unforgiving, wrote me only once," she wrote in her autobiography (1975, p. 45). He later did forgive her and presumably grew proud of her.

It is sobering to hear how many women experience their fathers as extremely stingy. A friend of mine needed only a small amount of money to end her schooling, and she begged her father to help her, but he had a new wife and her needs proved to be more important than his daughter's. And what does a daughter think these days when a divorced father does not contribute any money to her support?

I first discussed the father who neglects his daughter, humiliates her, or abandons her in some way. Equally difficult are relationships with binding fathers. At first it is deeply gratifying to be spoiled by one's father, to receive so much time, attention, and maybe even gifts from this deified man. Eleanor Roosevelt's father sent her a pony to demonstrate his love for her; it is a pity that she was afraid of horses.

Sometimes such a father treats his daughter like a son. He starts very early to share his interests with her. We hear that Virginia Woolf (Bell 1972) discussed literature with her writer-father; Shirley Chisholm (Chisholm 1970) shared her father's political interests; and Jane Addams (Addams 1910) had a father who taught her above all to live by high ideals. Many well-known women had close, loving bonds with their fathers in childhood, and the nature of these bonds strongly influenced their later careers. Since there was up to the current generation of mothers a dearth of strong women models, it is not surprising that research finds that successful women experienced closeness to and a strong identification with their fathers (Henning 1973). There was also great pressure to achieve, since it would have been unthinkable to disappoint the father's expectations (Lozoff 1973). He may even have counted on his daughter to fulfill his own disappointed ambitions.

Such a relationship may be experienced as deeply gratifying and may remain a happy memory. Helene Deutsch (Deutsch 1973) ascribed her vanguard battle to get permission for women to study law at the University of Vienna to her love for and identification with her father. In her autobiography, written at the age of eighty, she proudly talked of his love. " . . . even before he knew whether the baby was a boy or girl, he had already fallen in love with the large radiant eyes looking up at him. For many years his enchantment persisted. He was devoted to me and accepted me fully, not as a substitute for a boy but as his spiritual heir, as well as his beloved girl with the beautiful eyes" (p. 38). Yet, even this father was angry at her efforts at liberation and turned away from her in early adolescence. Helene too was afraid of her intense tie to her father and left home early, soon after starting a love affair with an older man, a political leader.

This was fortunate for Helene Deutsch, because in the eyes of many daughters, no other man can ever measure up to her father. If the father is in reality an exceptionally brilliant and attractive man, like Sigmund Freud or Bertrand Russell, it could easily become a hopeless quest ever to find a match for him. This can be seen in the following passage, with which Bertrand Russell's daughter ended her book about her father. "He was the most fascinating man I have even known, the only man I ever loved, the greatest man I shall ever meet, the wittiest, the gayest, the most charming. It was a privilege to know him, and I thank God he was my father" (Tait 1975, p. 202).

In defense of rejecting fathers, fathers may be frustrated if they believe they have failed to shape their daughters into conforming and compliant women, as suggested by Helene Deutsch (1945). We can also imagine that rejection is the only way fathers can manage to free their daughters from bondage, or perhaps to protect them from their inappropriate sexual desires.

Indeed, there are fathers whose ardent love leads to selfish possessiveness and irrational hostility against all other relationships in their daughters' lives. The subject of sexual exploitation would lead us too far afield, but it is sometimes the natural result of such an exclusive, possessive father-daughter relationship. For such an exploitative father the daughter becomes merely a narcissistic extension whose main purpose is to meet his needs and wishes. She has no separate existence in the father's eyes. Such daughters can escape their fathers only with an abrupt and hostile break, which leaves guilt and pain. (Meiselman 1978; Brady 1979; Allen 1980).

Being a favorite daughter can thus be a mixed blessing. This situation often involves the mother, in that most intense relationships are part of an emotional triangle (Bowen 1976). The mother may be in the background or in the foreground; in either case she is a party to the father-daughter relationship. The daughter may feel that the father's needs preoccupy the mother at the daughter's expense (Mead 1972; Woolf 1927). In other frequent situations daughters bitterly accused their mothers of having barred access or otherwise alienated them from their fathers.

An especially painful situation arises if the daughter feels that she is loved at her mother's expense, which seems to occur quite often. Some men who grow up with an erratically "good" and "bad" mother, whom they can never learn to identify as one and the same mother, later need a good and bad woman in their lives. Such a man may shower his daughter with love, while he neglects or mistreats his wife. Sometimes the daughter may become entangled in an alliance, and lifelong hostility against her mother may follow. Helene Deutsch and Eleanor Roosevelt both felt that their fathers were victims of controlling, malicious mothers and that they themselves had secret pacts with their fathers. Some daughters are later saddened when they think in retrospect that their mothers were perhaps not as weak, unfair, or insignificant as they had seemed in their childhood. "My mother was dead for five years before I knew that I had loved her very much," wrote Lillian Hellman (1969, p. 7). And Svetlana Alliluyeva wrote, "She was afraid of spoiling me because my father petted and spoiled me enough as it was. Of course, we had no idea that we owed all our games and amusements, our whole happy childhood to her. We only realized it later when she was no longer there" (1967, p. 3). In a book in which German women write about their fathers, Ilona Lorincz (1979) wrote how much she loved her good-natured, cheerful, irresponsible father and how oppressed she felt by her eternally depressed and anxious mother, and then she added, "Only after I grew up did I recognize her reserved and quiet strength of character, her cleverness, her intelligence and kindness. . . . She was the rock of our family. It was she who enabled my father to follow his whims" (p. 77). Watching how her own father humiliates her mother with words, with unfaithfulness, or sometimes even with beatings can become increasingly unbearable to a growing daughter, and her acute loyalty conflict may end in hatred against both parents (Reinhold 1979). A client told me how her mother had given up on her father in disgust. When he came home drunk, the daughter had to get him to bed and sometimes had to sit with him in the kitchen, listening for hours to his self-pitying stories.

There are fathers who, sober or drunk, beat the whole family, mothers and children; daughters of these men live with the same dread and hatred as their mothers. Other fathers may not physically beat their families, but may terrorize and tyrannize wife and children emotionally, leaving their daughters with unforgettable repellent memories about how men behave.

Some alcoholic fathers win their daughters' hearts. Such a father may be charming and seductive while sober, playing and laughing with her, and bringing her gifts, even when there is nothing to eat in the house. Eleanor Roosevelt had such a charming father. Of course there was enough money in the family, and neither did she have to sit in the kitchen with him. Instead, he left her with doormen at fancy drinking clubs and forgot her there (Lash 1971, p. 51).

Shall we be angry at these men in our lives or pity them? I know that fathers are just one piece in a round world. Many of these fathers were treated badly by their mothers (and fathers?), suggesting that men and women participate in their common betrayals. Fathers may act badly because they are unemployed, or they suffer from haunting war memories, or they are treated with contempt by the outside world. Even if a father counts nowhere else, he is boss in his own family, and there at least he can act out his rage unpunished.

Pity is a saving and yet a treacherous force. Men exploit women's capacity to feel pity for the men they love. When their wives die, strong fathers suddenly become lost and helpless. They clutch at their daughters, as Virginia Woolf's father did, with the expectation of being cared for. Even if the father was unjust, stingy, drunk, brutal, or sexually seductive, he is now a poor old man who needs his daughter to love and nurture him, and rarely will she deny him such help. He is her father and she wants to love him and be loved by him. Indeed, in old age there may be a last chance for this to happen.

When I was a young woman I felt deeply sorry for my father, who had been disappointed by life in many ways. I dreamed that

I would some day take very good care of him. For years, during the war, I saved my lunch money to send him food packages to Europe. He regularly wrote back: "It is raining; I do not feel well; could you not send me some smoked sausage that is less salty?" After many years I turned my back on him. We no longer corresponded during the last years of his life. One day they wrote me that he had died, and I never looked up from reading student papers. I had gotten over my need to play Cordelia to old King Lear. These are cynical words meant to hide my pain and regret that I abandoned my father in his old age.

What happens to the many daughters whose fathers did not love them well enough? I have already touched on a few situations, but each daughter finds her own solution. Daughters who were too deeply betrayed by their fathers or too outrageously exploited seem fated to hate men. Such hatred can be expresed in many different ways. There are daughters who will "fall in love" with equally exploitative, abusive men and amass ever more justification for their hatred; some other daughters will enjoy controlling men and competing with them; others will express their rage freely and directly; and there are yet other daughters who turn their backs on men, preferring women in work and in love. (Meiselman 1978).

We have learned that everyone identifies to some extent with both parents, even in very hostile relationships. We find daughters who are as diligent and ambitious, or others who also take to drinking, just like their fathers (Beckman 1975). Other daughters are more identified with their mothers and find a similar husband, one who admires and respects them, or who drinks and beats them (Hanks and Rosenbaum 1977; Beckman 1975).

There are also women who seek a relationship that is the opposite of the one their mothers or they themselves had experienced. The father was a tyrant, and they marry submissive men. The father was a drunkard and they find very sober husbands. The father was a philanderer and they marry faithful and devoted men. They may feel safe and well cared for initially, but they may soon find the relationship dull, empty, and passionless. They long for the charming scoundrel who had brought so much color and excitement into their childhood.

In spite of what Freud (1914) thought, being loved is after all not the only important thing for women. There is also the problem of being able to love. Feelings of love and passion for the opposite gender grow out of intense love experiences of childhood. If love was connected with sadness and yearning, with the feelings of being badly treated, with being neglected, betrayed, or perhaps even beaten, then it becomes difficult to love a kind and considerate man. Of course it is not difficult for such daughters to find men who will treat them as badly as their fathers did.

The fairy tale I told earlier described the ardent love between daughter and father in her childhood, and how the gradual independence of the daughter hurt the father very deeply and moved him to abandon her. The daughter then became very unhappy and unsure of herself; yet she could draw on her picture of that early blissful relationship, and this might have helped her to find it again.

My friends have reproached me that this is a harsh and unforgiving essay. Yet after expressing rage, we get in touch with our love and we are able to forgive.

Ten years after my father died I came across May Stevens' (1977) article on her work and her working-class father. She had painted a series of ugly pictures around the figure she called Big Daddy in which she expressed her hatred for our patriarchal society and the values for which her father had stood. "The portrait of my father, undershirted, before a blank TV screen turned eventually into a symbol of American complicity in Southeast Asia" (1977, p. 113). Here is an excerpt from the poem "Letters from Home," which she wrote upon her father's death.

MY FATHER TIED PACKAGES WITH WHITE WAXED STRING IN A SMALL TIGHT NET KNOTTED AT EVERY INTERSECTION SO THAT YOU WERE SURPRISED WHEN BEING CUT OPEN THE STRING CASE DID NOT STAND ALONE. THEY BORE ME PRESENTS THOSE BOXES CAUGHT IN STRING CANNED GOODS TO PARIS FEAST FOR POOR STUDENTS ELECTRIC BLANKETS ENERGY GONE PILLED WOOL PENCILS SAYING BETHLEHEM

STEEL COTTON DUCK STOLEN FROM HIS PLACE
OF WORK FOR ME TO PAINT ON BOXES OF JELLO
CONDENSED MILK. AND ONCE HE ARRIVED IN
QUEENS IN THE DEAD OF NIGHT WITH AN OLD
WASHING MACHINE WITH WRINGER ON TOP. HE
HAD A NEW ONE. . . .

I cried. By then I had found letters in my mother's estate in which my own father expressed concern for my well-being. My mother had never shown me those letters. By then people had told me that he had talked about me in loving words. I had not known that. My father and my life had parted ways when I was fourteen years old. I did not feel his protective presence during the war years in Europe. It felt as if he did not care enough, yet in truth, he was powerless to help. He did not help me to get an education. It felt as if he did not care enough, yet he may have been as poor as I was. My father passed his law examination in Vienna with great distinction, an unusual honor. He was apparently a man of intelligence and talent. He had wanted to be a writer and had written two books, which received no recognition. How hard it must have been for my father to be the son of Sigmund Freud and still grow into a man of substance and self-respect. My heart tightens with pain when I think of my father's hurts.

I had to look up the date of his death in a book someone had written about his father. It was in 1967. Thirteen years later I went to London, where he had lived and died, and I started the long and painful task of mourning and reconciliation. This essay is one step, albeit an angry one, in this process.

References

Addams, J. (1910). *Twenty Years at Hull House*. New York: Macmillan.
Allen, C. V. (1980). *Daddy's Girl. A Memoir*. New York: Wyndham Books.

Alliluȷ va, S. (1967). *Twenty Letters to a Friend.* (Translated by Priscilla Johnson). New York: Harper and Row.

Beckman, L. J. (1975). "Women alcoholics: A review of social and psychological studies." *Journal of Studies on Alcohol* 36:797–820.

Bell, Q. (1972). *Virginia Woolf.* New York: Harcourt Brace Jovanovich.

Bowen, M. (1976). "Theory in the practice of psychotherapy." In P. Guerin (Ed.). *Family Therapy.* New York: Gardner Press.

Brady, K. (1979). *Father's Days.* New York: Seaview Books.

Chisholm, S. (1970). *Unbought and Unbossed.* New York: Houghton Mifflin.

Day, I. (1980). *Ghostwaltz. A Memoir.* New York: Viking.

de Beauvoir, S. (1959). *Memoirs of a Dutiful Daughter.* New York: World.

Deutsch, H. (1945). *The Psychology of Women.* vol. 2. New York: Grune and Stratton.

——. (1973). *Confrontations with Myself.* New York: Norton.

Dworkin, A. (1974). *Woman Hating.* New York: Dutton.

Ekstein, R. (1980). "Daughters and lovers." In M. Kirkpatrick (Ed.). *Women's Sexual Development.* New York: Plenum Press.

Freud, S. (1914). "On narcissism. An introduction." *Standard Edition.* vol. 14. London: Hogarth Press, 1957.

Hanks, S. E., and Rosenbaum, C. (1977). "Battered women: A study of women who live with violent alcohol-abusing men." *American Journal of Orthopsychiatry* 47(2):291–306.

Hellman, L. (1969). *An Unfinished Woman. A Memoir.* Boston: Little, Brown.

Henning, M. M. (1973). "Family dynamics for developing positive achievement motivation in women: The successful woman executive." *Annals New York Academy of Sciences* 208:76–81.

Hill, M. (1980). *Charlotte Perkins Gilman.* Philadelphia: Temple University Press.

Lang, M. (1979). "Hundertprotzentig." ("One-hundred percent-wise"). In M. Lang (Ed.). *Mein Vater.* (My Father). Reinbeck bei Hamburg, Germany: Rowohlt.

Lash, J. (1971). *Eleanor and Franklin.* New York: Norton.

Lorincz, I. (1979). "Stecknadel in der Seele." ("Pin in the soul"). In M. Lang (Ed.). *Mein Vater.* (My Father). Reinbeck bei Hamburg, Germany: Rowohlt.

Lozoff, M. (1973). "Fathers and autonomy in women." *Annals New York Academy of Sciences* 208:91–97.

Mead, M. (1972). *Blackberry Winter. My Earlier Years.* New York: Morrow.

Meir, G. (1975). *My Life.* New York: Putnam.

Meiselman, K. C. (1978). *Incest.* San Francisco: Jossey-Bass.

Reinhold, C. (1979). "Der Spieler." ("The player"). In M. Lang (Ed.). *Mein Vater.* Reinbeck bei Hamburg, Germany: Rowohlt.

Roosevelt, E. (1937). *This is My Story.* New York: Harper and Row.

Stevens, M. (1977). "My work and my working-class father." In S. Ruddick and P. Daniels (Eds.). *Working It Out*. New York: Pantheon.

Tait, K. (1975). *My Father Bertrand Russell*. New York: Harcourt Brace Jovanovich.

Woolf, V. (1927). *To the Lighthouse*. New York: Harcourt Brace, and World.

19 / The Heirloom

SHE was at first quite surprised to be asked whether she knew anything about a certain Abigail Harrison, who had been analyzed by her famous grandfather in Vienna. She had once read some interesting articles by a psychoanalyst of that name, but had not known that the writer had been analyzed by her grandfather. How absurd that people expected her to know her grandfather's patients. But then Harrison's biographer, a woman academician like herself, wrote to her suggesting cautiously and tactfully that the woman might also have been her father's friend. That changed the situation. Suddenly the Daughter heard her mother's voice spitting out the name of Harrison with venom, that bitch Harrison her mother would say, although she had said it in German.

Wishing to help a colleague, the Daughter wrote to the biographer communicating this memory. The biographer needed to know whether Abigail Harrison and the daughter's father "did or didn't." It seemed to be of the essence to find that out. The Daughter had taken it for granted that her father must have had a florid love affair with that woman Harrison, who had been one of the evil, unknown figures of her childhood, and she wondered why the biographer seemed so hesitant to accept that as a fact. Just a few years before her death, her own mother had told another biographer dealing with her grandfather and his network that her husband had had an affair with one of his father's patients. She had undoubtedly referred to this Harrison affair. It had thus become established that her father had had love affairs with his father's patients. Why dispute facts?

The Daughter became intrigued with the possibility of revising history. She wrote to her old Fraeulein in Vienna, who was the only person alive who might know what had really happened. Fraeulein seemed doubtful. She reported that they had gone mountain climbing together, but that the Harrison woman had been positively ugly and thus was definitely not her father's type. The Daughter did not know whether her Fraeulein had ever seen Abigail Harrison, or whether this was another secondhand opinion. She now remembered how Harrison's unappealing looks had also been mentioned in her childhood. An ugly, rich American, that had been Abigail Harrison's identity. The Daughter could even evoke her impression that her father's interest in that Harrison woman was motivated by her money.

Fraeulein's response had seeded doubts in the Daughter's mind. Without further evidence, the case had remained open. Some time later, the biographer had the incredible good fortune to come upon a package of letters in Abigail Harrison's estate, including some letters that the Daughter's father had written to her after she left Vienna, before and up to the time of the Anschluss. The biographer wanted to know whether the Daughter saw these as the letters of a lover or a friend. It was a strange experience for the Daughter to read these letters that her father had written to a woman to whom he seemed to have turned for solace in times of hardship and loneliness. The Daughter remembered her father as a man with a talent for self-pity, and she herself had received many letters from him with similar themes of bad weather, concerns about his health, and money worries. But his letters to her had been devoid of the deep affection apparent in the letters to Abigail Harrison. The latter were indeed love letters, but not in the conventional sense. Could it be possible that her philandering father, that lifelong playboy, had actually loved a woman to whom he was not sexually connected? Her father's older sister had once before her death told the Daughter that her father had loved neither his own mother, his wife, his sisters, nor his children. He had loved only himself. Perhaps her aunt had been wrong after all, perhaps she had only felt personally rejected and was therefore angry and unfair. His younger sister had never said such condemning things.

At the end of the academic year, the biographer took a three-hour drive to the Daughter's home to discuss the matter of Abigail Harrison's sexual life once again. The biographer explained to the Daughter that Abigail Harrison had been greatly loved by all her students and colleagues, who had given the biographer interviews as one way of honoring the memory of their beloved teacher, colleague, or friend. The biographer felt that she owed it to all those people to do justice to her subject. The Daughter could see in the biographer another woman as conscientious and attentive to details as she was herself. She also realized that Abigail Harrison had been loved and respected by her students in the same way that she felt connected to her own students, and she started to feel a spiritual sisterhood with this woman who may or may not have had sexual relations with her father.

The Daughter kept on the upper shelf of her bookcase, which covered the whole width of her large living room, the collected works of her grandfather, along with all the single books by him in various editions that she had inherited from her mother. She took down a well-worn book in a blue-green hardcover, one of two in its edition, labeled with her grandfather's name, and the title of *Vier Krankengeschichten* (Four Case Histories). The first few pages dealt with the history of the Schreber case, but the rest of the pages were blank, covered with pasted-in photographs of beautiful women. It was the book in which her father collected his lovers. Perhaps as a publisher of his father's books, her father could produce such a disguised book. The Daughter thought she and the biographer could examine it together to see whether Abigail Harrison was included in the collection.

The Daughter explained to the biographer that her parents' departure from Vienna coincided with their decision to break up their marriage. The two children were distributed between father and mother, and she and her mother went from Vienna to Paris, while her father and her brother went with the famous grandfather and his whole family to London. The family goods had been shipped to Paris as a first station, and while the plan had been to ship on her father's share to London, her mother had not followed that plan but had kept everything in Paris. It was in this shipping of furniture and other possessions that this particular book had fallen into her mother's hands. The Daughter remembered when her mother, who never spared her much, had shown her that book. But she had been only fourteen years old at the time, and had both forgotten and not forgotten about it. After her mother's death, going through her old letters, the Daughter had found an angry letter from her father, demanding his photobook back. But the mother had kept the book faithfully all her life, and when the Daughter went through her mother's books she had found it. Now she kept the book just as faithfully in her own bookcase, among her grandfather's books.

On the inside cover of the book was a blue letter, which her mother had stored in that book, and which the Daughter continued to keep there. It was a letter addressed by a woman to her father just after he had left Vienna. The letter too had gone via Paris by express mail, been intercepted by her mother, and never reached its destination.

"What a desperately heartbroken letter" the biographer said after they had read it together. The Daughter was puzzled about that reaction. Even now, forty-six years later, the feelings of the bereft woman who had written that letter were a matter of no consequence to her. The Daughter remembered her mother's intense rage when reading this letter to her. It meant that her father had been involved in a passionate love affair in the middle of the catastrophe of the Anschluss when, as the Daughter well knew, her mother had risked her own life to protect him. The Daughter, who had just ended a forty-year-long marriage, was hardly an expert on love letters, yet she thought that it was as desperate and passionate a love letter as could possibly be written. It was certainly not the kind of letter that her father had written to Abigail Harrison. Of course it was a letter he had received, rather than one he had written.

It was impossible to tell which photo, if any, belonged to that love letter. There were women there in all poses, mostly blonde, in contrast to her own and her mother's black hair. They were mostly fully dressed, although quite a few wore bathing suits. Her father must have enjoyed going to the beach with his women lovers. Her father was included in a few of the photos. In one photo he carried a woman in his arms, and in another photo a woman rode on his shoulders, again in bathing suits, on the beach. The biographer was amazed how the Daughter's father had been able to collect so many beautiful women. The Daughter explained how her father's older sister had also told her that her father could not go down the street without women turning around. It was the Daughter's opinion that her chaste and ascetic grandfather had delegated the fulfillment of sexual pleasure to his oldest son. Finally they found two photos that the biographer tentatively identified as being Abigail Harrison, loosely filed at the end of the book, rather than being pasted in like most of the other photos. She was not in a bathing suit. In one photograph Abigail Harrison's enigmatic expression was framed by a black cloak and a Garboesque hat, and in the other she posed stolidly in a Viennese dirndl. In neither of the photos did the Daughter recognize the rich ugly American of her mother's vituperations. The biographer borrowed the two pictures to identify them more surely.

"What happened to your father after all these romantic adventures?" the biographer asked. "When he was sixty years old he hired a thirty-year-old woman of modest education to be a clerk in his store. She had come to London to seek her fortune. Soon after, he asked her to come and live with him, and she ended up taking care of his store, his house, and eventually when he got ill, of his old body. Unlike his wife, she had no personal ambitions, no particular pretensions, and happened to be a warm and loving woman who wanted only to take good care of him. Although she was only half his age, she became his good and caring mother, perhaps a much better mother than his original one, not to mention his demanding, spendthrift, and ambitious wife." The Daughter reflected that her father's mistress, with all her modesty and submission, had had more pride than her own mother. When she had sought out the mistress ten years after her father's death, she had been welcomed with much affection, perhaps especially because she looked like her father. The mistress had told her with pride that her father had announced one day that he would not be home for dinner because one of his old flames was in town. She had told him not to look for her when he did come home. The Daughter's father had either loved his young mistress too much to let her go, or his adventures had become less essential to him. In any case, he had chosen to come home that evening ready to be taken care of in full comfort for the rest of his life.

The Daughter reflected how wounding it must have been for her mother to find a book like that. It had been a major goal of her own young womanhood to find a husband who would not produce a similar book. To her mother's deep satisfaction she had married an antifather, a man who was totally loyal and faithful and would treat her with respect. But he had not evoked her deepest passion; as the years went by her attention became absorbed in her work, which became much more compelling to her than his devotion. She felt that she had become a hard and unloving woman professor. Eventually her husband had found a warm and loving woman of modest education and no personal ambitions who wanted only to take good care of him. The Daughter knew that he had found his good and caring mother, perhaps a better mother than his original one, not to mention his ambitious and queenly wife. How strange that history should repeat itself in this particular way. But on a deeper level the Daughter knew that history had been in her hands, and that she had been above all a loyal daughter who had needed to share her mother's fate. It had never been in her life script to grow old with a man at her side.

The biographer must have seen how hard it had been for the Daughter to look at this book again, at this time in her life. As she turned the pages of photographs of blonde women and reread the passionate love letter to her father, she relived her mother's pain. The biographer put her arms around the Daughter's shoulders.

It came to the Daughter that she had found the answer to their common quest. The Daughter remembered how she had once loved a man the way Abigail Harrison must have loved her father. She had loved that man profoundly and expressed her love in many ways. Her future biographer might ask herself the same question about that relationship. "It is too bad," she said, "that the world dismisses love affairs that are not sexually consummated as unimportant, mere infatuations or fantasies. Abigail Harrison and my father didn't have a sexual affair, but they loved each other. Her love for him might well have been the great love of her life, and the absence of sex between them is almost irrelevant." The biographer laughed in relief. Her problem was solved. The Daughter walked outside to the car with her and they embraced each other to affirm their meeting.

Back in the house it was time to put the book away. The Daughter wondered to whom she would bequeath this heirloom. On the one hand, she should perhaps continue the tradition of passing down the book from mother to daughter, yet her son looked strikingly like her father, and she had noticed that women turned around when he strode through the streets. Perhaps the book should rightfully go to him, after all. Some day she would have to decide this.

20 / The Legacy of Anna Freud

I HAVE pondered for a long time what particular perspective would best illuminate Anna Freud's identity: her father's daughter, or a pioneer among feminists, a label she would have rejected. I am going to focus on that very conflict of her divided self. Was Anna Freud above all her father's daughter, or was she primarily her own woman?

No doubt this particular focus reverberates with conflicts in my own life. It is the problem of balancing loyalty and commitment to family and tradition with one's desire to strike out alone, stand on one's own feet, and raise an independent and perhaps even rebellious voice. This dilemma can become particularly acute when one is a member of a prominent family, but I think it is a universal conflict.

There are many people, for example, who are raised in a strong religious tradition or some other belief system that may appear less compelling as they grow older; yet to stray from the dogma will be experienced as a major betrayal by their kinship group. Others fervently join social movements or espouse an ideology, belong to a oppressed minority group or to a particular institution or community that may both give meaning and direction to their lives, yet may also lead to acute loyalty conflicts if disagreements with the "party line" should arise.

Women and men can moreover experience loyalty conflicts around parental legacies. Anna Freud's first independent and completely original contribution in 1936 was the formulation of a new defense mechanism called altruistic surrender. In it she offered, in an obviously autobiographical case example, a far-reaching glimpse into her own life script. There is no question that the young governess in the example is Anna Freud herself. I need to present this example of altruistic surrender to you, in excerpts, because it introduces our heroine and sets the stage for my major thesis.

A young governess reported in her analysis that, as a child, she was possessed by two ideas: she wanted to have beautiful clothes and a number of children. . . . But there were a great many other things that she demanded as well: she wished to have and to do everything that her much older playmates had and did—indeed, she wanted to do everything better than they and to be admired for her cleverness. Her everlasting cry of "Me too!" was a nuisance to her elders.

Remember that Anna was the youngest of six children in her family and the playmates are really her siblings.

What chiefly struck one about her as an adult was her unassuming character and the modesty of the demands which she made on life. When she came to be analyzed, she was unmarried and childless and her dress was rather shabby and inconspicuous. She showed little sign of envy or ambition and would compete with other people only if she were forced to do so by external circumstances. . . .
[Yet] When her life was examined in more detail, it was clear that her original wishes were affirmed in a manner which seemed scarcely possible if repression had taken place. The repudiation of her own sexuality did not prevent her from taking an affectionate interest in the love life of her women friends and colleagues. She was an enthusiastic matchmaker and many love affairs were confided to her. Although she took no trouble about her own dress, she displayed a lively interest in her friends' clothes.

"Your lovely dress matches your silvery hair," she would say admiringly as a greeting to me. No one had ever made me feel as beautiful as Tante Anna did.

Childless herself, she was devoted to other people's children, as was indicated by her choice of a profession. . . . Similarly, in spite of her own retiring behavior, she was ambitious for the men whom she loved and followed their careers with the utmost interest. . . . (II:125) The patient felt that the fact that she was a girl prevented her from achieving her ambitions, and, at the same time, that she was not even a pretty enough girl really to be attractive to men. In her disappointment with herself she displaced her wishes onto objects who she felt were better qualified to fulfill them. Her men friends were vicariously to achieve for her in professional life that which she herself could not achieve, and the girls who were better-looking than herself were to do the same in the sphere of love. Her altruistic surrender was a method of overcoming her narcissistic mortification (II:131). The analysis . . . revealed clearly . . . the formation of an exceptionally severe superego, which made it impossible for her to gratify her own wishes. Her penis wish, with its off-shoots in the shape of ambitious masculine fantasies, was prohibited, so too her feminine wish for children and the desire to display herself, naked or in beautiful clothes, to her father, and to win his admiration. But these impulses were not repressed: she found some proxy in the outside world to serve as a repository for each of them. (II:125)

Later in the chapter Anna Freud used this same mechanism of altruistic surrender to explain certain phenomena of the parent-child relationship:

We know that parents sometimes delegate to their children their projects for their own lives, in a manner at once altruistic and egoistic. It is as if they hoped through the child, whom they regard as better qualified for the purpose than themselves, to wrest from life the fulfillment of the ambitions which they themselves had failed to realize. Perhaps even the purely altruistic relation of a mother to her son is largely determined by such a surrender of her own wishes to the object whose sex makes him "better qualified" to carry them out. (II:131)

I believe Anna Freud's comments on a mother's needs to delegate life tasks to her son is a disguised reversal of her own experience.

Other writers (Stierlin 1977) have expanded the concept of delegation to include any urgent task, creative or destructive, pro- or antisocial, which a parent may pass on to a child. In this scheme parental delegates are children who are less free than others to choose their own paths, finding their inner peace only if they carry out their parental mission, perhaps at considerable sacrifice.

I thus want to examine to what extent Sigmund Freud's need to delegate the extension of his life's work to his daughter, and Anna Freud's readiness for altruistic surrender, shaped her life. To what extent was Anna Freud her father's loyal delegate, and to what extent did she find her own voice? What can we learn from her about solving this difficult human conflict between loyalty and independence? In the course of my effort to answer these questions, the reader will notice how I solved a similar conflict.

The issue of whether Anna Freud was primarily her father's daughter is inevitably raised in connection with her work. The verdict of her two biographers and her many admirers tends to be that she was much more than that. They call her a powerful and original theorist in her own right. She is praised for the clarity and rigor of her metapsychological thinking. After reading all eight volumes of her collected works, I have come to my own opinion.

Let me state at the outset that, unlike Anna Freud, I do not believe in objective observations, eternal verities, or absolute truths. I am not a psychoanalyst but a teacher of human development and psychological thought systems, and I can give you only a very personal, biased, and subjective opinion.

We must first remember the nature of Anna's bond with her father. He was her father, psychoanalyst, mentor, and prophet. To him, she was his daughter, colleague, secretary, alter ego, and intimate nurse during the sixteen years of his illness with cancer. No doubt she was the person he cherished most in the world. Rarely are two human beings connected in so many different, insoluble ways.

Anna had loved her father passionately and reverently since early childhood. We have another glimpse of little Anna's life from a reminiscence she confided in a letter to her lifelong friend, Muriel Gardiner. " . . . [This] happened on a summer holiday when the 'others' all went off in a boat and left me at home, either because the boat was too full or I was 'too little.' This time I did not complain and my father, who was watching the scene, praised me and comforted me. That made me so happy that nothing else mattered . . . "(Bulletin of the Hampstead Clinic 1983, p. 64).

It is my impression that nothing ever mattered to Anna Freud as much as gaining, maintaining, and preserving her father's love, respect, and his gratitude and hope in her.

People sometimes ask why Sigmund Freud, who had three talented sons, chose a daughter as his heir. Yet Freud offered the obvious answer: he needed someone who would nurture, protect, develop, and guard his most precious child, psychoanalysis. He naturally turned to a woman, a daughter, for this care-taking function. His was a very wise choice.

It is recorded that Freud started to discuss psychoanalysis with Anna formally during walks they took together when she was fourteen years old. I imagine that more informal talks or conversations about psychoanalysis were background music for Anna during her entire childhood. She thus absorbed the language, culture, and thought system of psychoanalysis by early adolescence. While she could shift with admirable ease, albeit regret and bitterness, from the German to the English language, she never needed nor wanted to transcend her other mother- or rather father-language of psychoanalysis.

We know that both language and culture can give form and direction to one's thoughts, while simultaneously blinding one to other perceptions. I shall try to document the areas in which I perceive Anna Freud to have been enchained, the areas in which she found herself in conflict between her theories and her observations, and the areas in which she threw off her shackles and demonstrated her incisive, penetrating mind and her most exceptional leadership qualities.

The Loyal Daughter

Most striking is that Anna Freud clung tenaciously to Freud's drive theory, the belief that human beings are motivated and driven by sexual and aggressive instincts, and the concomitant belief that the strengths of these instincts, the so-called economic factor, is one valid way of explaining varying emotional reactions and behavior. Against increasing evidence, Anna Freud continued to maintain that infants were initially withdrawn and self-contained and had to be lured through oral drive satisfaction to becoming attached to their mothers; or that the wish to learn or to play was a mere sublimation of libidinal or aggressive instincts.

Sigmund Freud naturally operated within the epistemology of instinct theories, energy mechanics, and linear causality prevalent in the scientific paradigm of the nineteenth century. Anna Freud, however, grew into maturity in a new scientific era. Her major professional growth took place in England, where proponents of the object relations school rejected the view of human beings as passive organisms driven by mysterious forces.

Object relations theory has been empirically validated, refined, and extended by very exciting modern infant research, which sees infants as born with the predisposition to relate to other human beings, to learn, to explore, and to look for meaningful patterns. It is quite possible, of course, to call such inborn predispositions instincts. Development is further postulated as a transactional circular process between an infant who is fully human and ready for social interactions from the day of birth, and his or her care taker.

Only Anna Freud's loyalty to her father can explain her disinterest in these findings of cognitive psychology and academic infant research. This neglect is all the more strange in a woman who vigorously wanted to create one child development-focused discipline in order to combat the segmental approaches to children's needs, and who declared herself ready to find a common language for this purpose.

Anna Freud's understanding of adolescence was also primarily tied, and in my opinion limited, by her overriding belief in the importance of libidinal drives. The thrust of her classical paper on adolescence deals with the adolescent's defense against the sudden onslaught of "quantitative increase in drive activity and drive quality" and his desperate defense against incestuous impulses. I say "his" because I am uncertain whether she included girls in this conceptualization. Not only is Anna Freud's emphasis here primarily on sexual development, bypassing adolescent concerns about identity development and dependency conflicts, but she also places all of adolescent pathology in the young people's inner space, with very little interest in their social environment. During a Hampstead Clinic discussion of a clinical presentation, she was troubled when some clinicians suggested that the source of pathology might be located in the adolescent's family, and she pointed out that the parents were clearly well-meaning, middle-class, and benevolent, overlooking that none of these qualities negated a possible pathological family system. Yet I shall demonstrate later that she often had very acute recognition of pathological family processes.

Anna Freud also showed little interest in the adolescent spurt in cognitive development or in Piaget's seminal ideas in general. Her own opinions on cognitive development could be viewed as simplistic, because she understood both the wish to learn and cognitive development as the derivative of or the defense against drive activities: " . . . The intensification of intellectuality during adolescence is simply part of the ego's customary endeavor to master the instincts by means of thought. . . . this would explain *the fact* (my emphasis) that instinctual danger makes human beings intelligent" (II:163–4).

Her adherence to drive theory also led Anna Freud to draw the same dichotomy as her father between individual and society and between the need for renunciation of instincts for the sake of civilization. She wrote that "socialization demands from the child a certain amount of alienation from and turning against what he feels legitimately to be his innermost self (VI:175) . . . it restricts, inhibits, and impoverishes his original nature" (VI:176). It is my view that children can survive only in a social and human environment that affects them from the moment of birth, and that the concept of original nature remains a hypothetical construct. The above statement elevates some people's feelings of inauthenticity and self-alienation into a cultural necessity.

It is striking however that Stern (1985) similarly observes a degree of alienation from one's innermost authentic feelings in the second year of life. He attributes this to the acquisition of language.

We would of course have expected Anna Freud to *start* with her father's ideas, but it was striking to me to what extent many ideas expressed as late as 1970 mirrored and repeated concepts written forty years earlier. Early in life she had been handed the truth and she faithfully held on to it in many ways.

It seems clear that psychoanalysis was truth rather than theory for the daughter of Sigmund Freud. Many greatly admire the simplicity, economy, and clarity of her theoretical language. Yet at times this very simplicity exists because she treated hypotheses as facts. She wrote, for example (all emphases mine):

"Since 1922, when Freud's paper appeared, we have *known* what lies behind this solution; . . . " (IV:249) Or

" . . . it has also become part of everyday knowledge that this unconscious includes the instinctual life; . . . " (VIII:215) Or

" . . . psychoanalytic investigation *established* that we forget nothing except what we wish to forget. . . ." (I:81)

This is indeed the language of certainty.

We also find that psychoanalytic concepts were so real to Anna Freud that they became mathematical equations for understanding human behavior. Libido and aggression had to be mixed in particular quantities to produce mental health. Anna Freud also followed her father's lead in reifying id and ego to dramatize conflicts within a person. Let me use a quote from her article on adolescence to illustrate these two points.

We have seen that the basis of comparison between puberty and the beginning of one of the periodic advances in psychotic disease is the effect which we attribute to quantitative changes in cathexis. In each case the heightened libidinal cathexis of the id adds to the instinctual danger, causing the ego to redouble its efforts to defend itself in every possible way. (II:171–72)

Below is another example from a discussion about children's anxiety.

This anxiety denotes the ego's concern for the intactness of its own organization, at whatever level; it is due to economic reasons, i.e. to the uneven distribution of energy between id and ego; and it gains an intensity whenever the strength of the drive derivatives increases or ego strengths diminish for any reason. (VII:175)

In my view, this is the language of Anna Freud when enchained and enslaved. And while you are still pondering what
these sentences mean, I will present a reflection from her war
reports during the London blitz that Anna Freud wrote in her
individual voice, showing her marvelous humor, originality, and
observational powers.

This passage was written after a bomb fell about thirty yards
from one of the houses of her residential nurseries.

A bomb at a great distance may be an object of horror; a bomb which
settles down so near to one's own household, on the other hand, is
somehow included in it and soon becomes a familiar object. It is true
that on the first day an unexploded bomb is contemplated with respect
and suspicion. When it delays exploding, the reaction in the people around
is not, as one should expect, one of thankfulness and relief. The reaction
is rather one of annoyance with it, which develops into contempt for
the bomb as the days go by. The bomb is treated more like an impostor
who has forced us into an attitude of submission under false pretenses.
In the end, when no one believes in its explosiveness anymore, it sinks
down to the position of being a bore. (III:45)

Anna Freud's imprisonment in a psychoanalytic metapsychol-
ogy that Freud himself once called mythology is all the sadder
because it was so foreign to her way of thinking. She was actually
a reality-oriented and earth-bound woman. When once invited to
speak about a utopian psychoanalytic institute, she declared that
she preferred to think about reality rather than utopia, and that
even as a child she had never enjoyed improbable fantasy stories.
I believe it was her keen interest in the details of everyday living
that made her such an excellent organizer of psychoanalytic associations and administrator both of the Hampstead Therapy and
Training Clinic and of the Residential War Homes. It was in these
roles that she showed most clearly her wonderful good judgment, tact, and a sure sense of proportion.

She took care of 120 children in residential settings, during the
four years of the London blitz and every detail of the children's
lives was of concern to her: How could the children's waiting
time for breakfast be eliminated? Would cucumbers be an adequate nutritional substitute once apples could no longer be found?

Where could they find resources to build an infectious isolation hut so that no children under their care would ever be sent away? I shall return to her war years' accomplishments later in this paper.

This concern with practical reality which strikes me as a typically feminine trait, did manifest itself, albeit in a limited way, in her theoretical orientation. Her first seminal work, *The Ego and the Mechanisms of Defense* (1936), focusing on the ego, the more conscious part of the self, expressed this preference. It was instrumental in shifting the course of psychoanalysis from an id psychology to an ego psychology, suggesting that Anna Freud was a primary architect of modern ego psychology.

Her interest in a reality orientation was also manifest in her discussion on transference, where she consistently emphasized the very important *real* relationship between patient and analyst.

Later, in her years as Director of the Hampstead Child Guidance Clinic and Nursery School, Anna Freud focused her interest on establishing a psychoanalytic child development psychology, an area that would become her own distinct contribution to psychoanalysis. Her interest was in normal development. In line with psychoanalytic tradition, she had a strong vision of assessing the total child rather than merely describing symptoms without understanding their underlying meaning.

She devised a metapsychological profile that calls for a thorough, systematic investigation of every aspect of a child's ego, id, and superego functioning and includes the child's total life space as well. Although the profile includes Freud's stages of infantile sexuality, it also transcends them. She proposed that such an assessment tool could and should be used for every child who was brought to a child guidance clinic for therapy. On its basis a recommendation would be made for the kind of treatment that the child should receive. In most instances child psychoanalysis was suggested but occasionally simply guidance or education for either the child or his/her parents was deemed sufficient. This was one of many ways in which she put into practice her strong convictions regarding the complementary nature of theory and clinical practice.

The most innovative aspect of this metapsychological profile was its developmental lines. Anna Freud did not invent the construct of developmental lines, no more than Sigmund Freud invented the unconscious, but she developed the idea in great detail and her name has become associated with this concept.

Following is an incomplete list of her suggested developmental lines:

From dependency to emotional self-reliance and adult object relationships;
From suckling to rational eating;
From wetting and soiling to bladder and bowel control;
From irresponsibility to responsibility in body management;
From irresponsibility to guilt;
From egocentricity to companionship;
From the body to the toy and from play to work.

There were important developmental lines for the sexual and aggressive instincts, and sometimes lines for symptoms, like lying or fearfulness. Each child was to be evaluated where he or she stood on each of these lines, and decisions could then be made about the child's emotional health or his or her readiness for certain experiences, such as entrance into nursery school. It is curious that Anna Freud, who could draw so much information from a short observation or a mere conversation with a child, recommended such an exhaustive and no doubt exhausting clinical intake procedure.

A sign of mental health would be "a fairly close correspondence between growth on these individual developmental lines" (VI:84–5), while unequal progress along these lines, such as uneven correspondence between ego development and drive development, would signal developmental disturbances.

I think the major problem with these lines is that they have no basic common organizational or transformational theme, making any expectation of parallel development unjustified and impossible to determine. The lines seem to be chosen haphazardly and from very different conceptual levels. Some lines are observable and concrete, other lines intrapsychic and very abstract. At times there is the expectation of progression in terms of gradual differentiation and integration; at other times there is need for internalization, or alternately, perhaps mere acquisition of certain skills. Lines have arbitrary way stations and value-laden goals.

Although Anna Freud's focus was very much the total child, the lines convey a piecemeal image of development. She wrote, for example, that "individuation is hindered where the child's readiness to separate does not coincide in time with the mother's readiness to detach herself from symbiosis with him" (VIII:128). This sentence illustrates Anna Freud's railroad track image of development. Will the two or more trains arrive at the station at the same time? Transactional thinking suggests that the infant's and the mother's readiness to detach themselves will develop in their mutual interaction: they are not independently developing capacities.

Both the diagnostic metapsychological profile and the developmental lines that form an important part of it pervade the last twenty years of Anna Freud's writing; the need for a "reasonable harmony between the child's ego, the urgency of his impulses, and the demands of society" (I:116) is first expressed in a 1930 paper.

The whole scheme, albeit cumbersome, has some utility for developmental assessment. Many intuitive flashes of very modern cybernetic thinking alternate with mechanistic formulations. Seeing the child as whole rather than focusing on a particular symptom is a systemic and holistic idea. Her dictum that all behavior is "the best possible solution of conflicting influences which is available to the child at a particular moment in time" (VII:7) is an example of the cybernetic principle that development proceeds by restraint. Equally interesting is the idea that trauma has different impact on the child, depending on his or her developmental stage. In adolescence, for example, "withdrawal from the parent is a developmental task which does not bear to be interfered with by actual removal of the object" (VIII:73). Although the developmental lines are linear or at best interactional, rather than circular or transactional, she suggested wisely that development does not proceed in a smooth linear fashion, but normally vacillates between progression and regression. Her insistence that child disturbances must be understood as developmental deviations and their severity assessed against the child's potential for self-righting is a great original contribution that has become a basic axiom of child psychiatry.

Anna Freud's diagnostic assessment scheme has received much verbal recognition, yet few researchers have continued the work on developmental lines, probably pointing to some sterility in the overall framework.*

Conflicting Pulls

We are now ready to focus on the conflicts created for Anna Freud by the discrepancy between her own observations and her theoretical beliefs, and to observe the ways in which she handled such conflicts. We find that she sometimes overlooked such discrepancies, but at other times commented on them with surprise and slight unease.

Our first example will be Anna Freud's view of the aggressive instinct. She wrote in 1930:

> For centuries people have remarked on the cruelty of children, blaming it on their lack of understanding. . . . But . . . our observation teaches us something different. We believe that the child tortures animals, not because he does not understand that he is inflicting pain, but precisely because he wants to inflict pain. (I:100)

She then repeatedly and insistently referred through the years to infants as "animallike creatures" (I:111), "almost unbearable in their behavior" (I:111), with natural instincts of "violence, aggression, and destruction" (IV:62), "capable of the unrestricted cruelty of savages" (IV:438), betraying in this last comment as little sophistication about savages as about infants.

I shall never forget the uneasiness I felt as a young mother when my rather mild-tempered two-year-old little girl did not show the anal-sadistic tendencies expected of that age group, and I used practically to goad her to misbehave, so she would match Anna

*I would like to thank Dr. Robert Kegan and Dr. Gerald Stechler for our conversation on this subject.

Freud's image of a normal toddler. Nor will I forget my pride when I introduced her to my aunt, who observed her for a little while and commented in praise that she was rather better behaved than most psychoanalysts' children. Did she herself intuitively and secretly not believe in anal sadism?

Indeed, the same Anna Freud who wrote the above quotes described in exquisite detail episodes of helpfulness, tenderness, and altruism among children as young as eighteen months, whom she observed in her residential war nurseries. Finally, in 1971, at the age of seventy-six, her view of the willfully malicious child began to change in her writings, as illustrated here:

In fact initially these toddlers are completely oblivious of the effects of their aggressive actions and demonstration is needed from the side of adults to bring them to their attention. This, *to my mind* (my italics) invalidates the assumption that to inflict hurt is the basic purpose of the aggressive act. Rather, we have to conclude that only the aggressive action itself is primary, while its result is accidental initially. (VIII:72)

Anna Freud might have rid herself of drive theory if she had lived another ten years. Notice, too, that this statement, which basically questions psychoanalytic theory, is not written as a statement of truth, but as a mere hypothesis.

She similarly found herself in a dilemma when she noticed superego formation among children who had grown up in a concentration camp without consistent, reliable adult figures, and who had therefore not gone through the Oedipus complex.

It remains an open question . . . whether the social reactions learned in a group remain mere ego attitudes or whether they are incorporated into the structure of personality to form part of the superego which, according to present knowledge, is built on the basis of the emotional ties to the parents and the identification which results from them. (IV:162)

It was also surprising to Anna Freud, in light of psychoanalytic theory of gender development, that little boys were growing into a male sexual identity without any visible fathers or even significant father-figures in their life.

Anna Freud had a persistent theoretical belief that young children are neither capable of nor interested in companionship with other children until they are about three years old, even while she gave us a precise description of real friendships among toddlers.

Another discrepancy between theory and observation is particularly curious. It concerns Anna Freud's objection to children having more than one attachment figure in their lives, because she thought it would create an unmanageable loyalty conflict. This belief was in contradiction to her observation that her children in residence were able to love both their mothers and their primary care takers. Moreover, it was in contradiction to her own experience, since the Freud household had always had two mother figures, Anna's mother and her maternal aunt.

Rather than explore the radical implications for child development of these many detailed pioneering observations, she merely uneasily suggested that the children in her residential nurseries grew up under abnormal conditions and therefore developed unusual behaviors.

Anna Freud was eloquent in describing the importance of early mothering to the young child, and the pain, anguish, and sometimes even psychic damage that early separation can create. Her observations helped to shift the theoretical focus of child development from the Oedipus complex to the attachment experience, and we know the influence of this theoretical emphasis on child care policies throughout the Western world. It is my opinion that in her final and widely publicized conclusions, in *War and Children* and *Infants without Families*, Anna Freud overstated the incidence and extent of separation anxiety during the war separations and understated the evidence in her own data that children were capable of adapting quite happily to the best possible model of institutional life. I believe she did this in deference to the theories that emphasized the importance of development within a family setting.

Women have always been ready to ignore their own experiences for the sake of scientific theories. For example, they knew that their infants could hear and see but did not insist that this was so before the scientific community discovered these same facts, or they were willing to ignore the actual nature of their sexual functioning until they were given permission to feel what they felt. I believe Anna Freud, in spite of her uniqueness, acted like most other women when she ignored her own observations in favor of her father's theoretical framework. There was even clear evidence from her descriptions that a number of children were better off in her care than in the homes from which they had come. Her final summary is much more negative about institutional life than her individual reports would have warranted. In actuality, she demonstrated that a well-conceived and well-staffed children's institution *could* be a satisfactory substitution for family living. I am writing this from the perspective of a social worker who has accumulated grave doubts about our foster-care system. From the same social work perspective I am also critical of her firmly held "continuity of care" and "psychological parenthood" principles, which are to be evoked in legal custody, foster-care, and adoption disputes, at the expense of other equally important principles.

Here again Anna Freud was quite capable of contradicting her own principles when faced with an actual case. I told her of a Native American boy caught in a dispute between a very secure Caucasian potential adoption home, where the boy had made a good adjustment, and the boy's maternal aunt, who had come forward to claim his custody; Anna Freud sided with the aunt, feeling that in the long run he would feel more rooted in his own family. In stating this (for her) astonishing preference she therewith transgressed her principle of psychological parenthood.

The recent controversies on Freud's early seduction theory all point to his great reluctance to blame parents, perhaps due to his sense of loyalty to his parents, or perhaps due to his disbelief in his own revolutionary findings of parental abuses. He left his daughter and the rest of the world two contradictory legacies: instinctual development on the one hand, and interpersonal development on the other. We have already seen how Anna Freud mirrored this in her writing, without coming to a resolution. She certainly tried to carry on the tradition of not blaming parents, at least not excessively, which lead her to write ambiguous but benevolent statments, such as the following, written in 1954 and repeated in some similar form during the next ten years:

By rejecting and seducing, the mother can influence, distort, and determine development, but she cannot produce either neurosis or psychosis. I believe we ought to view the influence of the mother in this respect against the background of the spontaneous developmental forces which are active in the child. (IV:349)

As administrator of the war nurseries she did everything possible to preserve and enhance contact between parent and child, a goal that invariably took precedence over bureaucratic considerations. Parents could visit any time, stay overnight if they wished, and take over as much of their children's care as they wanted. Parents were also given first choice for the positions of child-care worker, air raid warden, cook, and so on, an inspired decision that solved their staffing problems. Anna Freud even respected the parents' rights to make serious mistakes, to lie to their children for example or punish them unfairly, without staff interference. In her war correspondence we find numerous passages in which some misguided parental behavior is described with an undertone of regret and disapproval, but always with a measure of detachment. The notes of irony that sneak into her reports invariably cause me delight. For example, in describing some estrangement between parents and a child manifest during a visit, she tells this anecdote:

Little Sonja refused to look at her father whenever he tried to approach her, whereupon he telephoned us in an excited manner and declared: "I do not like the goings-on in that Country House." But, luckily, Sonja cried when the parents visited next, at the moment of parting from them, and that completely helped the situation and restored the father's confidence in us. (III:229)

Thus Anna Freud's demonstration of respect for parental rights was genuine and unswerving. She frequently declared that all development was naturally subject to neurotic conflict, despite the best efforts of devoted parents. Moreover, even the best mother needed to frustrate the child for the sake of socialization and would therefore become a target for the child's hostility. This theory helped her to remain sympathetic to parents. Yet the recent criticism that Sigmund Freud or Anna Freud relegated all accusations against parents to the realm of fantasy is unjustified. Anna Freud made it clear that a child's fantasies needed to be disentangled from actual parental persecutions, for which there was often clinical evidence (VII:121). She took a very clear stance on the little child's powerlessness and on parental responsibility for deviant happenings in the family:

It is never the strength and energy of the child that affects abnormal fulfillment of emotional wishes, but the abnormal behavior of the adult who exploits the child's wishes for the satisfaction of their *own* lusts. In actual life it is as a rule far more important to protect the child from the father's violence than the father from the child's hostility. (I:93)

Moreover, Anna Freud's sympathy did not blind her to pathological transactions.

There are parents whose attachment to the child depends on the latter's representing for them either an ideal of themselves or a figure of their own past. To retain parental love under these conditions, the child allows his personality to be molded into a pattern which is not his own and which conflicts with or neglects his own innate potentialities. Some mothers or fathers assign to the child a role in their own pathology and relate to the child on this basis, not on the basis of a child's real needs. Many mothers actually pass on their symptoms to their young children and subsequently act them out together with them in the form of a *folie a deux.* . . . Parents may also play a part in *maintaining* a child's disturbances. . . . Some parents, for pathological reasons of their own, seem to need an ill, disturbed, or infantile child, and maintain the status quo for that purpose. (VI:47, 48)

Anna Freud even agreed with modern system thinkers that "a patient's pathology [may be] part of a pathological family or professional setting and cannot be altered without causing major upheavals and break-up in the external life situation" (V:75). Again, as with the aggressive instinct, her viewpoint became increasingly interactional in later years: "Much that used to be considered innate can be shown to have become acquired during the first years of life" (VII:149), she concluded in 1968.

I have emphasized Anna Freud's understanding of pathological family transactions because it shows her acute clinical perceptions and because they are in such contrast with the delegated drive theory and with the earlier mentioned more naïve stance toward family dynamics.

Historians credit Anna Freud as one of the original creators of child psychoanalysis, and she could thus be viewed as "mother of child psychiatry." We can judge her work not only by her own quite entrancing early case histories and theoretical writings, but also by an astonishing memoir written by Peter Heller, who was analyzed by Anna Freud when he was a child, and by her clinical notations on the case, which she generously passed on to him before her death. (Bittner and Heller 1983) My views are quite similar to those of Guenther Bittner, a German psychoanalytic therapist, expressed in one chapter of Peter Heller's book.

In this case, Anna Freud was relentless in her oedipal and sexual interpretations and therefore missed other crucial areas. The child Peter was the overvalued yet also neglected child of two separated parents, and Anna Freud's emphasis on his competitive feelings with his father and his sexual feelings for his mother not only often had a narrow focus, but also frequently seem quite irrelevant, both to myself and to Peter Heller, in retrospect. Only toward the end of the three-year analysis did she transcend her theoretical framework and connect with his abandonment anxieties. She never seemed to recognize or to address his realistic concerns about finding a haven in chaotic prewar Vienna.

I see her interest in and encouragement of Peter's precocious literary talents as enabling his creativity; but the author and commentator suggest that the patient remained persuaded throughout his life that his interest in books and literature was a mere defense against forbidden impulses, and that he therefore associated them with shame rather than pride. However, Anna Freud showed much respect toward Peter and even toward his parents. She seemed sparing with her interpretations and followed her own stated principle against assaulting a child with intrusive symbolic interpretations, a practice followed by the rival school of child psychoanalysis led by Melanie Klein. She wrote that the goal for child psychoanalysis was to help the child express the most important and perhaps traumatic events in his past life "in words and conscious thought, relieving him of the necessity of expressing his memory . . . in abnormal behavior" (III:100). She also consistently emphasized the ongoing educational functions of a child psychoanalyst.

On another level, Peter Heller's book can be seen as an ambivalent love epic to Anna Freud. His child analysis was the most significant event of his childhood and cast its shadows through many subsequent years. His first wife was a daughter of Dorothy Burlingham, which came as close as was possible to marrying one of Anna Freud's children. He experienced his great love for his child analyst as a form of "enslavement, tyranny, and benevolent dictatorship" (Bittner and Heller 1983, p. 297), against which he had to fight all his life. Both Heller and Bittner raised the question: Does psychoanalysis swallow up life? Heller's appraisal of his child analysis is extremely ambivalent, each negative sentence being followed by an opposite sentiment, and we come to understand that this book was his attempt to make peace with his adolescent passion for Anna Freud. He may not have accomplished this particular goal.

We can see from the case of Peter Heller that Anna Freud's intent to remain somewhat detached and unintrusive did not always protect her patients against excessive attachment. Anna Freud seemed quite unaware of having such an overpowering effect on her patients and other people in general. The child in her did not fully realize her own importance to others. Although I consider this a frequent problem of very strong women, we must remember that her father may also not have anticipated that the Wolf Man's identity would become that of Freud's most famous patient. I once told Tante Anna that I had avoided psychoanalysis, fearing that I would become overly dependent, and she reassured me that this was a completely unfounded concern.

Bittner also felt that Anna Freud was most successful clinically when she stepped out of her theoretical framework and used her psychological intuition. It is my thesis that this was also true in other situations.

I was present throughout the whole year of 1979/80 at the weekly case conferences of the Hampstead Clinic, and Anna Freud usually made some concluding comment that was central to the whole case. It is my firm contention that her comments tended to be extremely pragmatic, based on sound human judgment and a generalized clinical intuition rather than on any particular theoretical framework. This may also explain why our clinical views were usually in close accordance and why she praised me quite generously for my own contributions to the discussions.

Let me end this section with Anna Freud's amusing stand on psychoanalytic innovations. She was very exasperated with bureaucratic rules of the psychoanalytic institutes in the United States, especially in relation to candidate selection. She urged for an inclusion of mavericks among psychoanalytic candidates and recommended an open learning environment "where controversies can be fought and lively discussions enjoyed" (VII:88), while simultaneously bitterly deploring "the revolution and almost anarchy in the field of theory and technique." She would have liked to recruit for psychoanalysis independent and creative minds who would resist innovation and maintain the model of psychoanalysis as it was set down by her father.

Her Own Woman

I have so far suggested to you the many ways in which Anna Freud's legacy from her father interfered or conflicted with her independent thought. I now joyfully turn to the equally significant ways in which she fully expressed her own uniqueness and creativity.

Anna Freud led a very unconventional life for a woman of her generation. She eschewed the three realms commonly associated with women: sex, marriage, and motherhood, and thus assured us that one can be a woman of great substance and even considerable femininity without that trilogy. She shared her life not with a husband or lover, but first with her father, and then with a woman friend. It is my conviction that her most passionate love was reserved for her father, but her bonds to her life-partner, Dorothy Burlingham, were also very deep and lasted from young adulthood to the latter's death only two years before her own. We notice that these two central relationships encompassed both her personal and her professional life. She once wrote that she made little distinction among her personal, social, and professional identities, here again anticipating a feminist call for less sharp divisions between private and public spheres. Anna Freud was angered by feminists who reviled her father, yet she unmistakably led a feminist life.

I need to qualify the statement that she eschewed motherhood, since Anna Freud, while not a conventional mother, embodied the highest principles of motherhood, the care for children's welfare. Remember the governess in the altruistic surrender example? "Childless herself, she was devoted to other people's children" (II:125). I have already suggested that she was guardian/ mother for psychoanalysis, but beyond that, her motherhood extended to all the children in the world. She wanted children to have lives that would not be oppressed and exploited, restricted, impoverished, or damaged by an uncaring adult world. It was her fervent hope that by spreading the wisdom of psychoanalytic insight she could improve children's lives in their families, clinics, schools, hospitals, and courts. It was in this role of mother/educator and advocate of children that she spoke most clearly in her own voice and that we can celebrate her wholeheartedly.

It was during the war years, just after her father's death, while Anna Freud administered the residential war nurseries for young children whose families had been bombed out or who could otherwise not take care of them, that she could most fully practice her motherhood capacities and that she also came into the period of her greatest intellectual freedom. She was, during those years, less a psychoanalytic ambassador and care taker and more her own person. If you wish to get in touch with the most deeply humanistic aspects of Anna Freud, you must read the fifty-six monthly reports that she wrote to the Committee of American Foster Parents' Plan for War Children from February 1941 through the years of the London blitz, to December 1945. Her leadership of these children's homes during the war years was truly extraordinary and almost heroic, and I am glad that she received a high British distinction for her services. Whenever Tante Anna enganged in a life review with me, it was always those years that she recalled.

Anna Freud's love of children is best captured by the exquisite clinical vignettes of individual children she offered. It is hard to select just one. In the course of the fifty-six war reports, many children, all with their own unique individuality, spring to life. One hangs eagerly and hopefully on their fate, watching them grow during the war years. I think Anna Freud's early case histories and her later vignettes of the residential nursery children have the same compelling immediacy as her father's famous case histories; they are written with compassion and unsentimental tenderness. Here is Tony, admitted to the residential war nursery on an emergency basis:

As a bed-wetter he had been handed from one billet to another (five or six changes in all) and no further place could be found for him. He is a delicate little boy of graceful, charming appearance, friendly but noncommittal, rather frightened and lost, without emotional contact with anyone.

A year later Tony reappears in the process of learning to love. Here are some fragments:

The first period of his love for Sister Mary was by no means a happy one. He treated her as his possession, but his early experience had already taught him how easily possessions can get lost. This tinged his affection for her with continual fear and insecurity. He would cling to her desperately, would be violently jealous when he saw her handle other children, and would demand her sole attention which he could not get. Once, on a walk, when other children took her hand, he called out excitedly: "That is my hand!" He wavered continuously between expression of his devotion for her and of anger and resentment. . . . But in spite of all this violent display of emotion, he was at that time not yet able to run toward Sister Mary when he saw her. He would only look at her and smile shyly. Only when she lifted him up would he throw his arms around her neck and then look suddenly completely happy for a moment. (III:243)

I think Anna Freud could empathize with children's pain and passion so deeply because she had preserved the vulnerable, passionate child within herself. In Tony's passionate love for Sister Mary, we sense the abiding love of the child in Anna for her father.

Yet it was not passion or even love, but respect for the integrity and uniqueness of each child, that was the essence of good motherhood for Anna Freud. Even in the tender description above, we see not only empathy, but also a measure of detachment. She was as concerned about the results of loving too much as about loving too litte. Her concern about overlove as a form of intrusiveness was a pioneering idea, opposed to the somewhat exclusive emphasis on deep attachment of the object relations school.

She warned parents not to overindulge their children, lest they create anxiety in the children about impulse control or give the children unrealistic expectations of the outside world, making all other relationships disappointing.

Her ideal was to steer a "reasonable middle course between gratification and frustration, between strictness and indulgence, between abandonment of threats, force, and physical punishment and maintenance of moral guidance and the need to transform instinctual drives" (VIII:274). She stood for as much self-regulation and non-interference as was practical in every area of child rearing, whether it was eating, toilet training, or autoerotic activities. She advocated to parents and teachers the promotion of self-discipline rather than coercive obedience. Physical punishment of children was unthinkable in her scheme of things.

Her respect for children made her abhor every kind of lie and deceit, including those in the sexual area. Respect was also involved when she urged parents to treat the sexual and emotional love that children had for them and the ensuing crisis of disappointment with tact and understanding, preserving their children's self-esteem and self-confidence. I think it is extraordinary that Anna Freud, from a theoretical basis of drive theory, stressed as long as fifty years ago the most modern principles of current childhood education: self-regulation; promotion of autonomy; avoidance of physical punishment; the harmfulness of intrusiveness, excessive attachment, and above all deceit; and respect for the uniqueness of each child. It is my belief that she did not derive these principles from her theoretical position, but from her intuitive understanding of and affection for children.

Anna Freud's main identity of her later adult years was that of a psychoanalyst and the head of the Hampstead Child Therapy Clinic and Training Course, which has now been renamed The

Anna Freud Centre. It was in this capacity that she became a consultant to other disciplines that deal with children.

Her special concern always went to children of deprived background, and her nursery schools, both in Vienna and London, as well as her residential war nurseries, were especially designed for such children. Having started her career as a school teacher, she often addressed herself to that audience, urging them to be helpful, appreciative, and inspiring. They should never scold or shame children, and understanding must replace harshness. Many of her educational principles guide nursery school education throughout the Western world.

Anna Freud also eagerly extended her teaching to nurses and pediatricians. She pointed to the close connection between body and mind in the infant; to the inevitable repercussions of not only physical illness but also medical procedures on the emotional life of the child; to the harmful effects of restriction of motility; to the trauma of giving up developmental gains during hospital care; and to the importance of regular parental visits.

Although Anna Freud was of course faithful to psychoanalytic theory in her educational advice, she was quite adept at fitting the theory to her humanistic child-rearing principles. If a child was unduly aggressive, for example, she would say that the trouble was not with excess of aggression, which might have led to suppression. Instead, she attributed the problem to the fact that insufficient libido had not diluted the child's normal aggressiveness. The remedy was an infusion of kindness and understanding to increase libido supplies, and sure enough, the child improved (IV:153).

The idea that the wish to learn was a derivative of sexual curiosity could also be utilized creatively. She described enthusiastically how she succeeded as a young teacher to make learning very exciting for children by harnessing the subject matter to the child's instinctual concerns (VIII:310). There is testimony that she was a wonderful and much-loved young teacher.

We have heard that the psychoanalytical framework made her less judgmental about parents. This was even more in evidence when it came to children's misbehavior. Hate, jealousy, and death wishes against siblings and parents were expected and natural, to be understood rather than condemned. In actual practice, the roots of naughtiness were always sought in the child's unhappiness. In the residential nursery, emotional problems were never viewed as a nuisance, but as a challenge "to use and apply theoretical knowledge to solve the practical problems presented by each child" (III:77).

It was part of her respectful stance to be ever alert to the possibility of emotional exploitation of children. "Children should on no account serve as outlets for the uncontrolled and therefore unrestrained emotions of the adults," she wrote, "irrespective of whether these emotions are of a positive or a negative kind" (III:598). Anna Freud taught her students, whether they were in training to be child therapists or child-care workers, to approach each child not with "love for which there was no real basis, but with an insatiable curiosity to learn more about the problem of child development" (VIII:299). She thought every child should be "regarded by the professionals as an important representative of his own species" (VIII:299). She considered her own stance of curiosity about understanding children a primary motivating life force.

We have heard that Anna Freud did not make a sharp distinction between her personal and professional life. I believe that she carried a measure of the same serene, interested, and curious detachment into many of her personal relationships. Her memorial tributes reflect not only the intense love people had for her, but also her ultimate reserve and people's yearning to be closer to her. James Robertson, a psychoanalyst who worked with her during the war years and who was also a fervent advocate of children, made comments that could perhaps stand for many others:

During discussion her concentration narrowed to the matter in hand, everything else excluded. If one's ideas appealed to her, one would leave feeling valued and invigorated. Her attentiveness and friendly interest were such that one could have imagined oneself to be in a special relationship with her. But then one would remember that others were having a similar experience of her wholly committed attention, and that they too enjoyed the privileges of experiencing the genius of this unique woman. Anna Freud was admired, loved, and even venerated by a great number of people in Europe and America, but although in that sense she was known by many, Anna Freud remained a very private person. (Bulletin of the Hampstead Clinic 1983)

We thus hear that Anna Freud, like many of us, was both a very public and a very private person. His voice contains both great love and also pain. These are the feelings that Anna Freud evoked in people. She was intensely loved, not because she was her father's daughter, but because of her own radiance. Her memorial tributes are truly extraordinary. They mention her "noble formidable qualities," "her humility," "her moral courage," "her serenity," "her unwavering loyalty," "her candor," "her charm," "her directness," "her vitality," "her kindness," "her joyous commitment." Others said; "She stood head and shoulders above the rest of us"; "she was a great teacher;" "she was a noble human being;" "she was the incarnation of many virtues that made her stand alone;" "wherever she was, whichever room she entered, whoever was present, young or old, we all felt the extraordinary presence of a remarkable and unforgettable personality." These are the words by which her colleagues and students and others close to her remember her.

I have come to the conclusion that Anna Freud needed to protect herself because she was the kind of human being who might have been overrun, exploited, and perhaps used up by people's need and wish to love her too much.

I was among those who had that wish, although it seemed presumptuous and hopeless to gain a place in the heart of a person who was so intensely loved by so many people, and most especially in a heart that few people had ever been allowed to enter.

I had admired my aunt from a geographical and an emotional distance all my adult years; she had always been my ego ideal. Then I took my sabbatical year in London, perhaps to seek a last chance to still encounter her. I came to love her at the end of her life with a depth of passion and devotion that I have seldom experienced. I set out to woo her with imagination and extravagance, and she opened her heart a little to me, perhaps because she was already starting her last life stage and I reminded her of her sisters and brothers, whom she had loved very much. After her death on October 7, 1982, I deeply mourned her for two years. Sigmund Freud has written that we cope with loss by taking the lost object inside ourselves, and if it were not too presumptuous I would admit that the spirit of Tante Anna is strangely inside me and that I notice that people sometimes treat me a little like they treated her, even though I do not measure up to her in any way. These years of remembering Tante Anna, of thinking and writing about her life and her work, allow me to put her memory to rest and to keep it alive forever—the two things we need to do with people we have loved and lost.

I approached the task of reviewing her life's work with the respect and honesty that I admired in her. Blind adulation would not have been respectful. I come to the conclusion that Anna Freud had a divided self, being both her own woman and her father's daughter. As her father's delegate she was bound within the psychoanalytic language and culture, while her own self had penetrating powers of observation, sharp clinical insights, and great talents in writing and speaking. Psychoanalytic theory became an intellectual fetter that obstructed to some degree her insights and clarity of thought and led her to superimpose an ill-fitting theoretical framework on her brilliant, finely tuned perceptions. As the years passed, she became increasingly but never entirely her own person. I do not see her true greatness in her theoretical formulations. I see her greatest strengths in her wonderfully sound human judgments, her intuitive clinical insights, her integrity and humanistic values, and in her organizational skills. She had above all extraordinary charisma and the kinds of attributes we associate with a great leader.

Although Anna Freud was able to make creative compromises and found a measure of integration between her two selves, she did pay a price for being her father's delegate. I have repeatedly expressed my disappointment about this limitation. This was wrong of me. We must respect the choices that people make. Tante Anna never regretted any aspect of her life. She had been a loyal daughter and she had led a creative and fulfilling life that had enriched innumerable people around the world. She died at peace with herself. We admire her loyalty to her father. We celebrate her life.

Resources and References

The Writings of Anna Freud. (1973). New York: International Universities Press.

Vol. I   (1925–35) Introduction to Psychoanalysis.
Vol. II   (1936)   The Ego and the Mechanisms of Defense.
Vol. III   (1939–45) Infants without Families.
Vol. IV   (1945–56) Indications for Child Analysis and Other Papers.
Vol. V   (1956–65) Research at the Hampstead Child-Therapy Clinic and other Papers.
Vol. VI   (1965)   Normality and Pathology in Childhood.
Vol. VII   (1966–70) Problems of Psychoanalytic Technique and Therapy.
Vol. VIII (1970–80) (1982) Psychoanalytic Psychology of Normal Development. London: Hogarth Press, and the Institute of Psychoanalysis.

Bittner, G., and Heller, P. (Eds.). (1983). *Eine Kinderanalyse bei Anna Freud (1929–32)*. Wuerzburg, Germany: Koenigshausen and Neumann.

The Bulletin of the Hampstead Clinic. (1983). Anna Freud Memorial Issue, Vol. 6, Part 1.

Dyer, R. (1983). *The Work of Anna Freud.* New York: Jason Aronson.

Peters, U. H. (1984). *Anna Freud: A Life Dedicated to Children.* New York: Schocken.

Stern, D. (1985). *The Interpersonal World of the Infant.* New York: Basic Books.

Stierlin, H. (1977). *Adolf Hitler: A Family Perspective.* New York: Psychohistory Press.

21 / Mother and Daughter: An Epitaph

MY mother died a few days ago—a painful death of lung cancer. I need to write an epitaph for her life. I want to bear truthful witness to how I, as her only daughter, have perceived her life and how I have experienced it.

Because her life has ended I must understand what I can learn from it. I want to share this learning with you as a way of making peace with my memory of her. This is an essay about one woman's struggles. It is about my mother, and perhaps yours as well. It is about the mother-daughter relationship. It is about a particularly painful example of this most primordial of all relationships.

My mother was eighty-four years old when she died. Her life, which spanned this entire century, reaches back to Vienna, then capital of the Austro-Hungarian Empire. She survived two world wars and two emigrations, twice narrowly escaping the gas chambers of the Holocaust. In many ways she was the quintessential central European assimilated Jewish woman, with all the strength and determination, pettiness and mistrust characteristic of that generation. A victim of her oppressive female upbringing, she also transcended it to a considerable degree. My mother would not have survived if she had not been a fighter—and a fighter she remained, to her last painful breath. I do not remember my mother laughing or smiling. Living was a grim business for her.

Cancer was eating her body, but she refused pain killers in order to preserve her fine mind, which became her prize jewel after she lost her beauty. A few weeks ago I sat near her bed while she held my hand and screamed in pain the childhood diminutive of my name, over and over, all through that day. "Sopherle, Sopherle." She was the only person who has ever used that particular diminutive of my name. It is now gone from my life, but it will ring in my ears, perhaps forever.

I did not gladly hold her old hand. I could not find the words of comfort that I might have found in my heart for many others. I sat next to her bed with an icy and armored heart and waited for the day to pass to return to Boston, to my friends, family, community, and work, waited until I could flee in terror lest her spirit invade me and defeat my lifelong struggle to be separate and different.

The touching itself was fraught with discomfort. Except for perfunctory kisses, my mother and I had not touched each other since I was an adolescent. The screaming of my name on that last day when I saw her fully conscious was her last complaint to me, yet once more, the last time that she asked me to take away some unbearable pain, arousing the familiar defensive rage to ward off overwhelming feelings of dread, guilt, and helplessness.

It started when I was a very little girl. My earliest memories of my mother are those of a crying woman who turned to me for physical and emotional comfort. I see her as she told me of my father's daily unkindnesses that caused her the same sharp grief, day after day, year after year. She loved my father in her own way, and she could not let go of that love. She was never good at letting go. After they separated, she continued to share with me, through the years, the unkindnesses, injuries, and insults of the rest of the world.

My parents were poorly matched. Neither of them could give the other anything he or she needed or wanted. My father looked for women who were either his servants or his sexual playmates or preferably both. My mother was neither. She, on the other hand, craved love and admiration, first for her beauty and later for her achievements and her intelligence. Perhaps she might have developed in very different ways if her husband had been able to meet those needs. Perhaps such a man could have stilled some of her profound self-doubts, and she could have become more generous and less bitter. But she chose a man who was dashing and handsome and the son of Sigmund Freud—a man who loved no one but himself. It is not easy, however, to be the son of a famous man. Perhaps, after all, he too did not love himself very well.

If she could not have any sort of love from him, she wanted at least the accoutrements of an affluent bourgeois life: expensive clothes, servants, big parties, elegant travel. And there was never enough money. My mother was greedy, and my father was withholding. The more she wanted, the less he wanted to give her, and the less he wanted to give her, the more she wanted—the familiar, symmetrical escalation of married life.

Viennese Jews, having a precarious anchorage in their society, were excessively preoccupied with money as the only safety one could count on. Money became the focus and symbol of my parents' alienation and eventual constant warfare. I saved pocket money and offered it to my mother to still her laments. Sometimes she even accepted it. Money worries were mentioned at least once in each of the telephone calls during the thirty-seven years that I lived in Boston and she lived in New York City. Even at a time when she had substantial savings and went to first-class hotels in Europe every summer, starvation fantasies continued to preoccupy her. A few years ago I pointed out to her that she had saved enough money to assure a comfortable old age, even if she were to live a *very* long life, and that *we* had enough money to guarantee her comfort as well. She answered, "Let me complain." She left substantial savings to her four granddaughters, leaving out her two grandsons, a truly triumphant feminist gesture that transcends her life.

Photographs standing in my mother's apartment attest to her great beauty, well into middle life. There were many men in her life who admired her and perhaps loved her. She was a woman who had a queenly air. She dreaded losing her beauty and waged a relentless war against encroaching old age.

She spent hours pulling out white hairs that threatened to flaw her raven-black hair until eventually she dyed her hair. She had at least two face lifts; she took every kind of hormonal youth therapy (and I believe that this might have caused her earlier cancer of the intestines); she traveled all the way to Bulgaria for some rejuvenation treatments. It is good for me to look at my mother's life, because in her own exaggerated way she reminds me that deep down we are all victims of similar social messages: we shall be worthless and despised once we are old and ugly. I watched through the years her determination to appear and remain beautiful, the glitter and commotion surrounding the care of her body, her face, and her hair while she was still a young woman, and the desperate attempts of her older years to remain youthful. I vowed, even as a little girl, to take another route. I have never used cosmetics, nor dyed my hair, and perhaps fortunately, I have never held the identity of a beautiful woman—and yet, the thought of becoming physically unattractive fills me with dread.

I used to think that my mother's need to display her beauty or boast about her accomplishments was caused by excessive self-love. Later I realized that on the contrary, my mother was racked by *lack* of self-love, which is really the essence of narcissism. My mother, as the oldest of three daughters in a Jewish family, should of course have been a son. Her early and first tragedy was that she was not well loved by her own mother. Her earliest memories, recorded in her autobiography written at the age of eighty-two, were all of incidents in which she was misunderstood, discouraged, and unfairly punished. Her mother had been a cold, angry, and dissatisfied woman who gave up a potentially brilliant career as an opera singer under the severe pressures of a conventional Jewish patriarchal family. Instead she had settled down to a dull bourgeois life, tyrannizing her husband and her three daughters, punishing them for her disappointment. Later, widowed, she would flee from Vienna to escape Hitler and join her daughters in France. But none of her daughters proved determined enough to protect their mother, and eventually she was shipped to Terezin to die.

The realization that lack of self-respect and self-love had been my mother's curse stunned me. I too have struggled with self-doubts. I too have needed public recognition to feel assured of self-worth. My mother's frightening example has helped me to overcome these self-doubts. When I was abroad alone on my sabbatical, I found that I loved myself well enough to reach out to women and men who interested me. I was able to create a whole network of valued friends in nine months, and I realized that I had won the battle for self-love. Perhaps we can all learn from my mother's example that selfishness and self-love are not similar, but opposite life positions. These two orientations get confused, and many of us have not dared to love ourselves well.

My heart beat with compassion when I read my mother's description of her young married years, which for me illustrate the powerlessness of a young woman of her generation. Arbitrary and unjust domination continued after her marriage, with the oppression now exerted by her husband and his large, awe-inspiring family. Her relationship to the Freud family was fraught with conflict and ambivalence. As a little girl I had received the impression that not only my father, but all his relatives except the great man himself, were her enemies. I do not know whether she was justified in feeling criticized and rejected by them. Later she professed great respect for "The Family" and even wrote an adulatory profile of her mother-in-law. She would have denied her early bitter antagonism if I had reminded her of it, which I did not do. When I told her a few years ago that I had received special recognition for a paper arguing against the intrapsychic psychoanalytic approach to social casework, she snapped, "The public has always rewarded Freud's enemies—you should be ashamed of yourself," and abruptly hung up the telephone. That was the only time I ever felt compelled to tell her about a paper I had written.

After leaving Vienna my mother bore the name of Freud with enormous pride, and it became an important prop for her shaky self-esteem and, curiously enough, a cornerstone of her identity. Her self-designed obituary for *The New York Times* begins: "Dr. Esti Freud, daughter-in-law of Sigmund Freud . . . " and never even mentions her maiden name, the name of her beloved father on whose grave her ashes are to rest.

My mother felt loved by her father. She felt herself to be his favorite daughter, and perhaps her energy and ambition were the product of her male rather than female identification, as was true of other successful women of her generation. It was indeed her work that was my mother's life-line and that eventually afforded her pleasure, independence, and at least a measure of self-respect. When I last saw her she said to me, "I had a good and interesting life. I loved my work and I loved to earn money."

At the age of twenty-eight, when I was two years old, she took charge of her life. She started to study speech pathology and worked in this field all her life in three languages, achieving considerable professional success in Vienna, Paris, and New York City. She obviously had great competence in her own field, and after she arrived in New York at the age of forty-seven, she not only became self-supporting within a relatively short time but slowly regained the affluent life-style to which she felt entitled. She far surpassed my father's professional success.

While working, she went to night school and successfully completed her doctoral studies over seven years. At the age of fifty-nine she became Dr. Esti Freud, Ph.D., and after that no one could despise her any more. As she became older, her work took over more and more of her life, and her difficulty in creating meaningful human bonds became less important. The emotional isolation that seemed so frightening to me did not often burden her. Once she had won the fight for professional recognition and for financial security, her later life became less stormy and more content.

She continued working, both in hospital settings and in private practice, until a few months before her death. Her mind and memory remained unaffected by age. For recreational pursuits she wrote abstracts of foreign language articles in her field. I am thankful to my mother for having been a positive model for me in the areas of work, ambition, and continued learning.

Because my mother worked and had an active social life, my brother and I were cared for by servants. We had a series of cooks and Fraeuleins, as was the custom for middle-class families in Vienna in prewar days. The last Fraeulein came when I was six years old, a young country girl who was able to manage my mother's mood swings, her temper tantrums, and her attacks of acute mistrust. She stayed with us until our family left Vienna, when I was almost fourteen years old. She is still alive; we are fond of each other, and I have visited her a number of times in the last twenty years.

History has neglected the importance of servants in the lives of European middle-class women. Servants were sometimes the only intimate friends in such women's lives. This was true for my mother while in Vienna, and it became true once again in her old age in New York City. Her most loyal and devoted friend was her cleaning woman, and it was her name that my mother called out when she woke at night from her comatose sleep. It reminded me of Bergman's movie *Cries and Whispers,* in which a servant is the dying woman's most warm and caring friend. Tolstoy's unforgettable story of "The Death of Ivan Ilyich," suggests that perhaps many men, as well, found their servants to be the only emotionally available, nonjudgmental, and caring persons. In our own servantless society we turn to mental health professionals to help us with our problems of intimacy in living and dying.

Although the drama of my parents' disastrous marriage overshadowed my childhood, I also have many happy memories of those days. My mother would have liked to become an actress, and I believe she had great talent, but like her mother, she did not have the opportunity and the courage to break out of the conventions of her social class. Her husband, just like my maternal grandfather, stood in the way of such unconventional forms of self-realization. But my mother taught acting to others, and she gave frequent musically accompanied poetry recitations. Our household was full of plays and poetry, perhaps awakening in me an early love of books that later became one of the mainstays of my life. I was in charge of helping my mother memorize the poems, and this was probably our most significant sharing. On the other hand, her anxiety as to whether the recitals would be well attended weighed heavily on me, as did her other concerns regarding set-backs in her work. There was anxiety over promotions, over adequate recognition, the number of private patients, sufficient numbers of students enrolled in her classes, unfair competition, bills getting paid on time, and so forth. In later years my mother kept asking me whether people paid me enough, and whether I had enough students enrolled in my classes. All these were her lifelong uncertainties, which existed in all countries and at every age, until she died. My premature exposure to parental anxieties has limited my tolerance for bearing my children's worries. I find myself alternately overreacting and under-reacting in response to the old familiar feelings of panic that assault me when I listen to their concerns.

Although Fraeuleins took care of our daily needs, there was no confusion about who was in charge of our lives. Sometimes my mother would pick me up at school and take me to one of Vienna's famous pastry shops; these were red-letter days. My mother and I also traveled together, and those trips were joyful occasions. My brother, on the other hand, went to summer camp. I was not only the favored child but also my mother's main love object, the person who could give her the affection that she missed from my father. I was her child, and her child alone. She formed an impenetrable wall between my father and me. When we left Vienna, my father and my brother and the rest of the Freud family went to London, whereas my mother and I went to Paris. I was also a great ornament to my mother. Although failing in school, I was winsome and obedient; I had learned to curtsy and was willing to be exhibited on suitable occasions. I was, my mother told me, an enchanting child.

My mother loved herself so little that other people's actions were forever seen as slights. Her life was surrounded by people who she believed had offended her. As a child, I needed emotional contacts of a kind that, I realized early, my mother could not give me, and I reached out to other adults such as teachers and private tutors. My mother would often befriend these people and then, to my despair, quarrel with them, and I would lose my friends. I learned to pray to our Jewish God: "Sh'ma Yisrael, please let my mother not quarrel with anyone tomorrow. Please God, let her quarrel with me, rather than with my father or brother or Fraeulein or my teacher." But I was always good and loved, and it was all the others who were hated.

It was only later, when we left Vienna and I no longer needed to become a lady, that I stopped being sweet, and it was our turn to quarrel often and bitterly. In self-protection I had closed my heart against her pain, the pain of losing her husband and her home, and again and again she accused me of having a stony heart. "You have inherited your grandfather's famous stony heart," she said. I was to be a Freud child, a member of that alien and hostile clan. I looked like a Freud and acted like a Freud. It was my opportunity to become separate and different, and although it was my mother's curse, it was perhaps also her greatest gift to me—her permission not to repeat her fate. I embraced it as my salvation.

Although I had already learned in Vienna that it was neither safe nor really possible to share my hopes and fears with my mother, we now became strangers. We each tried to survive in our own way in that alien and fearsome country—France before the war. After we finally came to the United States in the middle of the war, my mother settled in New York City, and I went off to school in Boston. I never returned to her home again, except for short yearly visits. I married early, making very, very sure, even at the unripe age of twenty-one, to find a husband who would treat me better than my mother's husband had treated her. Moreover, I would not surrender my total self to him. For the rest of my life I never had an intimate or relaxed conversation with my mother, except for one time. That was a few years ago, after her first cancer operation, when I wanted to thank her for what she had done for me. I almost succeeded in thanking her— not quite, but almost.

You might not think it would be difficult to say a few warm words to an old and dying woman—but it was. Closeness to her was a major threat for me. I was a little girl who might get devoured by this hungry woman.

In reality my mother made few demands on me. Perhaps, after not having rescued her own mother from destruction, she felt she had forfeited her right to my protection. I did remain her major significant other, which meant that she called me whenever she was particularly distressed. Through the years the sound of her voice became associated with upsetting news. But in fact she did not expect that I would do anything about her distress; she only wanted to talk to me about it. We had an unspoken contract that we would not ask each other for practical help of any kind. Once I had left her home, she neither offered, nor would I have welcomed, support, advice, affection, or major gifts. She did not ask for any of these things either. She hardly knew her grandchildren as they grew up. A whole year might pass without a visit in either direction.

And yet through all our distance and noncommunication we had remained poorly differentiated from each other. Remaining physically or verbally distant from another human being is not the same as being emotionally separate. If we have differentiated from a husband, parent, or child, we can meet him or her with love or anger, with compassion, tolerance, or with indifference. Their pain does not create unbearable burdens for us, and their opinions are merely their own perceptions, rather than longed-for praise or dreaded criticism. We are not responsible for their happiness; we do not project our needs on them; and we are no longer bonded to them through guilt, shame, negative or positive passions.

My mother generally did not perceive other human beings as separate from her own needs, least of all me. She never knew me as distinct from herself. She may have been plagued by self-doubts, but at least she had produced a perfect daughter who was at all times happy and successful. When I told her that I was pregnant with my third child, she looked surprised and said, "Don't you remember that I had only two children?" Any hint that my children were not perfect filled her with extreme anguish, and she would always say, "You never had such problems; you were a perfect child," and then we would quickly change the conversation.

But I too had not been able to free myself. I dreaded any intrusion on my boundaries, to the extent that I could not tolerate her asking me the most trivial question. Fortunately she seldom did ask anything, because we were, after all, mother and daughter, and she knew how I felt without having to ask. I believe my exaggerated need for independence is still related to my dread of being invaded by my mother. I cannot bear to be asked by my husband where I am going, what I did today, what I am planning, when I shall be returning.

When I had my first child, I was going to be a much better mother than my mother had been to me. I would be emotionally available to my child. I would not burden her with my sorrows. I would be a wise and calm and joyful mother. I would be the opposite in all ways of my own mother. It is the drama of our lives that opposites usually turn out to be the same. My daughter and I developed the same kind of excessive closeness that injured us both, and it is only with enormous determination and effort that we have disentangled our lives and can meet, forever cautiously, as loving but separate human beings. It is not always easy, but we try. Lack of differentiation is passed down through the generations.

Nevertheless, mistakes need not be fatal. We all do the best we can with our children, and most of us make disastrous mistakes. I do not follow in my mother's steps, because I am willing to confront the hurtful truths that are a necessary part of the intergenerational dialogue that leads to reconciliation. My mother did not understand about such struggles. She was closed to self-knowledge and closed to understanding others. She desperately needed to protect herself against any truth that might threaten her hard-won equilibrium. Only a few weeks before her death she told my children, who had come one by one to bid her good-bye, that we had an unclouded, loving relationship and that she hoped they would be equally close to me.

Although I had become a neglectful and unloving daughter, I believe that my mother forgave me because I had on some level fulfilled her missions. I am my mother's bound delegate—she allowed me to go out into the world, but I had to fulfill certain missions for her. And on this other perhaps more important level, I have been a loyal and dutiful daughter.

I believe that my mother gave me four important missions. First, she wanted me to experience worldly success, so she could be proud of me and feel better about herself. Second, she wanted me to lead a safely married and conventional life so that she would never have to worry about me. Third, she wanted me to take revenge on the Freud family, who had, she felt, treated her badly. And fourth, she wanted me to honor that name of which she was so proud. These were complicated and contradictory missions, but I accomplished them to the best of my ability. On her deathbed she said to me with satisfaction. "Your brother is a Drucker [her maiden name], but you have always been a Freud."

My mother survived the Nazi occupation of Vienna and she rescued my father from being shot. She knew where one hides money and who can be usefully bribed. She had no illusions about anything. She helped us survive the German occupation of France. She had the courage and strength to knock on endless doors for jobs, to sell her skills, to insist on being recognized. She started her career three times in her life, always fighting for status and a respected place in society, looking for useful connections rather than friends. I had a sudden insight only a few months ago, when she bitterly berated her grandson, whom she fiercely loved (perhaps because he looks like her husband), for not visiting often enough. I realized suddenly how deeply vulnerable my mother had always been to feeling unloved and how much of her bitterness throughout her life was merely a defensive reaction against feeling rejected by others.

She was a woman of fierce and ferocious independence. When I tried to guide a glass of water to her lips, she sat up in her semiconscious state and grabbed the glass into her own hands. She never asked for the slightest favor without tipping and overtipping, bribing when no bribes were called for. She regarded money, rather than people, as the sole road to peace of mind, happiness, and self-respect. Her stance toward life remained that of a survivor after such a life position had become unnecessary and impoverishing.

My mother had armored herself against any kind of pain and vulnerability. Although this armor protected her to some extent, it also shielded her from reaching others or being reached by them in genuine love or friendship.

I believe some Jewish people have this survivor attitude in their veins. At least for me it was a major life orientation for many more years than necessary. Surviving means a preference for safety rather than risk, for conformity rather than self-expression, for narrowly constructed self-interest rather than generosity, for anxious planning for future catastrophes rather than appreciation of the moment. It took me a long time to realize that I do not need to be a survivor any more.

My mother's spirit has entered me in many ways, and I must be forever on guard lest I take on her identity. She was a speech therapist, a teacher, and a lecturer, and I am a teacher, a therapist, and a lecturer: Professor Sophie Freud, Ph.D. She has bequeathed me her energy, her perseverance, her ambition, her fierce independence. My mother showed me how to work, but she could not teach me how to love well, either myself or others. I too have self-doubts; I too like to be in control. But I have had a privileged life, and I have not needed to fight the world in order to survive.

My mother rescued me from Hitler's gas ovens. She brought me safely to America—I owe her an enormous debt. Above all it must be said that my mother wished me well. She did not curse my life with malignant missions. I have had the opportunity, leisure, luxury, and talent to build around me a network of family, friends, colleagues, and students who give richness and meaning to my life. I shall never be emotionally abandoned by the world. I have exorcised my mother's ghost. I no longer need to fear that it will take over my life. May her ghost rest in peace.

Index